To Stella & Rabbi Cy Stanway
Best Wishes

Hershel

ALL THE WORLD'S
A STAGE

Hershel Zohn is also the author of

The Story of the Yiddish Theatre

1979

ALL THE WORLD'S A STAGE

MEMOIRS

by
HERSHEL ZOHN

Illustrated by
ANN ZOHN

Yucca Tree Press

All the World's A Stage: Memoirs. Copyright 1992 by Hershel Zohn. All rights reserved. No part of this book may be reproduced in any form or by any electronic or mechanical means, including information storage and retrieval systems, without permission, in writing, from the publisher, except by a reviewer who may quote brief passages in a review. Yucca Tree Press, 2130 Hixon Drive, Las Cruces, NM 88005-3305.

First Printing   1992

Library of Congress Cataloging in Publication Data.

Zohn, Hershel

    ALL THE WORLD'S A STAGE: Memoirs

        1. New Mexico State University-Theater.
        2. Theater-Russian playwrights. 3. Theater, Yiddish.
        4. Theater, Educational.
        I. Hershel Zohn. II. Title

Library of Congress Catalog Card Number: 92-061290

ISBN 1-881325-01-6

Illustrations and jacket design by Ann Zohn

This book is dedicated to a person whose name encompasses the alphabet from A to Z, namely – Ann Zohn.

ACKNOWLEDGMENTS

Carol Bernstein spent many hours typing
and retyping my manuscript.

Linda Blazer of the New Mexico State University Archives -
the first to encourage me with her enthusiasm
about the pages of my book that she read.

Lee Gemoets - for many hours of hard
and patient work.

Janie Matson - for her interest in the project,
and who subsequently labored diligently as
editor and publisher of this book.

Rio Grande Historical Collection - New Mexico State
University Library, Hershel Zohn Papers - UR1.
Photographs from this collection are cited as
(RGHC/NMSU Library).

All other photographs are from Hershel Zohn's
personal collection.

TABLE OF CONTENTS

Preface	xi
Prologue	1
Act I	
Scene 1 Sinyava	3
Tate	3
Education	8
Sinyava	10
My Family	11
Sinyava's Characters	16
Wars and Pogroms	25
Shulemka and Resistance	31
The Great Adventure	33
Scene 2 On the Way to Columbus' Medina	36
Beginning the Journey	36
Zlochev	38
Warsaw	40
Across the Ocean	42
Columbus' Medina	43
Life on the Lower East Side	45
Act II	
Scene 1 The Golden Land	47
Home and School	47
Pushcart Entrepreneur	50
Jeweler's Apprentice	55
Adventures into the Unknown	58
Bitten by the Theatre	60
The Depression	69
WPA and the New York Public Library	74
Federal Theatre Project	76
Prelude to War	78
Scene 2 Army Days	84
Furlough to New Mexico	92
Peace!	98

Scene 3 The Future?	101
Highlands University	104
New York University	106
University of Denver	108
In Search of Employment	114
Interlude	117
Act III - New Mexico A & M	121
The First Year	121
Hadley Hall Theatre	129
Earthquake	149
The Second Decade	169
Act IV	
Scene 1 The Far East Tour	182
Preparations	183
The Tour	187
Tour Schedule	196
Scene 2 The New Theatre	197
The Inaugural Production	198
Shakespeare Festival	203
Southwest Theatre Conference	217
Anton Chekhov	223
Act V - What's In A Name	251
A Telephone Call	259
Epilogue - From Kiev to Sinyava	271
Addendum	275
A - List of Plays	276
B - Ten Years Tributes	
Dave Rodwell	281
Louise Nusbaum	287
C - The Critic - Joan Quarm	288
D - Saroyan Article	291
E - Letters	293
President Gerald Thomas	294
Dr. John Glowacki	295
Southwest Theatre Conference	296
Mrs. William Erwin	297
Hanna Spier	298
Index	299

ILLUSTRATIONS

Lost in the Woods	23
Mama by window on the Sabbath	37
Ellis Island	43
Making Friends	46
What's in This Book?	49
A Windy Day on Hester Street	52
Hershel Zohn - Late 1940s	118

(The following photographs are contained in two sections of photographs placed approximately one-third and two-thirds through the book.)

Sholem and Bella Zohn
Hershel Zohn in *Shabtsai Zvi*, *Revolt*, and *Yoshe Kalb*
Vardi-Yoalit Theatre Studio group
Dos Shtetel, Vardi-Yoalit Theatre Studio - 1929
Seder for Jewish army personnel, 1943
Denver University, *Distant Drums* - 1948
Modern *Antigone* - 1950
Traditional *Antigone* - 1972
Death of a Salesman - 1953
Kathryn Gibbs and Frank Richardson, *Candida* - 1951
Bernice Beenhouwer, *Pygmalion* - 1951
Rhinoceros - 1963
Life With Father - 1953
An Enemy of the People - 1954
David Travis and Bill Alford, *The Lark* - 1957
Judy Pille, *The Diary of Anne Frank* - 1959
Martha Gold and C.O. Ward, *Hedda Gabler* - 1956
Teahouse of the August Moon - 1958
Leo Comeau and Pauline Plumbley, *The Hasty
    Heart* - 1952
Sally Hodges, *The Glass Menagerie* - 1957
Jackie Clark, David and Lee Dressell, *Medea* - 1959
Jack Soules, Robin Hayner, William Frankfather,
    Uncle Vanya - 1966
Anton Chekhov (1860-1904)

The Sea Gull - Mexico City, Summer 1957
Millie Hayner as Madam Arkadina - 1958
The Sea Gull - 1973
Inherit the Wind - 1959

The Three Penny Opera - 1964
Oedipus Rex
Romero and Juliet - 1964
The House of Bernarda Alba - 1964
Elizabeth Huddle, *The Good Woman of Setzuan* - 1967
Rock Campbell, *J. B.* - 1961
Maxim Gorki and Konstantin Stanislavski
Marcia Riegel and Clinton Kimbrough,
    The Crucible - 1972
The Lower Depths - 1972
John Bellamy, Ed Garrett, Marjorie McCorkle,
    Leo Comeau, *Twelfth Night* - 1955
As You Like It - 1963
James Earl Jones and William Barney, *Othello* - 1965
Carolyn Johnson, William Barney, Ada Shook,
    A Midsummer Night's Dream - 1960
Jack Soules as *MacBeth*
War and Peace - 1969
Zohn and Judith Pattison; Zohn and Mark Medoff,
    War and Peace - 1969
Tevye's family, *Fiddler on the Roof* - 1971
Zohn as Tevye in *Fiddler on the Roof* - 1971
Dedication of Hershel Zohn Theatre - 1978; Dr. Gerald
    W. Thomas, Ann Zohn and Hershel Zohn
Dedication of Hershel Zohn Theatre - 1978; Zohn,
    Charles H. Stubing, Jerome Brown
Bert Seamans, Claire Lewis, Kathryn Harry,
    Michael Myers, *The Matchmaker* - 1963
Mildred Hayner as Mrs. Dolly Levi - 1961
Tour cast of *The Matchmater,* Hawaii - 1963

PREFACE

Hershel Zohn's purpose for living has been to create outstanding theatre.

He has done it with his enthusiasm. And in his insistence not to settle for second-best: Whether it was with a script, or with the actors, or with scenery, lighting and technical effects or costumes. His confidence in pleasing his audience was the result of the way he drove himself and his cast to perfection through long hours of strenuous work. The reward was success, it was winning.

Now Professor Emeritus of Theatre at New Mexico State University (NMSU), Zohn has decided to write a book, in part, about the days that span his twenty-five year, one-hundred play career in a memoir called *All the World's A Stage*.

No production was ever too ambitious for Professor Zohn, including the stage adaptation of Tolstoy's *War and Peace* or Brecht's *Three Penny Opera*. Classics: Moliere, Shakespeare, Sophocles. Productions included great Russian and European playwrights such as Chekhov, Gorki, and Ibsen. The list goes on to include the best works in contemporary theatre, such as those by Arthur Miller and Tennessee Williams. Avant-garde theatre: Ionesco, Carlino, Sartre. Even current trends: Neil Simon. Anything rather than something insignificant, one of his colleagues teased.

With a dramatic career spanning the past seven decades— there have been decades spent as actor, professor, director. In a sense, he has played all those roles. Now he wants to do some serious writing.

His story begins in the Ukraine where his father is running a flour mill. But things there worsen during and after World War I. By the time the twenties arrive, the family has lost its main livelihood. Increasingly, Jews are persecuted. They are blamed for the hard times in Poland and Russia. Armies wander around fighting numerous enemies. Peasant outlaws begin to terrorize the populace. Pogroms are becoming a daily event. Tate, Hershel's father, can think of a way out: Emigrate to America, the golden land.

In New York there are more hard times, but at least you aren't fearing for your life. Hershel learns a trade as a jeweler.

But for Hershel, fascination, inspiration and perhaps escape come at New York's Yiddish Art Theatre. He is bitten by the bug; he succumbs. He works very hard to become a professional actor; he conducts research on the Russian and Yiddish stage for the theatre collection of the New York Public Library. He begins to spend the rest of his life enchanted by the theatre.

After World War II, he moves West to start a more formal education in theatre at the University of Denver. He performs at Red Rocks. He studies more theatre at New York University, Cornell and Northwestern Universities. On the way to continue his PhD program at Stanford, though, his personal life interrupted the process.

He begins to teach and direct at New Mexico A & M (later NMSU). The year is 1950. What started out as a year or two at a college in the middle of nowhere turns into a quarter of a century.

He directs and directs. Colleagues jokingly call him the Stanislavski of the Las Cruces stage. He finds enough local talent to bring it off. He starts to cultivate the taste of the Las Cruces theatre-going audience. Were a thousand NMSU students and members of the community participants in the one hundred plays Hershel directed?

Antigone is on stage at Hadley Hall. An important college official warmly tells Zohn after the performance that even though he didn't understand the play, he did like it.

The Drama Department flourishes. But it has to move out of the first Hadley Hall—the building is declared a safety hazard and a fire trap. The Playmakers have to move to a World War II vintage air mechanics building. They produce many inspiring works of the theatre: Period pieces, classics, theatre of the absurd.

After six years of barracks theatre, the administration approves the expenditure for the new theatre. Its lighting and sound effects will be state-of-the-art. Expensive, but worth the high quality of the works produced there. It will have a beautiful, heavy velvet curtain, dressing rooms—the works.

While the theatre is constructed, Hershel and his student acting troupe tour the Far East. The university was chosen by the American Educational Theatre Association to present the Thornton Wilder production of *The Matchmaker* to armed forces overseas.

The new theatre opened with Shakespeare's *As You Like It*, starring well-known actress Jacqueline Brookes. Not many years later, Professor Zohn charmed James Earl Jones into starring in the NMSU production of *Othello*.

Three years after Hershel retired in 1975, the theatre was named for him.

Since then, he has directed plays in Santa Fe, El Paso and Albuquerque and performed some of his favorite roles from Chekhov's *The Sea Gull*; Anski's *The Dybbuk*; and scenes from other plays. The role he is best known for in recent years is the one of Tevye in *Fiddler on the Roof*.

The theatre and Zohn are a pair of lifelong companions. During the course of a conversation, it is possible to hear Zohn quote Shakespeare, sing melodies from Yiddish and Russian folk songs and chant passages from the Bible.

Back in the sixties, when I first met him, Zohn inspired awe. I believe it was the sparks flying from his black eyes that commanded the respect of New Mexico State University freshmen drama majors, such as myself. The image stays with me of the bearlike archetypal Russian roaring down the aisle at theatre practice thundering: "This scene has no life—start over."

More than all of this, then, it is Zohn's love of the theatre that makes him outstanding. He is a cultural hero to me, in the sense that his work with The Playmakers helped create an aspect of my own personal culture. He brought me - and others like myself—the best there is in theatre. for, as he likes to point out, theatre encompasses all the fine arts; especially writing, music, painting, poetry and literature.

In *All The World's A Stage*, I believe you will find those things that have made Hershel Zohn his particular self: A person who dedicated his professional life to the theatre and teaching others about it.

Lee Gemoets
Las Cruces, NM
June 1992.

PROLOGUE

One spring morning, driving to school to meet my class, I suddenly heard a police siren. Looking in the mirror, I saw two sharp, red lights blinking like the eyes of a Mephistopheles. Traffic was at its peak, and when I finally managed to stop I had practically reached the theatre building. A policeman approached with the usual request, "Let's see your driver's license." I immediately presented my license without uttering a word. He glanced at it and asked, "Where were you born?" A thought went through my mind—what a strange question for a minor traffic violation, but the police officer repeated his question, "Where were you born, Mister?" It was the last day of school and, on that day of all days, I was determined to get to class on time—so I rattled off my reply: "Mestechko Staraya Sinyava, Podolsky Gubernya, Ukraina, Russiya."

The cop gave me a sarcastic look and said, "Are you trying to be funny?"

I said, "Sometimes."

I finally arrived at class and related the policeman incident. We had a good laugh and proceeded to review the course of the semester. My reply to the traffic policeman was correct, but in order to save time I had given my answer in Russian.

ACT I

Scene I

SINYAVA

Tate

I liked to address my father as Tate.¹ I felt much closer to him than when calling him Father or Papa. Tate owned a flour mill from which he tried to earn a living. Most of the time the mill owned him. When some part of the machine broke down, he traveled to far away places in Russia, like Baku, or even Danzig, Germany, in search of replacement parts. Once, Tate even engaged a trained mechanic, Taras, who spent several days working on the machines until he finally succeeded in making the mill run. When Taras was on the job, people

---

¹ A familiar Yiddish form for Papa. Pronounced Tah-teh.

gathered to watch him labor. He was an immaculate mechanic. In spite of the oil and gasoline around him, Taras had his white shirt sleeves rolled up to his elbows and managed to keep his attire neat and clean. He was usually quiet and in town no one knew anything about him except that he was a good and thorough mechanic. Taras was not from our part of the country.

When the mill was running, smoke came up from the chimneys and reached out for great distances into the open fields. Also, the noise from the machines could be heard far away. There was much going on when the mill was in action. Peasants from the surrounding villages parked their wagons, horses, and dogs near the mill as they waited for their wheat to be ground into flour. Most of Tate's customers were the peasant farmers of that region. Tate had some partners in the mill, but the responsibility for the various problems in the running of the mill was always his. They were, apparently, partners on paper only.

Tate spent many hours at the mill, often working late into the night. One night, while walking the two-mile journey home in the dark with his coat covered with white flour, a group of girls returning from a stroll in the little park saw a tall white figure approaching, and thinking it a ghost, ran screaming into their houses and locked the doors. Tate laughed softly and walked on.

At times my mother sent me to the mill with a small sack of wheat to have it ground into flour. As I reached the road outside of town, boys from peasant families would inevitably call out insulting slogans at me—one, which I can remember to this day, was *Zhyd parakhate*.[2] At other times boys would threaten me with a dead rat or throw stones at me and not let me pass.

When business at the mill was good, Tate would have a horse and buggy. That sometimes created an additional burden

---

[2] This was a terrible insult used against Jews. *Zhyd* is comparable to "kike," and *parakhate* meant sick and ugly. Many of the people were poor and their children had lice, so *parakhate* implied you were lice-ridden.

for my parents, especially in the springtime when the snow melted into mud. Once, when Tate allowed himself the pleasure of going home for dinner in his horse and buggy, he got stuck in the mud not too far from the house. He had to call my mother for help and both of them tugged with all their might and finally pulled the horse and buggy out of the mud so Tate could have his dinner.

Often, pleasurable things may end in sadness. This was true of my little dog Mekus. He spent most of the time at the mill. We always played and had good times together. One day I was shocked to learn Mekus had drowned. I missed Mekus for a long time and never had another dog to replace him.

I remember the many walks my father and I took from town to the mill. These walks left a deep impression on me, especially when it was warm and sunny in the wide open green fields. Tate, who was rather tall, and I would both be lost in the cornfields. Tate invariably began a melody and gradually took my hand, which was the signal for me to join in the singing. I enjoyed these long walks immensely and never wanted them to end.

As the mill began to deteriorate, my father was without work and without money and mother nagged him to find some way to earn a living. "There are seven mouths to feed," she complained. Tate would not say a word. He would go into hiding by climbing the broken ladder into the upstairs loft and get lost in the straw, next to the Passover dishes which were kept there from year to year, until he eventually fell asleep. When mother ultimately discovered him, Tate unwillingly descended to face his daily problems.

The cow was our bread provider at various times. Grasy was no beauty—she had lost one horn in a battle, the other one was rather shaky, and her tail was always in knots, yet her milk was famous all over town. Early mornings my mother and I would take her to the place where all the other cows from town were gathered and then taken to pasture in the open fields for the day. Toward sunset Grasy would return home by herself, unless she decided to run away which meant hours of searching by Tate before he finally found her. On good days, people who had to drink milk on doctor's orders waited patiently for my mother to finish filling two to three pails of rich, yellow milk. Mother earned a fair amount of cash from the raunchy animal, which helped her to feed the family.

Once a year our cow had to visit a bull, and it was my father's responsibility to take her. Naturally, I followed him. He paid the owner a half ruble and the excitable bull performed his job. At that time Tate covered my eyes with his hand, in order for me not to watch this sinful scene. Every year Grasy presented us with a calf. Like a puppy, the calf became my pet. After two weeks a butcher came to buy the calf. Mama and the butcher argued and bargained until they arrived at a price. And the skinny little man with a nickname of "Balobushka" put the calf over his shoulders and walked off with it. The cow immediately began to cry and cried incessantly while I ran after the butcher, also crying. I walked back and forth outside the butcher shop hoping to hear sounds from the calf. Every once in a while a cry came through and then I heard no more. I finally walked back home wiping my red eyes on the way.

Mama, as she herself would say, "worked herself to the bone." She would carry water from the well, chop wood, bake the weekly allowance of bread, cook the daily meals, do the special baking and cooking for the Sabbath, do all the mending and sewing and even take some time out to complain to my father. In better days though, Mama had Andrei, the water carrier, provide us with water. He was paid three *kopecks* for two trips to the well for four pails of water. Andrei had one eye, a constant smile on his face, and occasionally tried to get fresh with the women nearby, until he was slapped on his hands. Then he retreated smiling, taking the empty pails to fill them again with water.

The day of Sabbath was when Mama tried to relax from the six days of hard work. She lit the candles, Tate returned from the synagogue and sang the prayer over the wine and the whole family sat down at the table to enjoy the Sabbath meal.

Sabbath was a day of rest. Meals were prepared on Friday to be consumed on Sabbath. Tea with warm milk and cake for breakfast, a lavish noon meal after the men returned from the synagogue. Then the older folks would have a siesta while the younger ones played games, danced, and the older boys would gather in the only soda fountain store in town to drink soda water and crack peanuts.

As the sun began to set, Mama, her two youngest ones, and occasionally a woman from the neighborhood, would sit in a corner close to the stove. Mama told us stories or read a part from the Bible. As it got darker she chanted a farewell to the Sabbath, "God of Abraham, of Isaac and of Jacob, the beloved Sabbath is departing...." In the near darkness, Mama's voice and the words she uttered created a strong mood of nostalgia and sadness. I was glad when the kerosene lamp was lit and the mood changed.

Flashes of early childhood memories include remembering how nice it felt when I noticed my parents being kind and considerate to each other. I recall church bells ringing, the wind blowing, my cap falling off my head and me crying. It was considered irreligious to be in front of a church bare-headed, and even more so when the bells were ringing. And then, early one morning Mama came to my bed saying, "Wake up! Don't you know there's a war?" She had trouble getting me into my shoes, but as soon as I was dressed, I ran outside, joined other boys and we began to play soldiers. It was August 1, 1914.

* * *

Education

It was Tate's responsibility to find a religious teacher for me. I remember Tate wrapping me in Mama's shawl to take me the first time to *Kheyder* (Hebrew school). Nakhem der Melamed (Hebrew teacher) was a youngish man with a short blond beard, who spoke rather loudly when he tried to impress the Aleph-Beis (alphabet) upon the little children. He was not especially kind to us, but neither was he mean. My parents worried that I'd be scared and cry the first time, but I passed the grade like a trooper. If I was scared, I didn't show it.

Reb Eli, the teacher at my second *Kheyder*, had also taught my father when he was a child. *Kheyder* was held in the rabbi's home. At Reb Eli's, I recall there was a large table with a long bench on each side with him seated at the head of the table. He only had one eye, with a prominent white beard, and would, in the summertime, teach the boys in his long white underwear. He was angry most of the time and scolded us, and often put his hand under the table to pinch the boy nearest to him. But a "fun time" was had when he left the room for a drink of water or a glass of tea. His only daughter, Bruche, who was much older than the boys, would stick her head out of the bedroom and tease us. I recall that she was quite voluptuous, and performed various movements intended to excite us. The boys, in turn, responded with their own suggestive motions. She purposely continued with this "flirtation" until her father returned so he could see what his students were up to. The Rabbi selected two boys that he especially disliked, had each one lie on the edge of a bench, reached for the whip he had hidden under his seat, and began his thrashings counting up to seven, while his darling daughter laughed herself sick in the other room.

Fishel der Melamed was an advanced teacher. He was rather short, of course had a long beard, and was meticulously dressed. His hands were small and looked swollen, which was a part of his physique. Everything in his *Kheyder* had to be neat, proper, and exact, as he was teaching Gemara (commentary on Hebrew learning, such as Talmud or the Prophets). The instruction was in Hebrew with immediate translation of each sentence or phrase into Yiddish, which gave the impression Yiddish and Hebrew were one language. Of course, the students often made up their own "commentaries" (usually vulgar) when the Rabbi left the room.

Chaim Yosi was an outstanding teacher who taught me privately when I was about twelve, I assume preparing me for my Bar-Mitzvah. I took one-hour lessons from him early in the morning. This was in the same room where his two daughters were still asleep on the sofa with their bare arms outside of the blankets. Well, how could one absorb the teachings and wisdom of the prophets under such conditions? These were all Hebrew teachers.

When I was old enough, I attended Sinyava's one-room school for a short period. First there was an attractive young teacher who came from a large city. She was primarily interested in teaching reading and writing. After she left a middle-aged, red-headed man arrived from Poland. He stressed arithmetic with the class. He was extremely strict with the students. Once I recall the class was about to begin when I whispered something to the boy sitting next to me. The instructor approached and, with a good-size piece of chalk in his hand, began to pound on my head saying, "Once the bell rings not a sound." My head immediately swelled up and was swollen for about ten days afterwards.

One summer day, I sneaked barefooted to listen to a group of men who were standing in a circle in the plaza discussing the danger of war. When they noticed me, they chased me away by throwing a small stone in my direction saying, "Go home, you are too young to listen to all this talk." But instead I joined a group of boys running after caravans of wagons loaded with beets. Using sticks with nails on top, we removed one beet after another from the load until the driver realized what was happening in the back of his wagon. He let go with his long whip and we made a fast retreat. We considered this very adventuresome.

Sinyava

Sinyava is approximately three-hundred years old, and is seldom found on a map of the Ukraine. At the Jewish Scientific Institute (YIVO) in New York, I did find it in an old history book of small Russian towns. The 1897 census recorded a Jewish population of 2,279. The non-Jewish population was approximately the same size, but lived and farmed mostly in the rolling hills surrounding the town. A river runs alongside the town where people swam in the summer and ice-skated in the winter. Outside of Sinyava the fields are rich with corn (Ukraine is called "the bread basket" of Russia). There are low, rolling hills in the distance. Winter days are extremely cold. When the snow melts in early spring, a thick deep mud spreads throughout the town and causes many problems. Not only would people get stuck in the mud, but also animals—namely horses, as Tate had reason to recall.

Every *shtetel*[3] had the traditional "little red mill" on the river at one end of town. This mill operated on water power, but my father's mill at the other end of town ran by gasoline (when there was any). Entering the town from one side, one noticed two glamorous edifices. No one could get near these structures as they were surrounded by iron gates. In them lived the two wealthiest families in Sinyava. They very seldom talked with the ordinary people in town. Every Friday, though, the older owner of one of these two homes walked to the public bath house with

---

[3] Jewish settlement.

a set of fresh underwear under his arm to take a bath. This was a mitzvah for the Sabbath. Whenever Tate went to the bathhouse, I accompanied him. Friday was set aside for the men, and other days were allotted for women to use the facilities. In those days, there was no running water, even in such palatial homes as those mentioned above.

Needless to say there was no sewage system or inside plumbing. To relieve oneself, a person went to the river beyond a hill where there was a ditch for that purpose. Often small boys threw stones aimed at the people sitting there. Yet the place was surprisingly clean. After the Revolution the new government constructed a public outhouse in the center of town. However, sanitation was neglected, the stench became unbearable, and the project was a failure.

There were three churches and four synagogues in town. When the Revolution triumphed, and before the chaos of the Civil War, celebrations were held all over town. The clergy from the churches came out with large religious banners and Jewish men came out of the synagogues with Torahs—each group marching to meet the other. They stopped in the center of town, shaking hands and embracing as a symbol of friendship. The excitement in the community was so great that it even affected a young boy like me. Mama put me in my best suit, I shined my shoes with milk and to the synagogue I ran to listen to my uncle's inspiring speech about the need for Jews and Gentiles to live together in peace. This did not last very long.

My Family
Tate was tall with a black beard, religious but not fanatic. I don't remember him ever being angry. He was considered to be a learned man; he spoke softly and was very low key. The only time he raised his voice was in studying the Talmud with a friend or two when he disagreed with them on the meaning of a certain passage. I don't recall him ever arguing with Mama.

When she started complaining about domestic problems, he would just walk off to be by himself.

Mama was not a typical "nagger." She worried about the children and was concerned about them, and she just expressed her feelings to her husband. I've heard that she was considered a beauty as a young woman. She was fair complexioned, a few inches shorter than Tate, quite religious, and, of course, not as well-informed as Father. It was not expected that girls of her generation have a formal education. When it came to her daughters though, they were encouraged to learn, except there was no formal learning institution for girls, so they could not attend gymnasia. It should be said that Sinyava was a small town where requirements, styles, and even traditions were different than in the larger cities. Mama was very much aware of what was expected of her—to keep the family content and together.

My sisters, I must say, were entirely different from Chekhov's *Three Sisters*. The oldest, Esther, would inevitably keep a book in her hands to prove to Mama that she was occupied and should be left alone. In later days she became the leader of the family and was always concerned about each one of us. The second sister, Feige (Fanny), was the tallest; robust and strong, Mama expected her to do the weekly laundry and all the menial labor that Mama did not have sufficient time to do. The third sister, Malka (Mollie), was the prettiest of the group. She had a nickname of *"meshigene"*—"the crazy one."

We all had nicknames, which I refrain from listing here. They were generally uncomplimentary and originated from our own behavior. When Malka was in her adolescence she wanted to have a good time by playing games, dancing and generally enjoying herself. When Mama sent her on an errand she would return two hours later, instead of the quarter of an hour which it should have taken. My twin sister, Haye (Khaike or Ida), the youngest, was quiet and withdrawn, allowing her twin brother to hold the fort.

Sinyava

I suffered from rheumatism in my youth, as well as other ailments which befall children. Once Mama became so desperate that she took me to a Gypsy woman who broke a raw egg over my head and murmured something and told my mother that I would be well from then on. It didn't cure me, but I don't recall that it hurt me.

I remember my maternal grandfather. He had a spacious home in Sinyava. A good part of the house was full of honey barrels as he kept bees and sold the honey. Where the bees were kept, I don't remember. Reb[4] David Israel Leib was his first name (last names were seldom used). He was a quiet man, and when he spoke it was soft and kind. When returning from a trip, he brought me a tiny tin barrel of hard candy. Why he selected me of his many grandchildren to receive that gift I didn't know and didn't question the largesse.

When grandfather died it was evening. He was laid on the floor with many lit candles encircling his body. His four daughters and other female relatives sat on the floor, surrounding the corpse and wailing and lamenting, a scene which I now realize was similar to a Lorca or Irish play. It was Jewish tradition. All of the little grandchildren were placed in the same bed to watch something which we did not understand.

His youngest son, my uncle, inherited his business and ultimately became one of the richest men in town. Matchmakers came from all over with marriage proposals for my uncle. He finally considered a proposal to a daughter of a wealthy man from a larger city. Father and daughter appeared at Uncle's house. Presumably the father gave the impression of a man of abundance. He was well dressed with a prominent figure, his daughter too was tastefully groomed and attractive. They

---

[4] Reb is used as a title similar to Mr. and given, out of respect, to any older, learned Jewish man.

agreed on a wedding date and on their departure, the would-be relative gave me a gift—a *grivne,* a Russian dime.

I ran home to show it to mother; she told me to save it. She put it in a jar and placed it on a top shelf. When opportunity presented itself, and I was alone in the house, I climbed to the top shelf, grabbed the dime and ran away with it. It was getting dark, my parents realized that I was not anywhere near the house and Tate began to search for his lost son. An aunt finally remembered that she noticed me buying an orange and chocolate. Tate eventually discovered me with another boy on the outskirts of town sitting beside an old wagon. We were having a feast of an orange and sweets. Tate didn't utter a word, he took me by the hand and led me home. This incident was never mentioned by any of us.

Uncle and the wealthy man's daughter were married. Later they, too, came to the United States, and Uncle opened a laundry in Philadelphia.

Every other Sunday was market day in town. Peasants and merchants came from nearby villages to buy, to sell, to barter, to argue, to fight, to make up, to get drunk and to fight again. This continued until late at night. Next morning the center of town was a mess. During the market day the area was filled with every imaginable kind of merchandise, as well as horses and pigs and chickens. People found it difficult to move from one place to another because of the congestion. As boys, we were always on the lookout for ways of generating income. Several of us decided on a plan to make a few *kopecks*—cut hair from horses' tails and sell the hair to paintbrush makers. The owners of the horses realized what we were about and several men with whips, yelling and cursing, ran after us for some distance until they became tired and returned to their horses. We boys dispersed into our respective homes and didn't come out until the day after everything was over. We felt guilty and were embarrassed to show our faces.

Sinyava was a town divided. The carpenters and the barrel-makers; the tailors, the shoemakers and the hat-makers; the merchants, the storekeepers and the butchers all lived in the center of town, which contained the homes of the bulk of the Jewish population. The peasants and farmers lived up on the hills encircling the town. A very small jail, manned by two policemen and a captain was generally occupied by unmanageable drunkards and the occasional thief. The one telephone in town was primarily used to call out. A so-called hotel, with a few rooms, completed the town's business district. Professional drivers, with their decorated horses and wagons, took passengers to nearby towns and cities. I recall a theatre company coming to town for one evening and presenting what must have been a Goldfaden play. The townspeople would talk or even imitate the actors for weeks afterward.

Passover was my favorite holiday. Mama worked for weeks making a new suit for me. I felt so proud parading in the new suit. We would bring the pretty dishes, used only on Passover, down from the attic. And then the Seder (Passover ceremony). How I looked forward to it with anticipation, and yet with trepidation. The whole family surrounded the table with Tate, in a long white robe seated on a special high seat made of several stacked pillows, looking stern, and his youngest son seated next to him. Tate began by chanting the Haggadah (the story of Passover), "Why is this night different from all other nights?" Then came my turn to ask the *Feer Kashes,* the "Four Questions."

"Tate, I will ask you the four questions. The fir-st—q-u-es-t-ion—w-ill—I—a-s-k—y-o-u...." The stammering turned into crying. Presumably I was scared. My sisters giggled and Mama looked at me with sympathy. Tate finally helped me and somehow I completed my agonizing performance. Otherwise, it was a joyful evening with songs, anecdotes, reminiscing about prior Passovers, and the food which I had looked forward to for a year. I finally collapsed and fell asleep. When I awoke the next morning, I recalled the fiasco of the previous night and "rehearsed" by myself for many hours so this should not happen again. As a result, I asked "The Four Questions" correctly the next evening.

As I got older, I remember spending Saturday afternoons with other boys along the bank of the river doing all kinds of boyish mischief. When the river froze during the winter months, my mother bought me a special pair of boots to go skating, but I had no one to go with.

My best friend was called Shmilek. He was my age, but shorter than I (he took after his father, nicknamed "Wisele"). As arranged between us, whenever Shmilek came by our house he whistled; this was a signal for me to join him and we would walk and talk. What about? I don't remember.

Sinyava's Characters

Sinyava, like other small towns, had its special characters. For instance, who could forget Lipe Shprintsyak? Lipe liked to tell stories about his own experiences, so he claimed. A circle of several men would form, with Lipe in the center, as he spun his tales. "It was a hot day when I was on my way to the town of Pileve to buy some watermelons."

"How did you go to Pileve, Lipe?"

"With my feet," he answered. "Pileve has the best watermelons in this part of the country. I was only about two miles from Pileve as I approached the bridge which I had to cross. I saw that the bridge was shaky and weak like a man who has been fasting for several days. But I had to get to Pileve for my watermelons before someone else got them, so I hurriedly began to cross the bridge, praying at the same time. But the bridge was so weak that even praying didn't help. And as I was walking very lightly, all of a sudden, fast like lightning, and loud like thunder, the bridge split in half and put me in the river.

Don't forget I used to be a good swimmer in my young days and I said to myself, 'Lipe, don't give up. Show what you can do.' And I swam and swam until I got to the shore.

"Naturally, I was very wet and you don't approach a man who sells watermelons in my condition. The sun was quite hot, so I lay down on the grass and, within an hour, I was all dry like nothing had happened. When I approached the man with the watermelons, he said, 'How did you get here, the bridge split in half a while ago?' 'Leave it to Lipe,' I answered. 'I can perform miracles!' I came back with a peasant who drove on a road a distance away from the river." Lipe got his watermelons.

Lipe was simply crazy about watermelons. He once made a bet that he could eat five large watermelons at a time. He won! However, this was the end of Lipe Shprintsyak, as he died—supposedly from eating the five watermelons.

Froika, the carpenter, was our landlord. His family occupied half of the house and we rented the other half. I don't recall our family living in any other house. Our two families shared hideouts during the days of the pogroms. We often exchanged food. Some winter evenings Mama would take my youngest sister and me, and we would make our way in the darkness to get to the other half of the house. There, Esther-Leye, the wife of the house, would spend the evening relating all kinds of gruesome horror stories about devils and people returning from the dead. Her two attractive daughters, Lifshe and Sosie, often helped by contributing additional, graphic details.

I always looked forward to the annual eight-day holiday called Succoth.[5] Our part of the house had a succa which Froika, the carpenter, had built in our half of the house. We

---

[5] The seven-day Festival of the Booths is held in the fall to celebrate and give thanks for a bountiful harvest. It is traditionally held in a special, outdoor arbor which can be decorated with fruits of the harvest.

pulled a string and a panel in the ceiling, painted many colors, opened up and we ate under the sky. Because of this error in his judgment, each Succoth Froika had to come and ask permission to use our dining room. Froika had his buxom wife, Esther-Leye, bring in all the delicious dishes of food so he could eat in our dining room during the week of Succoth. When Froika ate, no one dared to interrupt him, not even his wife. Esther-Leye was a wonderful cook and my eyes were green with envy watching him eat during those holidays. We were not invited to share.

Froika was not considered a learned man, but was very religious, observing everything in great detail. He was a carpenter by trade and specialized in making funeral caskets. When a peasant from a nearby village had a death in his family, he would go to Froika for a casket. Caskets were stacked up very high outside his house.

Froika was also a man of few words. But when he did utter something, his wife and two daughters immediately jumped to attention and with fear carried out his request. He once sat outside smoking a homemade cigarette when a hoodlum on horseback, gun in hand, approached and ordered him to move. Froika said, "Who are you, ordering me to move? I am older than you."

"I'll shoot you if you don't move," said the Pogromchik (hoodlum).

"Go ahead shoot!" said Froika, and the Pogromchik left. Froika had a younger brother, Moishe the Shoemaker. He was friendly, kind, and talkative, and he disappeared without a trace. Such were the days.

Our neighbor Yosele the "Weasel," was a short man, about five-foot two inches, with a small red beard, many children and a huge wife who served as the breadwinner for the large household. Yosele considered himself a man of wisdom and spent his time arguing with God about why he was poor and others were rich.

* * *

She was called "Surke the Whore." Surke returned home after an absence of several months and a rumor spread through town that she was pregnant. One morning, as she stepped outside her house, a mob of people—old, young, men, women—was waiting for her. Surke, full of fear, began to run and cry The mob ran after her throwing stones and other objects at her and yelling, "Whore! Whore!" She ran to the bank of the river, apparently looking for a place to hide. As the mob reached her she fell completely exhausted and in hysterics. Some of them grabbed Surke and vanished with her. No one knew, or at least admitted, what happened to "Surke the Whore."

"Leibush the Cantor" was tall with a small beard, neatly and attractively dressed, and wore a pince-nez (which at that time was a sign of wealth and intelligence). He was always ready with an anecdote and a smile. Leibush had a magnetic personality and his voice had such warmth that it made people admire him. He was not a singer, but on the days when he prayed before the congregation, everybody sat and listened with pleasant expressions on their faces, especially the women. They loved him and he loved them in turn...he was quite a flirt with the women.

There are cantors who sing and then prayer men who just chant established traditional tunes. Leibush was a prayer man and people would rather listen to him than to a cantor. Leibush had a general store that his wife, Tsine, tended like a slave at all hours of the day. He traveled a lot and no one knew where he got the money for his travels or his gallant attire. People always looked forward to Leibush's return from one of his trips, because he livened up the town with his personality.

* * *

What was outstanding about Tevye were his natural pink cheeks. He could never grow a beard—just a few hairs where a beard was supposed to be. Wearing a long light caftan every morning, without fail, he walked swiftly to the synagogue carrying a prayer shawl and phylacteries under his arm. Poor Tevye, he just had no luck with his wives. They became sick a year or two after the wedding and died. It must have been funeral number five that I remember. Tevye was standing outside as a group of women were preparing his fifth wife for burial. People were waiting to take the corpse to the cemetery. Everyone was morose and Tevye, with his usual pink cheeks and a light smile on his face, strolled back and forth saying *"A welt mit weltelech,"*—"A world with little worlds."

Shifre, a middle-aged woman from a comparatively well-to-do home, became sick and died. However, her immediate family insisted that she was not dead. Sinyava's citizens gathered outside, some even managed to get into the house, all expressing amazement that here lay a dead woman who was actually alive. She was just sound asleep. It took a week to ten days before the family was finally convinced that Shifre was actually dead and allowed her to be buried.

Then there was Mute Motel—his mother was the widow of a cantor. Her younger son, Nisele, was the apple of her eye. He was charming and a good student, but more than anything else, he possessed a beautiful singing voice. When Nisele sang on the High Holidays, there wasn't a dry eye among the women in the sanctuary and at times even a man wiped a tear. Motel the older son, was tall, strong, and a water carrier. He couldn't talk. If Motel became angry at someone, that person would be lucky to survive the encounter. When upset, Motel pounded with his feet and the angry sounds which came out of his throat could be heard all over town. People were afraid to come close to him and the only one who could calm him was his poor mother.

* * *

It was before the Revolution that a group of the younger generation, especially the females, attracted into town a young man who liked to dance and teach dancing. Berchik was his name. He would show up in Sinyava at the different seasons of the year—generally late spring and early fall—assemble a number of young people (primarily girls), and teach them waltzes, quadrilles and the latest modes of dancing which he said were popular in the biggest cities such as Odessa or Kiev. A good time was had by all. When Berchik left town, it wasn't long before people began to look forward to his next visit, when he would again introduce them to new dances.

Weddings, too, were important events in town. Naturally, if the bride was from Sinyava, the wedding was held there. The parents of the groom and bride arrived at terms about the dowry and the various stipulations associated with the marriage, such as the length of time the groom could live in the bride's home and so forth. The prospective groom was granted the right to live in the bride's parents' home for a specific period of time. This allowed the groom enough time to become established in his work and financially able to provide his wife a home of their own. In reality, if the groom became a favorite of the family, they might live with her family indefinitely. It took months to make the bride's wedding gown. Much time was spent baking and cooking. Relatives came from great distances, and many guests from nearby towns were also invited.

In one instance, the musicians, called *Klezmer,* were already playing softly before beginning to parade around outside the house, when the fathers of the bride and groom who had been consulting in a private room finally appeared before the crowd. They announced that the wedding was canceled, because they couldn't agree on a certain clause in the dowry. The bride's mother almost fainted, and the bride wept softly as she ran out of the main room. The crowd scattered, leaving the house to avoid facing each other. Everything was anti-climactic. The *Klezmer* gathered their musical instruments and left, embarrassed, as if they were to be blamed for the fiasco.

However, within three and a half months Yanek the merchant found another young man for his lovely daughter Tamara. All the guests returned, the same wedding gown adorned the bride, the same *Klezmer* were also on hand. Once again, first playing softly and eventually more loudly as they began to lead the parade outside. All the invited guests, relatives, and bride in her long white wedding gown with a white veil over her face, marched slowly to meet the groom. Neighbors, hearing the music, came out of their houses nodding approvingly. What a wonderful accomplishment! Yanek the merchant was finally marrying off his oldest daughter! Children, and even dogs, ran after the *Klezmer* making noise, and everyone was having a good time because the town of Sinyava was having a wedding. From the crowd of well-wishers a song is heard:

> *There is great joy in town, there is a wedding,*
> *Yanek's oldest daughter is getting married.*

It was summer life.[6] People relaxed after the cold winter days. Some strolled in the small park, others swam in the river or just sat outside their houses.

One day, out of a clear blue sky, Malka, one of my sisters, decided to go to the forest to pick strawberries and asked me to go with her. Quiet reigned in the thick forest. Even the

---

[6] A Yiddish expression about the drastic difference between the winter and summer seasons. Doors and windows were kept open in the summer and life was good.

birds' chirping seemed subdued and strawberries grew all around us. It didn't take us long to fill a pail full of ripe red berries and we were ready to return home. But, as we were walking we realized that we didn't know the way out and instead we went deeper into the forest. We became frightened and began to yell, "Hey, hey. How do we get out?" Our hysteria was short lived because we approached an exit which was also close to the road leading home. We joyfully walked back carrying our pail of strawberries. Afterwards, when my sister related the story about our getting lost in the forest, the menage laughed, but all enjoyed eating the strawberries.

lost in the forest

We had one doctor in Sinyava. It was said that he was an aristocrat who had come from Poland. He limped and his office was outside of town. As I was doing my homework one evening, while holding a pencil I unconsciously put it in my ear. The pencil point broke and a piece of graphite remained in my ear. Although it was night time and a heavy rain had fallen, my mother and older sister Esther began to walk with me through the deep water to the doctor. We woke up the doctor, who finally came to the door with a heavy lamp in his hand. He was irritated at being awakened and after looking into my ear, he said, "Oh, it's there. After I put my instrument in your right ear, I'll make the piece of lead go straight into your left ear." We all laughed at his joke. Mama paid him and we resumed our "swimming" back home. It must have been about midnight.

I remember a small bedroom with two beds, one for my mother and twin sister and the other for Tate and myself. During the long cold nights, we went to sleep "at the same time as the chickens." We were wide awake by four in the morning when Tate would begin to tell his tales about America.

Tate sailed the ocean to the United States during the 1890's. He left my mother and three children in Sinyava to go to the *"Goldene Medina,"* "Golden Land" as it was then called, to make an "easy buck" and return to Sinyava a rich man. Tate had a job in the "Needle Trades." He worked twelve hours a day, six days a week in the "sweat shops," but hardly made enough to sustain himself. After four years, he returned to his family in the old country with pockets void of any gold. Yet he was nostalgic about the days he spent in America. One reason might have been that he had his mother, brothers and sisters in New York.

Lying in bed on cold early mornings he would describe those wonderful, unusual material things that people could possess in America. Things we could never find in Russia, let alone such a small place as Sinyava. We children listened to Tate and became so engrossed with his nostalgia for the New Land that a few years later, when we finally decided to leave, we were prepared and ready.

But before that day came we had to wait for the First World War to end, the Revolution to begin, and a Civil War which was accompanied by pogroms and all kinds of upheavals.

* * *

Wars and Pogroms

The Russian Revolution began in March 1917, on the tail-end of the First World War, with the overthrow of the Czarist government. The October Revolution saw the Communists firmly take control of the country. There was a period when there was no established government and chaos and terror reigned. Leaders came and went. German and Polish armies, as well as Russian factions, moved across the Ukraine, each trying to establish control of territory they claimed. Bands of hoodlums and bandits roamed the countryside preying upon Jews and Jewish settlements. Their destruction was called pogroms[7] and modeled after the first pogrom launched in Kishinev against the Jews in 1892.

It was 1917, three years after Russia had joined the First World War, and now it was gradually losing its fight with Germany. The Russian economy was at a very low ebb. Russians were dying of starvation and the armed forces lost strength from day to day. Many of the Russian people still remembered the 1905 uprising against the Czar. Much of that leadership, whether in prisons or in hiding or counting the days in Switzerland, France or England, were now ready to return to their motherland to overthrow the Czarist Government—which happened. But it was easier said than done.

Various parties and factions emerged—Bolsheviks, Mensheviks, and Nationalists—fighting each other. First it was Alexander Kerensky, a Social Democrat who established a government according to his philosophy. He was a diplomat and not a fighter, so his government was only temporary. Lenin and Trotsky arrived from Western Europe to start a Communist Regime for which they had planned and looked forward to for so long. However, their task was not an easy one. General Deniken

---

[7] A Yiddish word adopted from Russian, which means an organized massacre of helpless people, specifically a massacre of Jews.

fought the Communists from one end of the country and Petlura battled the Soviets from the other end. Petlura's goal was to separate the Ukraine from Russia in order to have its own form of government, one void of Socialism. History tells us this was not the first time the Ukraine had fought for its independence.

The Polish armies were also fighting the Russians. Chaos reigned. Some nights two battalions of the same army fought each other only a mile away from Sinyava, not realizing that they were destroying their own army instead of the enemy. Before the error was discovered many soldiers had lost their lives.

Once, a Soviet regiment was ordered to stay in Sinyava. Many of the soldiers were quartered in private homes. We had the mixed pleasure of having two officers—Ratnikov and Kachabei. The pleasure was mixed because our family was already crowded, but there was a safe feeling in having two Russian officers in the house. Ratnikov—tall and handsome, always had a smile on his face and flirted with the women; Kachabei—was short, serious and shy.

Early one morning, an alarm came that the army was to evacuate immediately. They jumped out of bed, instantly put their clothes on, and started for the door. Kachabei was somewhat slower than his partner and to this day I recall how Ratnikov yelled, "Kachabei, skorei (hurry) or I'll leave without you." Kachabei had no time to gather all of his baggage, especially one piece which was made of a fine leather material that he apparently picked up beyond the front. My mother didn't know what to do with it. She had many sleepless nights—should she use it or sell it? Then what would happen if Kachabei came back for his leather? Mama's sleepless nights were in vain. Kachabei never returned.

It was a tumultuous period. A period of uncertainty. A period of constant change. A period when one may wake up in the morning and be killed by noon. A time when, if one died a natural death his family was congratulated. An elderly man and his wife lived quietly by themselves. Upon retiring for the night they repeated to each other a quotation from the Bible, "We go to sleep in peace and shall awake in peace." Later that night two soldiers came into the little house, saw the couple asleep, drew out their swords and stuck the blades into the bodies of that elderly, beautiful couple. His name was Aaron Zohn, her name was Basia. They happened to be distant relatives on my father's side.

One day a soldier appeared at our living room door. Tate asked him what he wanted. He mumbled something and shot Tate in the forehead. As he fell on the floor, the soldier ran out of the house. Fortunately, Tate was wearing a cap and the bullet went through the cap and into the wall of the next room. After the soldier left Tate stood up like nothing had happened. During this encounter, I was hiding behind the stove and shivering from fright.

There were three brothers, eighteen, twenty, and twenty-three years old. All were tall, handsome, well-dressed, intelligent, and from a respectable local family. They were found shot to death in a ditch a few feet away from the house. They had hidden themselves in the ditch, thinking they would be safe there, but were all killed by two bandits. One can imagine how their parents felt.

The confusion, uncertainty, and killings continued. For instance, a Polish cavalry company was stationed in Sinyava. As they went out on maneuvers, people stood admiring the pretty horses. While the Polish soldiers sang songs ridiculing Jewish people, a soldier guided his huge horse out of line, pulled a sword from his scabbard, approached an elderly Jewish man, and cut off his beard as the other soldiers laughed.

Then the German army came, seizing anyone they saw, ordering them to clean streets by yelling *"Pootzen zei die gassen,*

Pootzen zei die gassen." ("Clean the streets.") Ukrainian warriors, who needed trenches for protection, would find children hidden in closets and take them to the open fields to dig trenches as the firing went on around and above them.

The First Soviet Regiment was famous for its atrocities. Its soldiers consisted of drunks, ex-prisoners, thieves and ordinary hoodlums. The government did not condone their actions, but did little to restrain them. They would get out of hand, especially when they were in retreat—robbing, looting, raping. They rode their horses wildly and waved guns in the air shouting, *"Bei Zhydov, spasai Russiya."* ("Kill the Jews, save Russia.")

As horrible as the fighting was, however, it was the pogroms during that period that plagued the Jewish population more than anything else. Small groups of "bandits" would, without any reason, come to a town, break into homes, take everything they liked and leave the houses in shambles. If the owners were not hidden in a secret place, such as camouflaged closets or basements, they were killed.

Local groups of bandits emerged during the Civil War. Each group had a leader. The leader of the group in the Sinyava region was called Schepel. We never saw him but rumor said he was young, short in stature, and he was determined to kill as many Jewish people in Sinyava as possible.

For several days Sinyava had anticipated Schepel's attack on the town. Older people decided to stay and face the consequences—but the younger ones would leave. Tate engaged a peasant from a nearby village to take my four sisters and myself by horse and wagon to a town called Ostropol where we would be safe. It was a Saturday morning when we said goodbye to our parents, not knowing if we'd ever see them again. I recall passing by our mill, which had been idle for some time. Young boys threw stones at us from the open fields. Some tried to stop us, but the driver was going fast and we lost them. Night began to fall by the time we arrived in Ostropol. It was a very hilly town and quite a climb to the houses on top of the hill. A family provided us with lodging without much trouble. There weren't enough beds and I offered to sleep on the floor—which I didn't mind.

That same evening Schepel and his gang entered Sinyava. One family managed to escape and joined us in Ostropol. We bombarded the people with questions as though they had come from a different planet. The head of the family pointed to his youngest son—a handsome and sensitive little boy (probably a future violinist if he ever grew up). "This is what happened—a patch of gray hair in about two hours time," as the father pointed to the gray hair on the little boy's head. My sisters and I were worried about our parents—were they alive or not? We finally received word from Tate that the house had been robbed but he and Mama were in a hiding place and they were alive. The town held a mass funeral for about forty people killed by the gang. During the service, bandits tried to approach the cemetery and kill some more, but they were driven away with rocks and stones.

I am not sure which army was in town that day—Ukrainian or the Polish—but they looked for people to dig trenches. Soldiers who came into our house went directly to the closet where I was hiding, took me to the trenches, gave me a shovel and said to get in and start digging. The enemy was not far away and bullets flew over my head. Naturally I was scared, and after some time, when a soldier was not near, I got out of the ditch and ran home.

We hoped the firing would stop during my Bar-Mitzvah. Alas, they didn't listen to us and Tate and I had to observe the Bar-Mitzvah in spite of the armies firing at each other. Mama was unable to bake cake for the people in the synagogue, or have anything special to eat that day. Hurriedly I put on the tfiln—phylacteries—(it was midweek).[8] I knew how, since I had watched Tate using phylacteries all these years. I then read a passage from the Torah and that was it. The few people who were there shook my hand congratulating me and we hurried home, so as not to be in a conspicuous place on the day of the battle.

Amidst all this upheaval an influenza epidemic swept the country. People died in great numbers all over Russia. I remember Aunt Rivka, my favorite aunt who earned a meager living by selling flour in a little basement. She had only one son named Grisha.[9] He must have been about twenty. He was handsome, well-read and intelligent. In those days he was considered an intellectual. Grisha was also very popular with the girls in town. It seemed they kept coming to him with questions about literature. Grisha became sick, his temperature rose rapidly while relatives and neighbors held constant watch, but, alas, Grisha expired. After his mother, gentle Rivka, watched her only son utter his last breath, Rivka went to the street, raised her hands to the sky—although short in stature she looked tall to the bystanders—and, in an inhuman voice, angrily exclaimed, "My son is dead! My son is dead!" Rivka kept repeating "My son is dead" as she walked through town announcing that her son had died, and seeming to accuse the heavens for her great loss. People watching her were overcome with sorrow.

As I recall that scene today, I compare Aunt Rivka to a heroine in a Greek tragedy.

* * *

---

[8] Phylacteries are used only during weekday worship.
[9] Hershel in Yiddish.

Shulemka and Resistance

Shulemka was probably one of the most colorful figures in town. He was not a Sinyaver, as he came from another part of the country. He looked quite impressive with a head full of bushy hair and a hoarse, but loud, voice. Shulemka considered himself a leader. He was a Bundist (the Jewish Socialist Party in the early twenties).

The Jewish people found it difficult to continue in face of the constant pogroms which had befallen Sinyava. Killings became a daily event. People were killed at random and one never knew who would be killed next.

That's where Shulemka came in. He called a meeting in the plaza of as many of the inhabitants as possible. In a highly emotional speech he urged us not to endure this situation any longer. "We must not stand by and allow the robberies and murders of innocent people any longer. If our neighbors, the farmers and peasants nearby, see what's taking place in our community and they do not protest and try to stop it, then we shouldn't be here. Let them realize how it is without us. I urge everyone to leave for Khmelnik as soon as possible." Everyone agreed. Within two days about twenty-five hundred people left—the entire Jewish population of the town, except for one woman who was sick in the little hospital and could not be moved. Some walked. Others, who could afford it, hired horses and wagons, and, taking some clothing and bread, we began the forty-mile exodus to Khmelnik. All this was due to Shulemka.

That day is still in my memory. We started the march to Khmelnik very early in the morning and didn't get there until late at night. A problem developed when we had to cross a river, but we finally made it with no difficulty, except for Shmel'ke. He was the town's madman who "philosophized." A man in his thirties with a red beard, Shmel'ke was shabbily dressed, and walked and talked to himself. He was also an epileptic. Children invariably teased him with questions. "Ei Shmel'ke, why aren't you married?"

"Well, it's this way," he answered. "The girl I would want, wouldn't want me, and the girl who would want me, I wouldn't want."

When it came to crossing the river he repeatedly chanted, "I am afraid that I'll be afraid to cross the river," until a person standing behind him pushed him in the water. Then Shmel'ke, too, crossed the river.

Upon our arrival at Khmelnik, many people, some of them relatives, were outside of town to greet us and take us to their homes.

Khmelnik was a much larger city with a railroad, bricked streets, a castle in the outskirts of town which had been built as a fortress many years ago, and a self-defense brigade with guns and ammunition. Even the women, armed with pots and pans, were ready for a counterattack.

Tate's older brother had a home in Khmelnik. We moved in with them for the duration. One afternoon an alarm was sounded that the peasants of a nearby village were marching on the city to have a "party" of robbing and killing. No sooner had they approached Khmelnik than they were met by the Self Defense League. Meeting this show of force, the villagers started to retreat. The Defense League followed them as far as their homes and torched the hamlet. It was a role reversal. Such were the times.

My father's brother was called Shmuel, or "God," because he was extremely religious. He was always studying privately in his room, and seldom spoke to anyone. When a woman faced him to ask a question, he would put a handkerchief over his eyes before replying. However, when it came to counter attacking the bandits, Shmuel "God" would grab a gun and join the Defense League.

There were periods of quiet when the population was left alone and Khmelnik residents and new-comers could catch their breath. During one of these lulls, Uncle Shmuel decided to go to a nearby village to purchase wheat for the household. As he was riding in the buggy, from out of nowhere a horseman stopped him and asked, "Are you a Jew?" Shmuel answered "Yes." The fellow shot him in his forehead and that was the end of Uncle Shmuel, "God." Such were the times.

The Great Adventure

After about three weeks in Khmelnik, we returned to Sinyava and the town gradually came back to life. Stores re-opened, people walked in the streets, children played, and my mother conceived an idea how to earn an extra rubel. She heard that Medzhibuzh, not too far from Sinyava, had an abundance of military pillowcases which could be bought at a very reasonable price. If she could only get them, she could sell them for twice the price. But how could that be accomplished? It was unlawful to conduct such transactions, to buy on the black market. Well, that's where I came in. I was sent to Medzhibuzh. My Aunt Ethel wrapped the pillowcases around me under my clothing, and put me on a wagon with about six other passengers on their way back to Sinyava.

It was on a Friday midsummer night. The moon was shining brightly. The other passengers talked very little and there was a certain tension felt during the trip. Naturally, I, too, kept quiet and was scared the authorities might stop us and start searching the travelers—that would be the end of me! Nothing happened. I arrived home almost at midnight. My family was very happy to see me, particularly Mama since it was her plan. I felt very important and was treated like a hero. Next morning my mother gave me corn on the cob which I cherished. I filled my pockets with corn and walked outside to meet my friend Shmilek and related to him the great feat I had accomplished the day before. Of course I went into great detail when describing the trip. His opinion of me doubled right on the spot.

I remember that in more subdued times I used to treasure Saturday mornings when I would drink tea with hot milk which had simmered all night and had special sweet rolls that Mama baked for the Sabbath. One such Saturday morning when I was having my tea, a fire broke out two houses away. Aunt Rivka, who came for Saturday morning tea, saw the fire was so close to the building and became concerned that it might soon reach us. In great fear she said to me, "Come sonny that fire may soon reach your house, quick!"

But I said, "Wait, let me finish the 'tai' with milk."[10] Well, my sisters teased me with my "tai and milk" for some time.

Although the nightmare of pogroms, upheavals and Civil War began to abate, Tate had lost the mill and there was little income except for occasionally making and selling a gallon of vodka. The state of the economy was critical all over Russia, so my parents decided to leave for America. We sold or gave away everything we had accumulated through the years, except for our clothes, of course. Esther, my oldest sister, was sent in advance to Galicia to contact our brother in America to send us money, if possible, for passage across the Atlantic. One clear day in the winter months of 1921, we were ready to depart by horse and wagon for a border town in Galicia. My parents said good-bye to relatives and neighbors.

I, too, wanted to have a last glance at my grandparents' large house where I had spent many happy hours. There was no one in the front of the house and I continued to walk slowly to the second section where the many barrels of honey were lined up in several rows. The lights were dim, but amidst the barrels of honey stood my cousin Ethel. Why she was there I had no

---

[10] I had a habit of pronouncing certains words with an "ai" sound.

idea. She was a year younger than me, rather pretty and smiled at me. I said, "You know we are leaving for America now," and suddenly kissed her. Ethel just stood there and smiled. I felt as I had committed a crime and hurriedly left the house to join my family to begin our long journey.

When I returned to the wagon, Tate said, "Where were you? We were about to leave without you. Get into the wagon."

My sister, Malka, who always liked to tease me said, "He looks like he had a taste of honey." I kicked her with my foot and I sat down next to Mama.

Tate was sitting next to the driver who held the reins in one hand and the whip in the other, waiting for Tate to give him the order to go. Tate looked to the left side, then to the right, and as he turned to the front he said, "Stepan, let's go!"

As we rode in the wagon, I sat there lost in thoughts about Ethel. I had a good, but strange, feeling because I kissed her—my first kiss. Ethel, I mused, used to tell me that she wanted to be a doctor when she grew up. Who knows, perhaps she'll come to America and I'll see her there, I thought. Then Mama interrupted me saying, "Have a piece of cake and stop dreaming."

Once the town was behind us Tate said, "Why are we all so glum? Why doesn't someone start a song?" Malka began a Russian song,

Prochai, Prochai!—Farewell, Farewell!
Prochai Dorogaya—Farewell, my Dear Ones
Prochai, Prochai, Prochai—Farewell, Farewell, Farewell!

ACT I

Scene 2

ON THE WAY TO COLUMBUS' MEDINA[1]

Beginning the Journey

The journey from Sinyava to the border of Galicia[2] was uneventful, except for a hoodlum running after us until he gave up, but still exciting to a thirteen-and-a-half-year old. We spent that night in a peasant's house. It was Friday afternoon on a mild, winter day when we stopped at a private home for the

---

[1] "Columbus' Medina" was a popular Yiddish song of this period. It originated in the Yiddish theatre and told how thankful we were to Columbus, and long live Columbus and his Medina (country). This was a country where we could eat white bread every day. In the old country there was seldom any white bread, even on Saturday when we celebrated the Sabbath.

[2] The country of Galicia, between the Ukraine and Poland, no longer exists.

Sabbath in a small town in Galicia named Lonywitz.³ I recall Saturday afternoon, mother all dressed up in her special Sabbath dress, sitting near a window, reading pages from the Bible, I assume pertaining to the Sabbath. Stillness reigned over the house to the point of boredom.

It felt good when Sunday came and we took off for Zbarazh, a good-sized city. (Every place seemed larger to me than Sinyava!) I was impressed by all the action; people walked briskly, like they were on their way to an important meeting.

Then came Monday—a very eventful day in my father's life. Tate took me by the hand and said, "Let's go son." We entered a clothing store and within a short time he came out a different man. His long black caftan, cap, and boots were replaced with a three-piece brown suit, shirt, shoes, and derby. Tate, indeed, was a different man. Afterwards we went to a small restaurant. We sat at the counter and Tate ordered tea and cake for us—a first for me.

As for Tate, he had broken a centuries-old tradition by rejecting the gabardine which had been worn by Jewish men from the Middle Ages to the twentieth century.

The big scene, however, came when father appeared before Mama in his new finery. She almost fainted and then tears and more tears poured forth as Tate sat smiling. Finally he said laughingly, "Don't forget, we are going to America." It took all

---

³ To the best of my recollection, this is the correct spelling of that small town's name.

of us a little time before we got used to our new "father." But not so with mother. Mama seemed skeptical and questioned the entire move—to leave the town where she was born and raised, to go to a new world thousands of miles away, to say nothing of crossing a turbulent ocean!

Tarnopol, our next stop, looked even larger than Zbarazh. It was towards evening, street lamps were lit, with sidewalks full of people; but what impressed me most were boys about my age running with bundles of newspapers yelling "extra, extra," calling out some sensational event of the day, enticing people to buy the newspapers. I found it very exciting. Little did I know that I would be involved in a similar occupation within a year or so.

Zlochev

We finally arrived at Zlochev, where we were to spend approximately six months waiting to hear from my brother in New York. Would there be enough funds to make the trip to the new land? America—called by emigrants "Columbus's Medina."

Zlochev proved to be a pleasant place to spend the spring and summer months. The clean streets, the park, the musical concerts and other activities made days and nights interesting. The place which we finally found to stay added much to our enjoyment. We shared the house with another family from Sinyava. Subsequently, several single people joined us, all awaiting their opportunity to leave for the United States. Within a short time our house became a center for emigrants.

It was like a small colony with two families occupying a large part of the house; our family of seven and the other of three, in addition to the few other individuals.

Oizer, the head of the smaller family, had owned an apothecary in Sinyava. He was short, with a small beard. Constantly keeping it smooth kept him busy. He talked softly, was well-versed in current affairs, and gave the impression of a dislocated man in search of a new home. His voluptuous blonde wife, Mindel, busied herself by carrying out household chores, but she was always sad, giving us the feeling that she was still mourning for her little boy, who had died not long before of pneumonia during the epidemic. Whenever I saw her, I was reminded of her little boy's funeral. Their daughter, Sima, about twenty, blonde, beautiful, and appealing was the female attraction of the colony. Every young man who stopped there for a week or longer was drawn to her. Sima, well aware of that attraction, loved it. Even I, who was so much younger than all the other fellows, followed her around like a puppy.

Two young men from this period who especially remain in my memory are Pinye and Reuben. Pinye, tallish, in his mid-twenties with a round face, did not speak much. When he did speak it was very slow and gave the impression that he deliberated upon every word before pronouncing it. He was interested in social issues. When he sat at a table with other people, he had a habit of rolling a tiny piece of bread between his fingers as he weighed his opinion about a problem. When Pinye did talk, he blushed, apparently because he was shy. Pinye loved to play chess, then he had an excuse not to talk. It was apparent that Sima had a crush on him, but Pinye did not show any interest in her. If Pinye had been religious he would have been a mystic. People invented stories about him. A year or two after Pinye had departed for the United States, we heard he had committed suicide. No one knew the reason.

Reuben was the opposite of Pinye—tall, dark, handsome, cheerful and an incessant talker. He filled the room with his presence. Reuben was an extrovert. When a theatre company visited Zlochev with one of its plays, he analyzed the stage production for days afterwards. Reuben wanted Sima to pay attention to him and, regardless of how hard he tried to impress her, she remained indifferent to him.

Generally, the little colony of emigrants in the Zlochev house had an abundance of activities to keep them busy. Singing, storytelling, anecdotes, and gossip made the long stay quite bearable. Also, strolling in the park, sitting on benches, and listening in the early evenings to programs of classical music were satisfaction for the "soul." Yet there was a restlessness and a sense of anticipation as everyone looked forward to the day when they would continue their journey to America. Every day we hoped the postman, with the long black mustache and cheerful voice in his blue governmental uniform, would bring us good news from our relatives in the United States. That momentous day finally arrived. We heard the postman's whistle, and calling our name, he announced a registered letter for us. It was from my brother in New York, informing us that he finally had accumulated enough cash to send us for our tickets to America.

Warsaw

Now we bade farewell to the friends we had made in Zlochev and proceeded on the next leg of our anticipated voyage, this time by train to Warsaw. It was my first experience riding on a train. Naturally I found it most exciting and wanted it to last as long as possible.

> *Warsaw the city of many colors*
> *Warsaw for you I am ready to die.*

This song we heard sung in theatres in Warsaw and later in New York. Warsaw stores displayed the latest styles in women's clothing, gold and diamonds glittered in the shining windows, wide avenues, street cars—everything was overwhelming.

Warsaw now became our residence while we waited until we could continue on our journey. As it turned out the wait was much longer than anticipated. Quotas to the "New Land" were limited, and for those with large families, it was especially difficult to obtain a visa. The word "visa" became very popular those days, with many people complaining, "Ah, Uncle Sam just doesn't want us." My father made numerous trips to the American Consulate, standing in a mile-long line, waiting, waiting, and nothing happened.

During this period I met a boy my age who was also from Sinyava, although I hardly knew him there. We even shared the identical first name. In Warsaw we became close buddies. Our mothers bought us new clothes—after all we couldn't arrive in America looking like *shleppers*. One day my friend and I decided to buy walking canes. It was the style in those days for even young boys like us to walk with canes.

Tate visited the consulate every day. Perhaps a miracle would occur and we would be issued visas. One day the consul became intrigued by the idea that there were twins in our family and he asked my father to bring the twins for him to see. Father immediately fulfilled his request. Later the consul advised Tate that our family was too large for everyone to get visas. Therefore, my two older sisters separated from our family and went to Canada. Eventually, they joined us in New York.

We were now a family of five and, once we were issued visas and left for Berlin, our journey to America began in earnest. In Berlin we were directed by an Immigration Aid Society to a big barn called "auditorium" where we spent the night. There were literally a thousand people lying on the floor. We finally found some limited space to rest the few remaining hours. We certainly were relieved to board a train the next morning for Antwerp, Belgium, there to wait for a ship to cross the Atlantic to New York.

* * *

Across the Ocean

Our funds were limited so Tate had to do a lot of running around to select a ship. The Cunard Line was the most desirable. However, for financial reasons, he had to choose the Red Star Line which had four steamers criss-crossing the Atlantic. It was our lot to get tickets for a ship called *Finland*.

Antwerp was a nice quiet city, but we didn't know anyone there and we were bored and ready when the day arrived for us to board the ship.

The five of us were assigned to a small cabin on the lower deck of the boat close to the boiler room. The white tablecloths at our first evening meal were a nice touch, although the food left something to be desired—just plain delicatessen. One of my sisters became seasick and spent most of the time in the cabin watching rats parade above her on the water pipes. The rest of us spent much of the time on deck, weather permitting. We sailed during the month of December when ocean waves, like moving mountains, were at their wildest and most turbulent. I was reminded of a Russian proverb: "Those who have not sailed the ocean, don't know what fear is." Since passengers were unable to stroll on the decks very often, many spent their time in the cabins, looking forward to the waves subsiding. There were even rumors that the *Finland* was old and damaged and could sink before the trip was completed.

Even in the most critical situations a bit of humor was heard. For instance, one Sunday afternoon, as many of the seasick passengers were stretched out on the deck, the ship's staff saw fit to distribute oranges to the children. One little boy asked, "Mama are we going to get oranges every Sunday." Sometimes it seemed we would never see land again.

After fifteen or sixteen days the voyage neared an end. For some reason, this ship, heading for New York, touched first on Canadian shores. Another rumor, running rampant towards the end of the voyage was, "that this was the *Finland's* last voyage." Finally, early one morning we began to see the lights of New York City. A spontaneous "hurrah" came from many. Dressed in my best suit, with my shoes shined to the hilt, I stood on the deck and watched the ship approaching slowly, but surely, to the pier. This maneuver took longer than one would have expected.

Ellis Island

Columbus' Medina

Upon debarking, we first had to go through customs on Ellis Island (called Castle Garden in an earlier day). Through the years tears have been shed by many who, for one reason or another (primarily health), were denied entrance into the country and were compelled to return to their former homeland.

Finally, my turn came to go through the interrogation. I was always a little pushy, and in my anxiety I found myself in line well ahead of the rest of my family. A man in charge asked me, "How much is nine plus five?"

My answer was swift and loud: "Fourteen!" The memory retains flashes of great clarity, but although I clearly remember shouting, "Fourteen," I cannot recall if he spoke in Russian, German, Yiddish or English. I am inclined to believe it was English. All I remember clearly is answering "Fourteen!" The man replied to me in German, *"Bizt ein finer knabe"* ("You are a fine lad.") and motioned me to go on. That was it. My parents and sisters were still in line.

Those who had completed customs were led to a huge hall where we remained until everyone from the *Finland* was inspected. We were not allowed to meet our relatives, who were outside, anxiously waiting to see us until all had been cleared. Inside the huge room we were treated to our first American "snack"—soft white bread with American cheese and bitter coffee with a little canned milk on top. Not being used to this type of food or coffee, I soon discarded it. My parents and sisters eventually joined me and we were elated that we all had "made it."

As we waited in the hall we glimpsed my brother through the large windows. I recognized him from the photographs he had sent us. He was tall, dark, unshaven (a habit in our family), wearing a stylish, tightly fitted overcoat, and pacing back and forth. After a long wait we were actually led out from Ellis Island across the river to the city of Manhattan. It took all of us a short while before we were able to relax in brother Jack's company; then we began to exchange questions and answers. A dozen years had elapsed since we had seen each other.

Our baggage consisted of a few small, straw suitcases. Jack led us to the Second Avenue elevated train to go to Attorney and Broome Streets (on the lower East Side) where my uncle's home was located.

It was a late afternoon in January, but not at all cold for that time of year. Whether it was the lateness of the day or the clouds, it was dreary and approaching darkness as we climbed the many stairs to the elevated railroad which would take us to the Broome Street Station. The train was not crowded yet and we all found seats. The trip did not take long. Soon the conductor announced our station and we got off.

Life on the Lower East Side

Tate's brother, whose house we were approaching, owned a delicatessen-butcher shop on the corner of Broome and Attorney Streets. Gossip said that Uncle became quite wealthy from that business. Yet he resided with his large family on Attorney Street, one of the dirtiest streets on the lower East Side. Later, though, he moved to a better section in that area.

Attorney Street was the subject for many anecdotes in the contemporary Yiddish theatre. A play called, *Poor Man Where Are You Crawling?* (*Kabtsen Vee Krikhstee*) about Attorney Street, and featuring the noted comedian Ludwig Satz, was quite popular during that period.

Back to Uncle—he was a loud talking man with a long gray beard and *peyess* (side curls) hanging down on each cheek. His children were very much afraid of him. If one of them disobeyed him, he gave him a beating to remember.

When we reached the house on Attorney Street, my two sisters, Feige (Fanny) and Malka (Molly), who had come to the States via Canada, were waiting outside to greet us. Traditionally our family did not manifest public affection towards each other, but on that day Fanny was so elated at being reunited with us that she kissed me on the cheek. I was so surprised that I nearly fell backwards. We entered the big rambling house and before long the place was full of Tate's relatives—brothers, sisters, uncles, aunts, cousins—all bombarding us with questions about the old country.

One of my father's sisters and her husband "kidnapped" me and took me to Rockway Beach to stay with them for a short period. On the subway trip to Rockway I fell asleep and dreamed that I was still on the ship. The dream was partly a reality. When I awakened and got off the train in Rockway, I saw that my aunt's house was near the ocean. "More ocean," I thought, "can't we ever get rid of it?" However, one had to behave like a gentleman when in a new land and not divulge his true feelings.

The elderly uncle began to teach me how to behave in a twentieth century American home. He gave me especially detailed lessons about the bathroom and how to flush the commode.

There were two male cousins in the family: One studying law and the other still attending high school. They immediately began to question me about Russia and the pogroms. Before long they paid me quarters to tell them stories, particularly about the Ukraine. The more gruesome the tales, the more they liked them, and the better my monetary rewards. This continued until I was taken back to the city to rejoin my family in the house my parents had rented.

Making Friends

ACT II

Scene 1

THE GOLDEN LAND

Home and School
    431 Grand Street—a top floor, and it was quite a walk up. Even the youngsters had to stop in the middle to catch their breath. It had no modern comforts whatsoever, and was still illuminated with gas instead of electricity. Gas lights were unheard of in Sinyava, but for goodness sake, this was America! It was a railroad apartment—four rooms in a row with access to succeeding rooms only through the previous room. Even so, it was grand to us.

* * *

During the first few weeks, Sinyava *"landsleit"*[1] who had lived here for years came on Sundays to pay us a visit. Mother had a bowl of apples on the table for guests. She continually pressed visitors to have an apple. She kept repeating, *"Nemt (take) an apple, nemt an apple."* My sisters reprimanded her after the guests departed. "Don't insist for people to eat the fruit if they don't care to. New York is not Sinyava," they continuously reminded Mama.

One of the first things we all did was Americanize our names. I became Harry Sohn, a name which stayed with me until after my army days, when I legally had it changed back to Hershel Zohn. Even my older brother Jacob was called Jack.

Three of my sisters easily found jobs in shops or factories, and my brother also moved in with us. On Friday evenings or Saturday afternoons many of our relatives came to pay us a visit. It seemed our kinsmen were all concerned about my future. Should I go to public school and eventually to college and, in due time, study medicine and ultimately become a doctor, or go to a Yeshiva—leading to the rabbinate; I became neither.

My Aunt Odel (Tate's sister) was a tall, slender widow with two children, and she always looked tired. She worked many hours a day for her brother who owned the delicatessen. Aunt Odel became my favorite aunt (just like Aunt Rivke in Sinyava). She took me to Public School 34 in the East Side on Broome Street to register for the semester.

The five months of school were enjoyable. I learned English, the United States Constitution, how to salute the flag, and wrote "compositions." My teacher, Miss Franklin, became interested in my development as a student. She liked my answers to questions. She must have been a humanitarian.

---

[1] Compatriot or countryman.

What's in this Book?

"What would you do if you were a doctor?"

Answer: "I would help the sick and make sure that they got well."

"What would you do if you were a policeman?"

"I would take care of the traffic and watch out that there are no accidents."

Really, one had to be a genius to answer such questions. Yet the teacher liked my answers so much that she read them to the class. In general I was a success in school, never missed a day and at the end of the semester I was promoted to 6-B. That was quite a jump for a "green" boy.

Father searched in vain for work until he finally decided to become a peddler, selling Uncle's (his brother's) deli products. Uncle must have thought, "After all, I helped him to come to this country. He should pay me back in selling my merchandise."

This did not last very long. Tate peddled with his push-cart during the cold winter months and before long he became bedridden with rheumatism.

One Friday afternoon after I came home from school I was informed there was a job for me at Chayefsky's Hat Factory. I lost no time in getting there and was told to do several errands before sunset. I was still not quite acquainted with Manhattan streets and got lost. Mama was worried. It was late and I had not returned. She urged my older brother to look for me, since he was the one who originally found the job for me. When he found me at the factory it was after sunset and that was the end of my first position.

Pushcart Entrepreneur

With public schools closed for summer months and father being seriously ill, it was up to me to take over his "business." With some help from mother, I sold sausage and salami on the busy streets of Hester and Orchard.

I cried when Mama had to wake me up in the early hours of the morning, and she cried in having to do that. Nevertheless, I dressed and ran to Uncle's delicatessen to take my little push-cart, filled with his delicious delicatessen, out onto the market streets prepared to sell. I was even provided with a sign for the small push-cart, printed in red letters "Here is being sold fresh wurst from a famous delicatessen."

The main problem in selling delicatessen on the streets of the East Side was that we didn't have a license, and it was almost impossible to obtain one. Whenever I saw a city supervisor approaching the market, I had to run with my pushcart; otherwise I would be arrested. This went on continually. I felt very uneasy not having a permit. Mama went to the supervisor's mother, begging her to influence her son to issue us a license, but to no avail.

I became friendly with an Irish policeman on duty on Hester Street. He always managed to warn me when a supervisor was approaching. I didn't know his name but I can see him vividly, red-headed, meticulously dressed in his blue uniform with silver buttons. Whenever we were not busy he would motion me to get closer to a store and would begin a conversation—what did I plan to do, would I resume school, would I look for another job instead of peddling, etc. When I replied to his questions with a "Yeah", he immediately corrected me. "Don't say 'Yeah', say 'Yes.'"

Because of our family's financial situation, I did not return to public school the next fall. New York law required one to attend school until the age of sixteen. In order to comply with the law and earn money for the family, I continued to work the pushcart through the fall and winter and was supposed to attend trade school classes in the afternoon and night school in the evening. Most of the time I was either too tired to attend school or fell asleep in class.

A Windy Day on Hester Street

The sign on the pushcart was very lightweight and the bitter winter winds had a good time with it and made it difficult for even a fifteen-year-old to handle. The pushcart was the smallest on the block. A glass case mounted on it contained the juicy wurst rings and salami. Financially this "business" did not do too badly. Mother would relieve me occasionally; otherwise I was by myself. One rainy, windy day the pushcart took off by itself and the nasty wind pulled it a few blocks downhill, west towards the river, while I ran after it trying to catch it. Mother ran after me, which made us seem like characters in a Russian fable.

The Bronx, during that period, was considered a well-to-do residential section. Very often women from the Bronx, dressed in expensive fur coats, came shopping downtown and, noticing a young boy at the pushcart, felt obliged to do a good deed by helping me make a sale. As they walked away from the pushcart they would say to each other, "Poor boy, we should buy from him more often."

There were all kinds of characters among the peddlers on Hester Street. One we called Motie. He was huge, in height as well as in width. He walked like a bear. His steps were slow and left an impression on the ground. When he picked up a fruit or a vegetable, the customer was reluctant to take it from him. His voice carried throughout the block. His pushcart was big and rickety. It seemed like an old wagon bought from a peasant. Always dressed in his worn-out pants, big old shoes, and torn shirt, his day started with the pushcart loaded with oranges, apples, pears, and bananas. Motie would yell "Buy! Buy! Buy women! A bargain! Fresh fruit, women!" He could be heard all over the place, as he was yelling "Buy! Buy!," even if he had only one or two bananas left. I wanted to talk to him once, but he wouldn't listen to me. He was busy yelling—"Cheap, Cheap, Cheap! Women, buy, buy, buy!" It was all in a rhythm which was an integral part of him. It wouldn't surprise me if the popular song from those days, "Yes We Have No Bananas, We Have No Bananas Today," was tailored after him.

Father's illness became severe. Every attempt to alleviate his pain failed, and instead of better he became worse. He was eventually admitted to Montifiore Hospital. Thereafter, everyone in the family visited Tate on weekends.

I wasn't content with either the trade or the night school. That was not the school's fault, since I had to rise early in the morning to care for my pushcart. I finally dropped public school and registered at Eron Preparatory School. The classes were crowded. All the students were older, and had full-time jobs during regular hours. They attended night school to prepare themselves for college and advanced studies, to eventually become physicians, attorneys, or accountants.

As for me, I didn't know what I wanted—I was confused. However, I became an avid reader—the novel, poetry, history, philosophy, and drama. I spent most of my free time in the library and when the library closed, I borrowed books and locked myself in a tiny room at home during hot summer evenings so as to be able to read one book after another without interruption. This led me to join the Jewish Teacher's Seminary where some of the outstanding writers and thinkers of the day lectured and offered courses in literature, psychology, Bible criticism, philosophy, history, and so forth. It was a prestigious school, with Albert Einstein as one of its board members. I found the courses interesting and exciting.

As for work, I gave up peddling with a pushcart and went in search of another job. Every morning one could see groups of boys walking on West Broadway, then to Seventh Avenue, and from Twenty-third to Forty-second Streets, eager to see if there were any signs out announcing "Boy Wanted." Sometimes one would get an errand boy job, or general work in a factory for a week or even longer. Salary was at a minimum, seven to eight dollars a week. Tate was still seriously sick in the hospital. My sisters worked when there was work.

* * *

We moved away from Grand Street. It turned out that the place was not only without any conveniences, but there were also rumors that one floor had a "house of ill repute."

We finally found a home at 203 Madison Street which was more or less livable. It was on the first floor, with a bathtub in the middle of a room and a coal stove in the kitchen. We still had to share a lavatory with another tenant, but nevertheless, it was better than before.

Jeweler's Apprentice

After constant searching and deliberations I found a place to learn a trade. The idea was, first acquire a trade where you can earn a living and then, go to school in the evening where you can gradually learn a profession.

My trade was in the jewelry business—as a chain maker. Actually, I wanted to be a diamond setter, but it was difficult to get an apprenticeship in that trade. Therefore, I had to settle on chain-making—platinum, 18, 14, 10-karat gold chains, particularly watch chains. It was a slow process to learn any trade. One first served as an errand boy or assistant while, at the same time, learning the trade.

The place where I began my jewelry work was owned by Mandel and Rabinowitz, located in the Wall Street district. Mandel came from Romania. He was plump, talkative, had dark curly hair, and his philosophy was to eat, drink, and be merry. He just loved to command me. "Harry do this, or that. Harry get me a corned beef sandwich with a lot of mustard and plenty of sour pickles." Once it was, "Take this package of candy and bottle of wine to a lady on East Sixty-seventh Street." An attractive lady answered the doorbell. She was extremely appreciative of my bringing her the package and invited me to sit down and have tea and cake with her. I excused myself and said, "I must go. I have a lot of work to do."

The other partner, Rabinowitz, hailed from England and came to work every morning carrying *The Morning Call*, a socialist newspaper. He looked pale and sad most of the time. It was also my responsibility to answer the telephone and doorbell. One day when I answered the door bell, two young, blonde girls were standing in the doorway. They were giggling and trying to make conversation with me until Mandel came over and said to them, "Nothing today." As they left he mumbled, "They were soliciting."

Another time when the door bell rang, a middle aged man with pince-nez and a small beard said he was a fund raiser for a certain cause. As I looked at him I thought it was Mendel Beilis whose picture had appeared earlier in the press in connection with the publicity surrounding a sensational trial which took place in Kiev. Beilis was falsely accused of killing a Christian boy in order to use his blood for matzoth during Passover.[2] The trial created quite a sensation in Russia and Beilis was finally acquitted. Because of all he had suffered from the false accusations and the trial, he was considered a martyr. A song, which I partly remember to this day, was composed about him and how he suffered in prison. Tears were shed by anyone hearing that song. People discussed the trial for years afterwards. To this day I believe it was Beilis in the jewelry shop then.[3]

Two of my co-workers in that jewelry factory were Sorkin and Edelman. Sorkin was a hard worker. He had to labor fast, said he, there was a large family to support. But he still found

---

[2] This theme has been used throughout the ages. Chaucer (1340-1400) used it as the subject of one of his poems.

[3] Bernard Malamud wrote *The Fixer* which described the "Beilis Trial." It was also made into a movie, although both the movie and book deviated from the actual events.

time to tease me. "Hey Mockie,[4] you like this country?" He would repeat this question every day. Of course he wanted to get a rise out of me but he didn't succeed. Edelman was a slender young man, elegantly dressed, and did the most delicate work in the shop, mostly in platinum. He was quite interested in sports, prize fights primarily. The day of a fight he would quit early, in order to arrive in ample time. Afterwards, he would talk about the fight for days.

I gradually learned the trade and later obtained a job in a jewelry shop on Eldridge and Canal Streets on the East Side. The owner had most of his family working there—daughter and sister in the office, his brother (a foreman), two cousins, a young son and his old father. Only an elderly man as the polisher and I were not members of the family. The owner would constantly tell me, "Harry, you shouldn't do this work, you must go to school and become a lawyer." I was seated next to his young son who had a habit of hitting me in my left rib with the pliers he held. I was forced to complain to the foreman (his uncle) who said, "Oh that idiot," and he moved me to another seat. One of the workers was a cousin, nicknamed Berile because he was short. His favorite subject was the British Labor Party. Berile was bright and directed his conversation to his neighbor, Pinye, who listened, nodded, and smiled. Sometimes Morris, the foreman, started a folk song and most of the others chimed in.

The jewelry shop building also contained various offices. In addition to something else.... One day when I came down in the elevator, the man operating it rather furtively said to me, "Would you like to have a good time?"

"What do you mean?" I asked.

"Com' on, go home," he said angrily.

---

[4] Greenhorn or a derivative of Max and applied to new immigrants.

I ultimately moved across the street to the Liberty Gold Chain Company. The boss was politically liberal, rather short, had a huge wife, and two grown children who all came to the office to sit quietly and, from a distance, watch us work. Most of the people employed came and went whenever there was work. We were hired by the hour. I made twenty-two dollars for a forty-four hour week, five and a half days. When the Great Depression came, jewelry, especially chains, was the first commodity to decline and go out of style. Yet, even with the market slump, I stayed with the firm for several years. Whenever there was no jewelry work, I busied myself at newsstands for the city subway system. But through it all, my main interest was the theatre. Many times I sneaked away from my job and ran to rehearse or audition for a part.

Adventures Into the Unknown

Finally, when I was about eighteen, I thought it was time to venture out from the city. This was considered very "daring" in the early days. I made a journey to Buffalo by train and then to Niagara Falls—all by myself. Dressing in a rubber hat and coat and going down to the Falls was fascinating! The beauty of the water and constant noise of the Falls were like music to my ears. Of course I wasn't the only one praising the Falls. There were many tourists that day, all marveling at it. I recall after I was through with the Falls (if one could ever be through with them), I found a little hilly green spot where I sat down and wrote a poem about nature—how beautiful it can be and how fortunate man is here to enjoy it. I came home to tell my mother and sisters about my "experience." I felt like a hero.

The Catskill Mountain region was a popular vacation spot for many New Yorkers and continues to be so to this day. One hot summer a close friend and I decided to have a vacation. An acquaintance suggested a small hotel in the Catskills. Soon after we arrived, members of the family who owned the hotel—sons and daughters—undertook to show us around without our asking them. "Do you see the beauty of that mountain? And how about the lake so clear, only a few yards away. And the rooms—aren't they gorgeous?"

Suppertime was a repetition of the same routine. "Isn't the food terrific? The chicken you are eating has just been killed especially for you." When we went for a walk in the evening, a staff member immediately appeared to accompany us. "Look at that moon and the stars, aren't they beautiful? They wouldn't shine like that at any other summer resort." The guests consisted primarily of mothers with young babies and during the night it was a chorus of babies crying.

The next morning we decided to leave after breakfast. The rate quoted to us upon arrival was eighteen dollars a week. We, therefore, thought three to four dollars for one day should be sufficient. We gave the owner of the "hotel" a ten dollar bill and asked for change. He made an obscene gesture and said, "This I will give you." An actual fight started. The owner's wife and daughter were screaming. He threw us down the few steps, first my friend, then me, and we rolled down to the sidewalk. Suddenly, out of a clear sky, a policeman appeared who seemed to be friendly with the hotel management. He took only us to jail in the police wagon, there to await trial. Since it was in the country, the court and jail were in the same room. After a long wait the judge finally arrived and listened to our complaints. Naturally we were strangers, and the hotel keeper and judge looked like buddies, so he reprimanded us and called us lawbreakers. He said we had no right to come to such a beautiful place and act like gangsters! We lost the case and had to pay a fine, in addition to the extra money to the hotel.

Once free, we were tired, thirsty, hungry, and angry and carried our luggage as we walked to the nearest lake. There we waited for a ferry to take us across the lake to board a train for a summer camp. When we arrived at the camp and related our day's experience to an administrator, he took us to the dining room and told the crowd of the "treatment" we had received in a hotel in the Catskills. In his speech he said we were the victims of the capitalist system. The crowd first booed and then applauded us when they were told that we would spend our vacation there. We had a good meal, were given a nice tent to sleep in, and the next day, and for the rest of our stay, we were treated like martyrs and also as good friends. I even participated in a program on Saturday night. In general, we had a great time in every way and regretted having to depart for the big city. The moral of the story—one shouldn't go to places where he doesn't belong.

Back in New York I related this incident to friends, one of them a prominent writer. After listening to this tale, he said he was going to use this material for a short story. Whether he ever wrote it, I don't know.

Bitten by the Theatre

Once I went to a Second Avenue theatre and saw an operetta, *The Golden Bride*. I couldn't get it out of my mind. This exciting experience sent me to see another play and then another. On weekends I would absorb no fewer than five different plays: Friday evening, Saturday and Sunday matinees, and evenings. I didn't discriminate at first—musicals, melodramas, comedies, serious drama. I even went to the Metropolitan Opera House to see Feodor Chaliapin in *Faust*. On another day, I saw the famous dancer Anna Pavlova. These were standing room only tickets, all I could afford.

Summer, when the established theatres were dark, I spent Sunday afternoons from one in the afternoon to eleven in the evening watching vaudeville shows which featured different stars. I even brought sandwiches to share with the musicians who played between the acts. I knew I had the "bug." I couldn't live without it. After performances I would stand near the back stage door, hoping to catch a glimpse of the actors as they came out from the dressing rooms. I even dared to stop one of the stars to ask him how I could get over my strong desire to become an actor, since it was so difficult to get into the profession. His answer was brief and succinct. "Could a drunkard stop drinking?"

During the twenties and thirties there were about twelve professional theatres performing in Yiddish operating in New York.

Maurice Schwartz, director of the Yiddish Art Theatre, was the most energetic and imaginative man in the theatre. His theatre lasted from about 1920 to 1950. It was one of the most prestigious cultural institutions of the period. Never, in my wildest dreams, had I ever expected to be on the stage of his theatre.

My opportunity came when I learned that an important event would occur at Schwartz's theatre. A special presentation of *Kiddish Hashem* (*Martyrdom*), a drama by Sholem Asch, would be revived in the author's honor. I had seen the play earlier and knew there were many characters. I accumulated all the nerve possible and approached the stage manager, inquiring if I could take part in the play. Before long I was wearing a beard and an eighteenth century costume with a long prayer shawl over me. The lighting was dim. It was a scene with many people on stage and I had to pray, cry, and beg for my life to be spared. I heard someone whispering to me "*Halt zich, Halt zich, yinger-man.*" "Very good young man, very good, keep it up, keep it up." I looked to see who it was saying such encouraging words to me, and it happened to be none other than Maurice Schwartz himself! (Once, at a meeting with young actors, he pointed me out as "a young Paul Muni.")[5]

---

[5] Paul Muni (1897-1967) began his career on the Yiddish stage as Muni Weisenfreund. When he was "kidnapped" by Broadway, he changed his name to Paul Muni and, ultimately, became one of the shining stars in Hollywood.

For the next six to eight years I was involved in various Yiddish Art Theatre productions, as well as being associated with other theatre groups. I auditioned for Eva Le Gallienne's Civic Repertory Theatre. In addition to the theatre, Le Gallienne had a studio for young people who might eventually join the main company. It was the only theatre in New York doing primarily Ibsen and Chekhov. Le Gallienne suggested I prepare a scene from *The Cherry Orchard* and *Hamlet*. Before the audition I asked for an interview. At the interview she mentioned Jacob Ben-Ami's name. "A certain resemblance," she said. (It so happened Ben-Ami was my idol.) At the audition I presented Hamlet's speech to the Players, and a scene between Trofimov and friends in the second act of *The Cherry Orchard*, which I can still recall.

> TROFIMOV: *We had a long conversation yesterday, but we came to no conclusion. Pride, in your sense of it, there is something mystical. Perhaps you are right from your point of view, but if one looks at it simply, without subtlety, what sort of pride can there be, what sense is there in it, if man in his physiological formation is very imperfect, if in the immense of cases he is coarse, dull-witted, profoundly unhappy? One must give up glorification of self. One should work, and nothing else.*
> GAEV: *One must die in any case.*
> TROFIMOV: *Who knows? Any what does it mean dying?*

She was pleased with my audition and wanted me to join her group, but I had to reject her apprentice program because it paid only in experience. I told her, "I had to eat."

* * *

With the passage of time, my attitude toward the stage also matured. It wasn't the glory or even the infrequent money; it was a means of expressing oneself, as in the other fine arts—writing, music, painting. Various theatre masters have developed different methods by which the actor can prepare himself for his life's work. Konstandin Stanislavski (1863-1938), head of the Moscow Art Theatre during the early years of the twentieth century, advocated "method acting." An actor must learn how to live and feel the character to be portrayed.

I joined the Vardi-Yoalit Theatre Studio to study the Stanislavski-Vakhtangov acting technique. We were a group of aspiring young actors working by day and learning the theatre profession by night. David Vardi, who had been with the prestigious Habima Theatre in Moscow, came to this country in the twenties. He was short in stature and performed excellent imitations and improvisations. After a Saturday night performance, in a room near the small auditorium, people gathered and drank tea as Vardi appeared on a small platform, put a handkerchief on his head, placed a finger near his mouth, and talked like a woman complaining about current events. He was a riot. He also appeared in a number of plays and conducted his studio using Stanislavski and Vakhtangov's[6] methods. His wife, Eva Yoalit, acted occasionally, but mostly advised her husband. In addition to training the group, Vardi also produced three plays with us.

During this time, I was a part of the *"troika."* The *troika* consisted of two friends, Malka and Velvel, and I. For a short period we were constant companions and co-actors in several Vardi productions.

---

[6] Although a disciple of Stanislavski and his realism, Eugene Vakhtangov experimented with "selective realism," or stylization. In other words, he was against having the "kitchen sink" on the stage. (See: Hershel Zohn, *The Story of the Yiddish Theatre*, for more about these men and their effect upon Yiddish theatre.)

The first piece was *The Golden Peacock*. The name of the playwright was kept a secret until the day of the first performance. We never learned the reason for this secrecy. The other two plays were Harry Sackler's *The Seer Sees His Bride* and *Mazel Tov* (Good Luck) by Sholom Aleichem. Naturally the latter was humorous and Sackler's was of a serious nature, dealing with a young man about eighteen, the descendent of great rabbis, who was coming to see his bride. Two of us rehearsed the young man's role. The Martin Beck Theatre on Broadway was rented for the first performance on a Sunday night. When it came close to the actual performance I was told that I would play the leading character later in the season. In the meantime, I was to do an improvisational role, which was not in the script, of an old man assisting the older rabbi. In his review, the foremost contemporary theatre critic expressed disappointment with the actor doing the young lead and praised the player appearing in the role of an old man. That's theatre for you. Nevertheless, I still looked forward to performing the leading character when it was my turn.

However, the Friday papers announced the Saturday performance to be the last of the season. Therefore, the *"troika"* decided not to perform that evening. An hour before curtain time we appeared before the entire cast and said because the administration had not been honest with us, we three refused to perform that night. The cast applauded our decision.

Many things can happen in the theatre, but insurrection of this nature is wrong. The very next day our collective conscience began to plague us. We had no peace. We could not eat or sleep. Within two weeks of our announcement we went to Vardi and Yoalit and asked them to forgive us. It wasn't easy. They said, "It doesn't matter, we don't blame you. We are leaving the country anyway. We are going to Palestine." That was the end of the Vardi-Yoalit Theatre Studio.

That also ended the *troika*. Our interest in the stage was mutual, but Velvel and I also loved Malka. On the other hand, if she offended one of us, the other came to his defense and vice-versa. Malka was attractive, intelligent and good company. At this time she was married to a sensitive poet who struggled to earn a living, and also was the mother of two "cherubs" as she called them. If Velvel and I noticed Malka flirting with a man, we were both jealous and attempted to teach her a lesson by ignoring her for a day. I don't remember seeing her again after the Vardi-Yoalit Theatre Studio folded, although Velvel and I continued our friendship. He was fortunate enough to obtain a good position with a newspaper. His friends benefited when he occasionally provided a free meal. Velvel was not only clever, but also generous.

"To be an artist one must suffer." I don't quite agree. But be that as it may, late one afternoon as I entered Cafe Europa without having had any nourishment that day, the smell of the food throughout the restaurant assailed me. A dizziness came over me and the next thing I knew Velvel was standing at my side with a glass of water saying, "Why didn't you tell me that you don't have money for food? Let's have supper."

I paid him back one day by being on a picket line. The staff of his newspaper went on strike. Velvel was in charge of a picket line one Saturday afternoon. Naturally, he wanted to have an impressive turnout, and I volunteered. Before long the police arrived, threw us all into a police wagon and took us to the police station where we waited for many hours before we were transferred to night court uptown.

Night court was quite an experience. Some people wanted to be arrested so they could spend a few hours in night court. It was a fascinating experience in observing humanity. The crowd was tremendous, and composed of all kinds of characters: robbers and thieves of all grades, prostitutes and pimps, drunks and vagrants. In general, individuals from society's lower depths were in the majority. But there were some who looked well-off who happened to be there for one reason or another.

Our group appeared before the judge and a lawyer, who talked on our behalf. Within a few minutes the charges were all dismissed and we left. Velvel seemed satisfied. It was very late at night when we left the courthouse.

Before long the picketed newspaper folded. Velvel lost his job. He was a good speaker and had a sense of humor. In due time he became a street corner orator and spoke in public places on behalf of the poor and downtrodden. Somehow we lost track of each other. Later I heard that he died.

Many immigrants who came to New York in the twenties first settled in the Lower East Side, but after decades of living in the same neighborhood, they looked for greener pastures—Brooklyn, the Bronx, and even outside the city altogether. We, too, left Madison Street and moved to Williamsburg, Brooklyn. It was quite a change—true luxury. This house had an actual private bathroom with shower and all. Furthermore, there was even an honest-to-goodness tree growing in the back yard—"A Tree Grows in Brooklyn!" However, we didn't live there too long. After my mother died we moved to the Bronx. Father was finally discharged from the hospital, almost cured. Three of my sisters and my brother were married (but they lived close to us), so it was only Tate, my younger sister, and myself in a small apartment. Before long I, too, left home to live in Greenwich Village.

I continued with my work in the theatre. I was engaged as a professional actor at the Bronx Art Theatre directed by Mark Schweid. There was a time when actors couldn't read or write, but Mark Schweid made up for all of them. He was a writer and well-versed in literature. He was, for many years, a member of the Yiddish Art Theatre and eventually decided to go out on his own. His first play was *Electric Chair* by Sholem Asch. When my name appeared in the dailies in connection with the Bronx Art Theatre, the "Kibitzers"[7] at Cafe Royal asked, "Who is he? Where does he come from?"

Cafe Royal on Second Avenue and Twelfth Street served the actors from the Yiddish stage as well as writers and theatre people in general. Broadway actors, producers, and their friends went slumming to Cafe Royal. It was a popular cafe in the city of New York. Numerous stories and anecdotes have been related about the cafe and its head waiter Herman. *Cafe Crown*, a play by Hy Craft about Cafe Royal, was first produced in the forties, then as a musical, and later as a Broadway play in 1988.

Second Avenue used to be the Broadway of the Yiddish speaking stage. At least four large playhouses on the avenue were constantly packed with people from all over the city. There were about eight Yiddish theatres in the other four boroughs. Broadway producers usually came to Second Avenue in search of talent and would ultimately "kidnap" a star to Broadway. Jacob Ben-Ami and Paul Muni were two Broadway stars who spent many years with the Yiddish theatre before going to the English stage.

Important figures from the literary world would come to see a Yiddish play, whether they understood the language or not. In addition to spotting an undiscovered talent, the Yiddish Art Theatre was one of the most interesting theatres in New York. The use of new methods and innovations made Yiddish theatre a mecca for those looking for something new and different. Some of the most significant plays from world drama have found a place on the Yiddish stage, generally presented in unique and original styles.

---

[7] Yiddish for meddler.

There are no more Yiddish-speaking theatres or Cafe Royals on the avenue. With their disappearance, the majority of the actors from the East Side gradually found work in the English-speaking theatre or Hollywood.

Plays that were successful in Yiddish were finally translated into English and produced on Broadway. However, *Yoshe Kalb*, which was a tremendous success on Second Avenue, failed on Broadway. The same critics who were ecstatic when they saw it in its original did not approve of its English version. *The Dybbuk*, on the other hand, which first premiered in Warsaw in 1920, has been playing in many different languages, including English, ever since. *The Dybbuk*, a mystical drama, has been performed in many translations in addition to being produced in two different films, two operas, and a ballet. *The Tenth Man* by Paddy Chayefsky, first produced in 1959 and revived in 1989, is a parody on *The Dybbuk*.

Another theatre which stands out from among smaller groups was the Artef. At first its aim was to be a theatre for the working class and to produce plays of social significance. It eventually drew attention from the English press and the New York theatre world. Its primary attraction was the production method. Benny Schneider, originally with the Habima, managed Artef according to Stanislavski and Vakhtangov's philosophies.

There were two groups in the Artef. The first one, formed at the very beginning, learned modern acting techniques, and the later group—mostly composed of experienced actors such as Jules Dassin and David Opatashu—worked mostly doing improvisations. I was a member of this group.

Artef occupied a small theatre on West Forty-Eighth Street and on Saturday afternoons after matinee performances well-known actors from the Broadway stage would come to the studio to observe our improvisation work. Occasionally the guests would express an opinion to the director.

Unfortunately, the Artef, too, had to discontinue its activities because of financial difficulties.

The Depression

The Wall Street crash in 1929 drastically affected the theatre. The Depression put millions out of work. People didn't have a dime for a loaf of bread, let alone to buy a ticket to see a play! I was lucky to get a job with the New York Subway System and ran a newsstand at various subway stations.

There was a great treat for music lovers in New York during the summer months. People flocked to Lewisohn Stadium in the evenings to listen to classical music directed by the finest conductors with the New York Symphony.

The waiting lines were long. Those waiting for tickets formed in two's. As I was standing, I became aware that on my right was a tall, very exotic-looking brunette. We chatted and complained about the big lines. Suddenly she said, "I don't have the patience to stay in line any longer," and added she was sorry not to be able to enjoy the music with me that night.

I uttered, "Perhaps another evening. Why don't I call you and we can go together if you would let me have your telephone number."

"That would be nice, here is my number," she replied and left in a hurry. I managed to get into the stadium and enjoyed Tchaikovsky's "1812 Overture" immensely. I was simply carried away by the symphony that evening. At moments I felt like marching along with the sounds of the orchestra.

I called her the very next day—no answer. The no answer continued for about a week and I began to think it was a hoax. She finally answered. We met the next day. We didn't go to the stadium. She informed me that she was a professional dancer. It turned out that she was well-known in her profession.

We went to the theatre, to restaurants, to dance rehearsals and recitals and I met her friends, all famous dancers. Soon she participated in a dance program at a Broadway theatre. One of her numbers was about a Greek goddess preparing for war. The number was well-received, yet after a performance while we were riding in a subway train, a group of young men recognized her and made unseemly remarks. I felt embarrassed and couldn't talk to her the next day. She volunteered to see a Broadway producer about getting me a part in an important play which was coming up. I asked her not to do that.

Days, weeks, and months rolled along, most of them exciting and tumultuous. I wondered if it was perhaps too much for a guy of my background; besides, there are more important things to do in life than running after a dancer.

She came from France, although she was of Russian origin. One day she announced she was returning to Paris to be with her mother. I went to the ship to say farewell and presented her with a book on Isadora Duncan.

Two or three years later I heard she was back in town. Not long after that, she was at the headquarters for unemployed actors and dancers. I was the "big shot" secretary-treasurer of our WPA workers group.

She came over with the usual, "Hello. How are you?"

I felt awkward and didn't know what to say. I blurted out, "Have you seen any plays lately?"

"Not since the last play I saw with you," she said.

"Well, well," I mumbled, as I walked away to answer the telephone. That was it.

Looking back, it is ironic, but life went on regardless. My mother was dying of cancer, I had fallen in love with a dancer, and there I was, selling newspapers, magazines, candy, and orangeade. Passengers waiting for the next train to come in demanded my attention: A man asked for an *Argosy Magazine*, a young lady wanted the latest *Love Story*. As I searched for the magazines, customers pushed me because the train could enter the station any second. As if this wasn't enough tribulation, suddenly the shelves lined up with magazines fell on my head and shoulders, and still there was a man demanding a cold drink! All the while my head was so filled with thoughts about my mother dying and at the same time thinking of the temperamental dancer, that I forgot to insert a paper cup under the dispenser and the juice went straight to the floor. The customer, disgusted with me and still thirsty, ran hurriedly into the subway car. All this was too much for me. I cried out in desperation, "God! Why do you do this to me?"

After my mother died I frequently visited the cemetery. Perhaps I had a guilty conscience, feeling that I was responsible for her early death because of the aggravation caused by my determination to become an actor. At least that was the opinion of my relatives. "Actors are like Gypsies," my mother would say. Still, I was resolved to pursue a theatrical career.

At the Yiddish Art Theatre in the 1930s, I recall a drama titled *Chains* by the talanted dramatist H. Leivick. The play took place in Siberia. We were doing a scene which depicted two soldiers having an argument. The older one yelled at the younger one (me), "You SOB." The script did not elaborate on that phrase and the scene continued.

Afterwards, my sister, who saw the play, asked, "How come you didn't reprimand that soldier when he insulted our mother?" Maybe this was why Mama felt as she did about the stage. It used the kind of "language" which her generation found difficult to tolerate.

I left the subway station job to join the cast of the triumphant production of Maurice Schwartz's *Yoshe Kalb*. This piece usually played to standing room only. The work was adapted by Schwartz from I.S. Singer's novel of the same name. Nahumtche, the principal character, is seduced by the young wife of old Rabbi Melech. Nahumtche, who is married to Rabbi Melech's daughter, is guilt-ridden and disappears to wander on the face of the earth crying out to God for help. "I beseech you at day and cannot find you, I cry to you at night and cannot hear you!" But wherever he goes, people deride him, calling him simpleton. He realizes that he must continue to wander in loneliness for the rest of his life.

In addition to the large crowds attending *Yoshe Kalb*, influential people—Albert Einstein, the German novelist Lion Feuchtwanger, Charlie Chaplin, and others—were guests at various performances. Theatre critic, Brooks Atkinson, wrote in his review in the *New York Times*, "No matter in what state the English speaking stage is in, Maurice Schwartz's theatre is full of life."[8]

I also performed in the English version of *Yoshe Kalb* when it was done on Broadway—however, as mentioned earlier, that production had a very short life.

It was in the early thirties when I was introduced to Roberta. She hailed from Geneva, upstate New York. Living here in the city with her little boy, she taught music in the public schools. She was short, yet she was like a ball of fire and so full of energy that she was ready to explode at any moment. She could play a Bach composition to an enthusiastic audience, conduct the university orchestra, publish two volumes of music, and change a tire on her little Dodge—in short, do almost anything.

I didn't completely move out from my father's house. I told him I was staying at a house downtown with a boy who made the potato salad I liked so much. I doubt if he believed me, for which I didn't blame him. In reality, I stayed on and off at Roberta's 67 Horatio Street apartment in Greenwich Village. Her younger sister, Dora, also stayed there, and other friends would come and go. 67 Horatio Street even caught the fancy of a writer who wrote a novel about that basement apartment.

---

[8] Hershel Zohn, *The Story of the Yiddish Theatre,* 1979. p. 186.

We traveled through the New England states, went on hikes, attended the theatre and concerts, and yet my stays at 67 Horatio were sporadic. I would leave for weeks to stay with my father and then return. This continued until she decided to leave for New Mexico where she had obtained a teaching position at Highlands University, Las Vegas, New Mexico. We corresponded occasionally and I learned about her work and how she and her little boy fared in the "land of enchantment."

In the summer of 1935 I obtained a different kind of position—a counselor in a children's summer camp. It was an interesting and exciting experience. A bungalow full of boys, ages eight to twelve, filled my days and some nights in taking care of them, seeing that they behaved, taking them to the dining hall and eating with them, taking them to the swimming pool, and reading them bedtime stories. And, if one disappeared, I searched for hours before finding him and bringing him back to camp. One, named Marvin, kept me very busy. On the other hand, there was Benjamin who was handsome, sensitive, considerate, gentle, and looked like a future violinist. (Wouldn't it be ironic if Marvin had become the violinist?)

I had a book of stories about the trials and tribulations of a dog called Labzik. Whenever trouble was about to erupt with the bungalow's occupants, I would bribe them by reading a story about Labzik. He was some dog. I just loved him. Due to the frequent battles in my bungalow, the other counselors created a pun on my name, calling it the "War Zone."

The counselors had a great time after the children were asleep. We met to sing songs and relate our experiences of the day to each other. The stillness of the summer night, the stars in the clear blue sky, the beautiful rich country around us, the lake, that wonderful moon at midnight, the country nearby, and the noise of the frogs gave us a feeling of fulfillment—and also an awareness that this situation would not last forever.

On weekends parents would arrive. We had entertainment of folk dancing and even theatre programs. One Saturday evening we presented scenes from Clifford Odets' *Waiting for a Lefty*—a currently popular play.

Everything must come to an end. Besides, I was getting impatient. I wanted to return to the city and get involved in something more specific.

WPA and the New York Public Library

When I returned to New York that September, three letters from the alphabet—WPA (Works Progress Administration)—were very popular among the unemployed. And there were many, many unemployed.

WPA was created by President Franklin D. Roosevelt with Harry Hopkins as its advisor. They were determined to provide work for all unemployed, including those in the Fine Arts. A Federal Theatre Project was established, along with music, dance, art, and writer's projects. Hallie Flanagan, a highly intelligent person, was in charge of the Federal Theatre. Head of Drama at Vassar College in New York State, she was well-versed in theatre, traveled widely, and sympathized with the unemployed in the theatre movement.[9]

Harry Hopkins was also very sympathetic toward the unemployed workers. It was the United States Senate and various administrators that were against the arts in the WPA programs.

To qualify for the WPA programs, one first had to be on Home Relief, which I was. I went to the WPA offices on Sixth Avenue and Eighteenth Street and had no problem reaching the man in charge.

"You want a job?"

"Yes," said I.

---

[9] Joanne Bentley, *Hallie Flanagan: A Life in the American Theatre*. New York: Alfred A. Knopf, 1988. This is a stimulating description of Hallie Flanagan's trials and tribulations with the Federal Theatre.

"Go to the Math Department of Higher Education" at such and such an address. "They'll have you teach math," and gave me a short note.

I asked no questions, but, instead of going to the Math Department, I made my way to the New York Public Library at Fifth Avenue and Forty-second Street. I asked to see the president and went directly to his office where I inquired about working in the Theatre Collection. I had always wanted to work in a place surrounded by books and records on theatre. He asked me where I was employed now and I replied that I had just been assigned to the Math Department. The president said, "It's OK. We will put through a request for them to transfer you to us and ultimately you will be with us officially."

The next morning I reported to the Theatre Collection of the New York Public Library. It was considered the most prestigious theatre library in the country. The Theatre Collection was situated in a corner of the very popular large reference room Number 305. The Theatre Collection was a library by itself. Research, employing about twenty people, was done downstairs. George Freedley, theatre historian and critic for the *Wall Street Journal*, was in charge of the collection. After interviewing me he said I would be assigned as senior research worker in charge of Russian and Yiddish theatre. My work consisted of collecting photographs, programs, records, reviews, notices, and periodicals pertaining to the Russian and Yiddish stage.

A considerable amount of information was already in the theatre library, but it needed to be classified and put in order. I also had to approach the theatres on Second Avenue for any records they might possess on the history of the Yiddish theatres.

I considered the work interesting and significant and learned much about the Russian stage. To this day, when I visit the library at Lincoln Center I check on those records compiled in the thirties.

* * *

Federal Theatre Project

Kappy and I were close friends. After Roberta left New York we rented her apartment on West Fourth Street in the Village. He, too, was on the WPA Federal Theatre project as a writer, so our interests were mutual. I also befriended Toby, a nurse, who had spent some time in Spain during the Civil War and could not easily forget its horrors. She related her gruesome war experiences to me. Our friendship lasted for some time.

After being involved with research and books for about eighteen months I was longing to become again a part of the live theatre and requested a transfer to the Federal Theatre Project. I became a member of the National Play Bureau, which was under the leadership of John Houseman. My work consisted of reading a play each day and recommending or rejecting it, and translating plays and contributing articles to a magazine, *Theatre Abroad*. I also became involved in live productions.

No sooner were theatre people hired, than the WPA administration issued pink slips firing them. Therefore, it was essential to establish an organization to take up their cause. A so-called union was organized for that purpose, which undertook to negotiate problems arising between the theatre people and the administration. There were huge demonstrations in the streets of Manhattan, especially Union Square. Arrests were made. Slogans were heard. "We can't eat pink slips. WPA must go on. Get rid of Ridder."[10] There were sit-in strikes. Delegations went to Washington. On one such trip we had a Negro actor in our group. We stopped at a luncheonette outside of Baltimore for coffee. The Negro actor was refused service. Naturally, we

---

[10] A WPA administrator.

all left and continued to Washington without coffee. In Washington we met with various senators and administrators; nothing was gained but we were heard and seen. Our visit left an impact on them.

While the commercial stage struggled for survival in the thirties, the Federal Theatre flourished. There were WPA theatres not only in New York and Los Angeles, but also in Chicago and Boston, in St. Louis and Denver, in Cleveland and San Francisco, in Philadelphia and New Orleans, and in many other cities.

WPA theatres performed not only in English, but also in Spanish and Yiddish, and probably other languages as well. There were theatres for serious drama and theatres for comedy, plus a theatre where the same play was produced in two different styles—realism and impressionism. Theatres for musicals and opera, classic theatre, theatre especially for children, puppet theatre, theatre in the parks, and theatre in tents abounded throughout the United States. People could see theatre free of charge or at a minimum price. There was even a suitcase theatre where actors carried their own costumes and props and ran from one place to another for their performances. There was scarcely a play in world drama which was not produced during those five years.[11]

At no other time in the history of the American theatre has there been such an abundance of live theatre, featuring plays of all periods and styles, as during the thirties. Yet, with a single act of Congress on June 30, 1939, the entire Federal Theatre Project was abolished.

The WPA theatre had been a bone of contention with the United States Congress since its beginning. "Why should dramatists and actors have the audacity to criticize world figures like

---

[11] Information obtained from an article written by the author and published in the *Las Cruces Sun News*, August 16, 1991.

Mussolini?" they argued. And they finally succeeded in killing the theatre.

Other countries have national theatres supported by the government, but not the United States, not even during the Depression Period.

The popular children's play *Pinocchio* was having a successful run at a WPA Broadway theatre when, on that famous but ugly Friday (the last day of June 1939), the cast was informed they would not be allowed to perform any longer. The wooden figure of Pinocchio lay in a black-draped casket as many theatre people formed a procession down Broadway, accompanying Pinocchio to his grave. It was symbolic, but also real. People wept and prophesied that there would never be such a significant theatre again.

After the Federal Theatre was liquidated I was still with WPA, wandering from one project to another—doing research at Columbia University just to kill time, then to the U.S. Geodetic Survey and sitting with a calculator measuring the distance from one village to another in the state of Wyoming.

Prelude to War

At this same time another World War was looming upon the horizon with Hitler and Mussolini raging all over Europe trying to conquer it, even if it meant first destroying it. There were very effective May First demonstrations during that period. I remember one slogan, "Hitler wants peace, piece by piece."

The thirties were also the period of the Spanish Civil War. Dictator Francisco Franco, with help from Italy and Germany, fought a war where a million people died. A great number of volunteers (unauthorized by the United States government) from this country went to fight Franco's fascist government. The talented Spanish poet and dramatist, Garcia Lorca, lost his life in that war. He was especially known for his plays, *Blood*

Wedding, *House of Bernarda Alba*, and *Yerma*. And his poetry—so much beauty, so much feeling.

It was barely twenty years since the end of the First World War and, now, another war was brewing.

It was the summer of 1940 when I took a six-week leave to visit California. For New Yorkers it was still quite adventuresome to take such a trip, and by bus!

I saw the Midwest and West, Northwest and Southwest, from Pennsylvania to Ohio, to Illinois, to Wisconsin, to the Dakotas, to Montana, to Seattle, to Oregon and then to San Francisco. There were many different experiences. Whether it was meeting people or seeing places, I generally stayed only a day in most of these locations. I watched wild animals in the fields of the Dakotas, went down into the mines in Montana, and then to the Golden Gate Bridge in San Francisco where I spent a week and was told that I had seen everything there was to see—an opinion with which I didn't exactly agree. This city was different from New York or the big cities in Europe. I have visited San Francisco numerous times since, but I still remember the impression that city left on me the very first time I was there.

While in California, I couldn't stop raving about a city between San Francisco and Los Angeles, Carmel-by-the-Sea. When I returned to New York later that summer, I realized that Carmel and Santa Fe, New Mexico were the two most beautiful towns in the United States—Santa Fe, for its architecture and mountains, and Carmel, for the background of the Pacific Ocean and the typical tall California trees. I still haven't changed my mind.

Los Angeles was quite different and yet I liked it, especially Hollywood. I settled in a room on Taft Avenue near Griffith Park, where I went every day to dream. I met a friend from New York and made new friends. I really questioned whether I should leave California where the sun always shines and warms you and the people are tall, blond, handsome, and happy, and go back to New York where it is cold, gloomy, and sad. But I felt I belonged in New York. "How could I die in California, so far away from New York?" I reasoned.

Two young men I had known in New York became quite friendly with me while I was in Los Angeles, and kept me up-to-date about the difficulties they had encountered trying to break into the movies. There was also a tall, impressive lady dressed in black, mourning for her husband killed in Spain, who occupied some of my time.

I left Los Angeles for Arizona and then traveled to Santa Fe and Las Vegas, New Mexico. There, I again saw Roberta and her friend Lini, a colorful person who had returned from Spain where she was a head nurse during the Civil War. In addition to Roberta and Lini, there were the writers and painters in Santa Fe, all people worthwhile knowing.

We visited villages and stayed in Taos—an interesting place famous for its artists.

I approached an Indian and asked if I could snap a picture of him. "Yes, of course." After I snapped the picture, he said, "Fifty cents please." Surprised, I paid. Back we went to Santa Fe and Las Vegas. After all the goodbyes, I began my trip back to the big city. Little did I know that this country of many colors would, in due time, be my home.

It had been quite a journey. There was much to absorb. And yet it was anti-climactic. I had a strange feeling in my stomach. A feeling of longing, for what, I didn't know.

Russia, England, and France in 1941 were at the peak of their struggle against the Nazis. Draft boards were busy registering American young men, just as I received a call for a part in a Broadway production which was to go into rehearsal. The play, called *Showdown*, portrayed the Russian people

The Golden Land

helping the Red Army beyond the front with everything necessary to fight the Nazis. The character I portrayed was Gurewitch, a tailor. He was a sympathetic man and even had a song about digging the trenches at night. There were favorable reviews and a very good audience reaction.

An agent who saw me in the play became interested in my being on a weekly radio show, and an appointment was to be arranged to meet the producer. The theatre presenting *Showdown* was dark on Sunday. Kappy and I were in our apartment listening to a radio program of Gogol's *Inspector General* when the show was interrupted with the startling announcement—"Japan had just attacked Pearl Harbor!"

We left the apartment to visit mutual friends and talk about this latest event. The streets were full of people with only one subject on their lips, (and yes, it was a rather jovial, lighthearted atmosphere), "There is War!"

Drafted!

Showdown closed soon after and I awaited news from the draft board. I didn't have to wait too long. No less a personage than the President of the United States informed me that I should report to the draft board on March 3, 1942 to be inducted into the Armed Services.

This reporting date allowed me about two months to sell or eliminate all my furniture and personal belongings and say farewell to friends and relatives before joining Uncle Sam's family. I am not what one would call a party man but the last weekend, especially, one could not absent himself from the various parties. Suddenly I had more friends than I was aware of before.

When I found time to be by myself I realized my life was about to change completely. In the midst of all the farewells to my relatives, my friends, my ambitions, my plans, my habits—my everything—who knew what awaited me in the immediate future? Would I come out of it alive? It was all so mysterious.

Also looming in my mind was the idea of war. Did I believe in War? When I was very young I used to romanticize it. I especially fantasized about the cavalry—riding a horse and waving a saber. But that was before I read *Le Feu* (*The Fire - 1916*) by the French novelist Henri Barbusse, about a squad of soldiers during the First World War. This completely destroyed all my illusions about war. This new perspective was reinforced when the popular novel *All Quiet on the Western Front* (1929) by Eric Maria Remarque appeared; it was also about the First World War. All this took me back to Tolstoy's *War and Peace*, which is now more than one hundred years old and is still a classic and no doubt will be for years to come. I began to see the ugliness and futility of war.

However, there will always be a war of which the general public is inclined to approve. This was the case with the Second World War. Hitler was out to destroy, to ruin, to kill everyone in order to conquer the world. *Deutchland uber alles*—"Germany today, tomorrow the world." So I went into the service without qualms. Without reservations.

Early on that fateful March Tuesday morning a heavy rain embraced the borough of Manhattan. I told the cab driver to take me to the draft board in Greenwich Village. The driver's response was encouraging, "Oh, I received a notice yesterday that my cousin was killed. I hope you have better luck." As I entered the draft board, a friend and popular night club singer, Paul Villard, was waiting to say goodbye. Someone at the draft board gave me my papers, plus twenty-five cents to take me to the railroad station. Paul and I embraced warmly as I left to take the subway to the Pennsylvania Railroad Station. That twenty-five cent coin bothered me. It was as though they had given me a quarter for my life. At the station many waited to say

Tate—Sholem Zohn
in his mid-eighties.

Mama—Bella Zohn
in her early sixties.

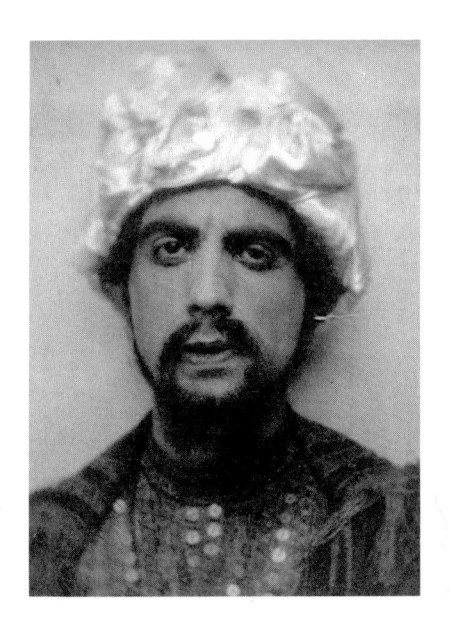

Zohn as 'The Sultan' in *Shabtsai Zvi*, c. 1933.

A revolutionary in *Revolt*, c. 1932.

A Hassid in *Yoshe Kalb*, c. 1932.

Vardi-Yoalit Theatre Studio, December 2, 1927. David Vardi (bow tie) and Eva Yoalit in center of middle row. Hershel Zohn to left of Vardi. Malka Tennanholtz, second from right in middle row. Velvel Draiarsh, fourth from left in back row.

Vardi-Yoalit Theatre Studio production of *Dos Shtetel*.
Zohn second from left, leaning out with hand to ear. c. 1929.

Above: Seder for Jewish army personnel in Washington, D.C. area, 1943. Zohn second from right. *Below*: Denver University summer production of *Distant Drums* at Red Rocks Ampitheater, Denver, Colorado, 1948. Zohn third from right (black hat).

Modern version of *Antigone*. First Zohn production
at New Mexico A & M—1950.

Antigone

Traditional version of *Antigone*—1972.

Above: Kathryn Gibbs and Frank Richardson in *Candida* —1951. (Courtesy: RGHC/NMSU Library)

Left: Bernice Beenhouwer in *Pygmalion*—1951.

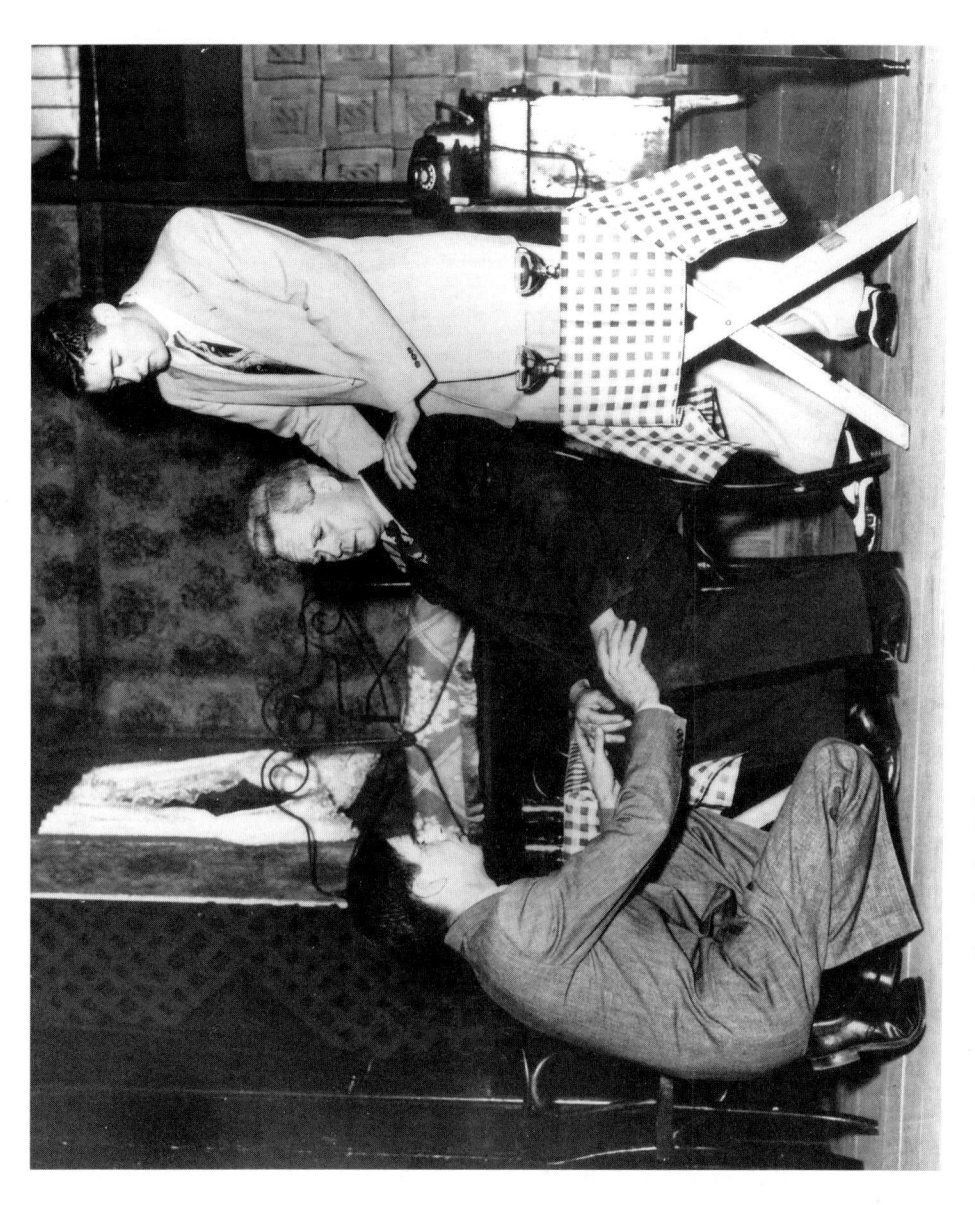

Death of a Salesman—1953. l. to r.: Bob Taggart, Leo Comeau, and Bill Wilson. (Courtesy: RGHC/NMSU Library)

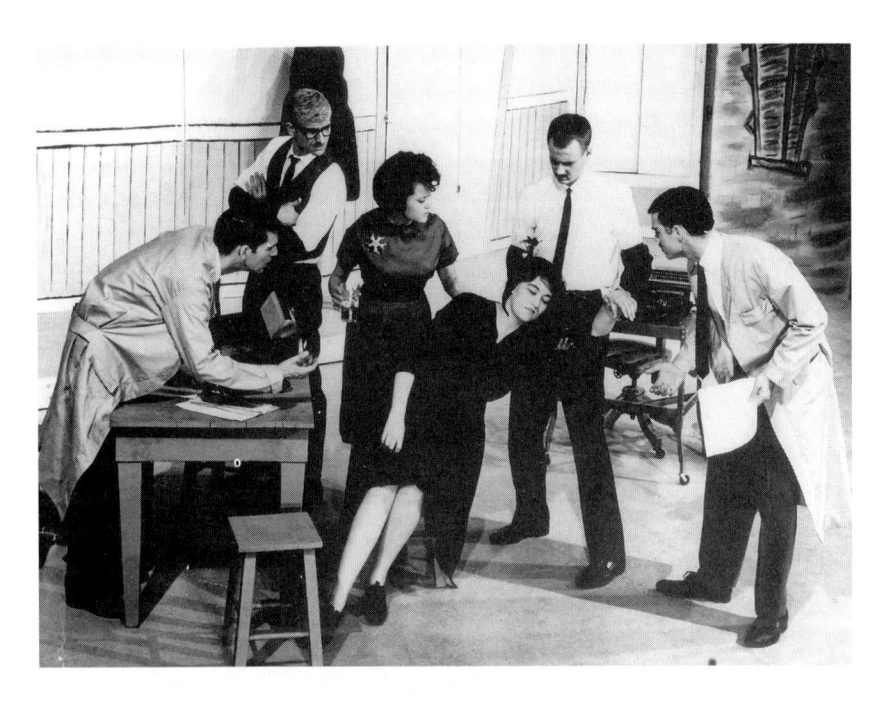

Above: *Rhinoceros*—1963. (Courtesy: RGHC/NMSU Library)
Below: *Life With Father*—1953. (Courtesy: RGHC/NMSU Library)

Mob scene from *An Enemy of the People* - 1954.
(Courtesy: RGHC/NMSU Library)

(Above l.): David Travis and Bill Alford in *The Lark*—1957. Judy Pille as Anne in *The Diary of Anne Frank*—1959. *(Below)*: Martha Gold and C.O. Ward in *Hedda Gabler*—1956. (Courtesy: RGHC/NMSU Library)

Above: *Teahouse of the August Moon*—1958. *Below l.*: Leo Comeau and Pauline Plumbley in *The Hasty Heart*—1952. *Below r.*: Sally Hodges in *The Glass Menagerie*—1957. (All courtesy of RGHC/NMSU Library)

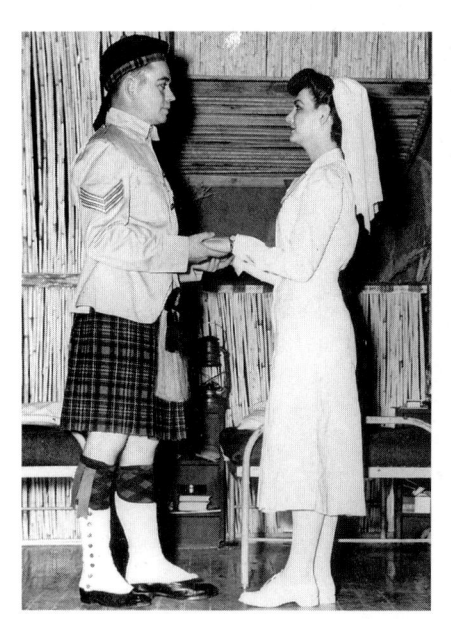

Left: Jackie Clark as *Medea*, with David and Lee Dressell—1959. (Courtesy: Jackie Clark) *Above*: Jack Soules, Robin Hayner and William Frankfather in *Uncle Vanya*—1966. (Courtesy: RGHC/NMSU Library)

Anton Chekhov (1860-1904).

The Sea Gull

(Above): Mexico City, summer 1957. *(Right)*: Millie Hayner as Madam Arkadina—1958. (Courtesy: RGHC/NMSU Library) *(Below)*: l. to r. Gloriette Thompson, David Long, Elizabeth Gaidry, James Post, Star Hayner, Philip Palmer, Mark Mandel in the 1973 NMSU production.

Inherit the Wind—1959. (Courtesy: RGHC/NMSU Library)

goodbye to loved ones. As the gates opened to allow us to go down to the train mothers, sisters, and girlfriends began to cry. Since I didn't have anyone there to cry for me, I was moved to tears and began to cry, too.

Down on the platform, before we entered the train, army guards checked us in one by one. When my turn came I was wearing a small soft "La Guardia hat," which was the style those days, and carrying a *PM*. This daily newspaper was considered a liberal paper then. One guard said to the other, "Here comes another one." I didn't know how to interpret that remark. Upon entering the train, I eventually found a seat and observed the various fellows who were to be my traveling companions—some drunk, others laughing, a few with tears in their eyes, no doubt from saying goodbye. One fellow asked another, "Did you say goodbye to your girlfriend?"

"Yes, I sure did, and how!"

The train then pulled out to take us to the Fort Dix, New Jersey Induction Center.

ACT II

Scene 2

ARMY DAYS

My transformation, from civilian to soldier, began immediately upon arrival at Fort Dix, New Jersey.

First on the agenda on that Tuesday came the famous G.I. haircut. Never in my life had I had such a close haircut. Then medical examinations from tip to toe and, ultimately, an interrogation by an army psychiatrist who apparently was a German refugee. He approached me with the standard question, "Have you ever had any sex?" I mumbled to the affirmative and he continued on the same line, "Mit a man, tsi mit a vooman?" I muttered to myself, "Drop dead."

I asked him what were the chances of my being assigned to heavy artillery, where you do the least walking? He replied,

"This is not a casting agency," as he continued to examine my employment record from the private sector. (I entertained my friends for a long time afterwards with the story of my encounter with the psychiatrist.)

Next they outfitted me with military clothes—but completely. Everything had to be G.I. When I looked into the mirror I hardly recognized myself. "Who am I?" I said. "Is that really me?" In addition, my trousers were so long and my shoes so tight that I could hardly walk at first. I filled my duffel bag with all my private belongings and followed the others outside.

It had been 7:00 a.m. on Tuesday morning when I left East Sixteenth Street, Manhattan, and it was raining "cats and dogs." It was now after midnight on Wednesday at Fort Dix, New Jersey, and the rain was still pursuing us. It looked as if the rain was sympathizing with us and didn't want to leave us alone. About two hundred of us were waiting, wet and tense. Why were we waiting? Who were we waiting for? I was reminded of a poem I recited during the Depression days: "I was waiting in the bread line, waiting and waiting...." In fact, I once used it for an audition.

All of a sudden a very common military phrase, one we would hear many times, split the air "ATTENTION!" We all straightened our lines and quickly picked up the duffel bags given us by Uncle Sam, as the same voice said, "Men, you can all go and _ _ _ _ yourself!" Laughter was heard from most of the men. That fellow had succeeded in breaking the tension.

It was about 2:00 a.m. when we were finally marched to a barracks and shown to our bunks. Wearily we got out of our strange wet clothes and lay down on the narrow army cots, when another clown yelled, "Does anyone have change for a fifty?" "Shut up you _ _ _ _ _." Crude language was rather common in the service.

Approximately three hours later (5:00 a.m.) a corporal ran into the barracks, turned on the lights, and yelled, "Everyone out for reveille in ten minutes." No shaving, no brushing your teeth, no shower—one hardly had time to get into his tight shoes and long pants. I recalled the popular song, *This Is The Army Mr. Jones*. Outside in the dark and cold we formed three lines. Our names were called. Two or three men were missing from the list and the corporal ran back into the barracks to search for them as we waited and shivered outside. The corporal soon returned with the missing men who finished getting dressed on their way to join the platoon.

As we marched, a voice yelled at me, "Ei soldier get in line." Can you imagine addressing me as "soldier"—*soldat*? Me—who was anti-military, a pacifist who couldn't forget the many evenings of reading anti-war novels—being called soldier!

Next we had to stand in line to get our "grub." Heaps of cold oatmeal, cold tasteless scrambled eggs, dried cold toast, and bitter coffee. Uncle Sam apparently tried to economize when it came to feeding his military. In the mess hall we soldiers sat at long tables. When one needed butter, which was usually on the other end of the table, you called for it. You were through eating by the time the butter reached you, with the result that you completed your meal without butter. This happened to me so many times that I gave up butter as long as I was in the service. Ultimately I gave up using butter, and to this very day still don't. "How come you don't use butter?" I am often asked. "Since I was in the service," I say.

After breakfast we again formed lines to "police" the area by picking up cigarette butts. Afterwards we returned to an office to fill out additional records, containing the same questions which had been asked several times before.

A very important event took place that first day in camp. Joe Lewis, the prize-fighter, was inducted into the army on that same day—although we never saw him again.

During that first week at Fort Dix, in addition to picking up cigarette butts every morning, we performed various duties.

Pity the soldier who was caught napping. Extra KP (Kitchen Police) was a common punishment. Between chow time (notice the military terms) we gravitated to the bulletin board to check whether our names were on the roster to be shipped out.

About a week later my name appeared on a departure list for Fort Belvoir, Virginia, an engineering base. The camp was just a few miles from Alexandria, Virginia, and only a short distance from Washington, D.C.

A military band greeted us as we came off the train and we were marched to camp accompanied by corporals and sergeants. We were assigned to Company C, 7th Battalion.

It didn't take long before we were each issued a rifle, bayonet, steel helmet, winter coat, and other soldier necessities. No time was lost in beginning training, which consisted of instructions and lectures, as well as running, jumping, and marching several miles a day. On normal days we had reveille before sunrise, with retreat about sunset. During the time between we were kept busy performing all kinds of chores. Then there were the three- or four-day bivouacs with obstacles, maneuvers, and all forms of exercises. Our sleeping quarters were in the open fields. Frequently, we would be awakened during the night and marched to another area to attack the "enemy." All of this was to condition us before we faced the real enemy.

My previous firearm experience was practically nil. I recall handling a real rifle only once in the Old Country when a cousin came to visit us during the Civil War, but never since. I had to learn how to take care of my rifle, how to clean it and above all how to shoot a rifle on the range. It was not easy for me. Psychologically I rebelled against the gun, but in due time I made peace with it and learned how to shoot. I even received a medal at the end of the training period. Rather ironic. Probably more to keep up the morale, I assume, since they were issued to most soldiers.

While in training we also had to serve on KP, washing dishes; a duty usually despised by the men when their turn came up. There were also other duties. For instance, I was assigned to fuel the furnaces in the Officer's Club cellar. It was a night session and I constantly fed the furnace with wood or coal to keep the fire burning, so the poor officers would stay warm as they danced with their ladies. The band continually played a contemporary, popular song, "Tangerine." "Tangerine, I wonder who is kissing her now." The longer it played, the angrier I became. Every soldier had a girl and my thoughts wandered. Yes, I wonder what she is doing now, miles away. It was after midnight and they were still dancing and repeating that song and I still had to shovel the coal. I was so irritated by it all, that I felt like running upstairs yelling at them, "Stop playing that song you bastards!"

My duty was to stay at the Officers Club shoveling coal until daylight. My face became black with coal dust, and when I finally returned to the barracks, a platoon Sergeant from the South yelled in my direction, "Who is that Nigger there?"

There were frequent speeches about equality and having no racial discrimination, yet one evening all the military in camp were ordered to attend a program at the stadium. One of the entertainers was a Black singer, but the Black soldiers were seated separately and way in the back. That was the forties in the South.

It was an early winter morning when I discovered that I could not make the walk from the barracks to the orderly room. I actually had to crawl on my hands to get there. Perhaps it was due to too much walking and running. Apparently my old arthritis had acted up. I was kept in the army hospital for five weeks. The only nice thing was a little blond nurse by the name of Miss Benet who would occasionally come to chat with me.

I was finally discharged for duty. By then the company I was with had already completed its training, and was shipped to another base and eventually overseas.

* * *

In the meantime I was assigned to work in the orderly room taking care of "Special Orders" and "General Orders" which daily arrived from Washington, and to make corrections on corrections. I soon became an "authority" on "Morning Reports" (something like a diary) which is a daily account of the enlisted men and officers in each company. Washington kept sending new rules and regulations pertaining to "Morning Reports," so it was difficult for First Sergeants to keep abreast of all the changes. These reports were basically the responsibility of the First Sergeant in each company. In due time, First Sergeants from various companies came to me with questions on how to write their "Morning Reports."

Gradually I became a member of the Cadre (military leadership unit) which usually consisted of a Commanding Officer (CO—a Captain), and an Administrative Officer. The enlisted men were—a First Sergeant, a Company Clerk (me), Mail Clerk (often these two jobs merged and were done by one person), a Supply Sergeant, and a Mess Sergeant with several cooks helping him, and occasionally two or three other men helping in the supply room. All served a company of four platoons—a total of two hundred fifty men.

Members of the Cadre frequently changed. They worked for a year or longer and then were transferred or shipped overseas. Others worked in military bases in this country throughout the war.

My first CO was a Captain Elliot. He was soft-spoken, sad-looking, and never laughed or even smiled. (Perhaps he had personal problems.) His wife lived with him on the post and came to see him frequently. She was an attractive young lady. Soldiers teased me that she was responsible for my getting the job of Company Clerk (which of course was not true).

Captain Dodge replaced Elliot. He was the opposite of his predecessor. He was loud, smiling, and frequently used two phrases: "Do you have change for a quarter, Sergeant?" or "What time is it Corporal?" He also had the unaesthetic habit of constantly picking his nose. Most of the officers hailed from the South, while the enlisted men represented every state of the Union.

Lieutenant Kinney was the Administrative Officer. He must have been about six-foot-six, with a big belly and a loud speaking voice. One day he came in with a list of six names of men who had applied for passes to observe the upcoming Jewish High Holidays (New Year). In the Orderly Room was the First Sergeant, myself, and one or two other men and Lieutenant Kinney. The Lieutenant delivered a diatribe about Jews reminiscent of a Goebbels or Goering. I sat there and listened until he finally finished. I said slowly, "Sir, I am Jewish."

"Oh," said he, "that's different." This is the usual excuse to get out of such a situation. The next replacement for Administrative Officer was a Lieutenant Mandell.

First Sergeant Patrick, a clean-shaven and neatly dressed man hailed from the Carolinas. He didn't seem to have any interest in the war, just carrying out his duties with as little effort as possible. These consisted of: a Morning Report of the daily happenings in the company including the number of officers and enlisted men present during the 24-hour period, how many new arrivals and from where, how many departures and where to, the number of meals consumed during breakfast, lunch, and dinner, the total number of soldiers on sick-call that day, and so on and on. Washington insisted on this Morning Report every day of the year, without fail. Rules and regulations for the report changed frequently and the First Sergeant was responsible for knowing them. He would have me, the Company Clerk, gather all the information and type the account every evening or early morning.

Sergeant Oswald was in charge of the Mess Hall. There were three cooks working with him. The cooks were all nice men with a sense of humor, hard working, all from Rhode Island, and all of Italian descent. Sergeant Oswald was in complete charge of the Mess Hall. He was huge—a voice which carried from one end of the Mess Hall to the other—yet good natured and laughed loudly. He would appear in the orderly room between meals and get into an argument with the First Sergeant. They would invariably end the dispute by Oswald, who was from Buffalo, New York, calling the Sergeant who was from the South, "Rebel _ _ _ _," and the First Sergeant calling Oswald "Yankee _ _ _ _ _."

One time our CO decided that his C-7 Cadre could stand some exercises before going on duty in the morning. We were getting sluggish, he said. Captain Stewart conducted the exercises by yelling, "One, two, three, one, two, three, left face, right face, about face...." Chubby Oswald from the Mess Hall apparently missed a turn as the captain yelled at him, "What's the matter Sergeant, are you pregnant?"

Oswald replied instantly, "Sir, the way I am being _ _ _ _ _ _ around here, I may as well be pregnant."

The Supply Sergeant was Bill Leadwill, also from the South. He was a military man who was primarily interested in having a good time on weekends, and frequently during the week. As soon as he was through with work, he left camp for Alexandria or Washington, D.C. for drinks and to pick up girls. He didn't discriminate. One day he felt there was something wrong with him and reported to the infirmary where the physician ordered him to be admitted to the army hospital for circumcision. "Oh Lordy," he kept repeating. "Who knows when I'll be able to see another girl." We in the company headquarters had a good laugh. It seemed the Sergeant was forced to abstain from having a good time with the girls for quite some time.

Members of the Cadre were entitled to weekend passes when the CO was in a good mood. Occasionally I went to Washington to visit friends; once in a blue moon I would even take a trip to New York to spend the weekend with my father and sisters. The passes were good until Sunday p.m. One time I took the liberty (intentionally or not) of staying over in New York until Monday morning. The army didn't waste any time instructing the Red Cross to find me. By the time the Red Cross approached my father about my whereabouts, I was already back in camp. However, the army considered me AWOL and was ready to punish me by having to work on a nearby road project. This punishment did not last more than two hours before I was dismissed by an officer and returned to my job. He laughed about my "crime and punishment" and said that I could go back to my usual work. His name was Lieutenant Pershing. He was the son of the well-known General John "Black Jack" Pershing.

My interest in theatre continued, especially when I became acquainted with a member of the WACS, Private Helen Tucker. She was majoring in drama before she enlisted and we occasionally met for coffee to chat about theatre and even went to see a play whenever an opportunity would arise.

Furlough to New Mexico

I finally obtained a two-week furlough. I decided to visit my close friend Roberta at Las Vegas, New Mexico, where she was teaching music at Highlands University. We had corresponded frequently but hadn't seen each other for three years, ever since my big adventure to the West.

The airport at Washington, D.C. was terribly crowded. Fortunately my name was called before long and I was ready to experience my first airplane flight. It was an old-type plane with long benches facing each other. No sooner had we taken off than it started to snow and we were compelled to land at a small airport in Delaware. We were stranded there for two days because of the heavy snow. There were three of us. There was a barracks to sleep in, a little luncheonette, a Coke machine, and a juke box for "entertainment." The other two soldiers kept calling me "Sarge," (although I was only a corporal) and said, "We want you to be the one to decide when we can leave." Somehow they wouldn't make a move without my approval. They were young, green and scared, and I was a few years older with two stripes on my sleeve.

On the third day the sun began to shine, the snow started to melt, and we were ready to go. There were several planes leaving in different directions and the three of us parted company. My lot was to go on a two-passenger plane headed for Dallas. It was a tiny little thing, and the pilot warned me he was going to say goodbye to his wife when we neared Pittsburgh. Once over the city he started maneuvering his little plane, waving goodbye to his wife, throwing kisses to her—to the left, to the right, forward and backward. With every turn he made I was sure I would fall out of the plane. But the pilot kept saying, "Don't be afraid, one more goodbye and we go for real." He kept his word, picked up speed, and we finally arrived in Dallas where I changed to another plane for Albuquerque.

As we waited, a non-commissioned officer couldn't stand to see soldiers sitting idle and ordered us to police the area by picking up cigarette butts. Before long an Albuquerque-bound plane was announced, and I thought, "To hell with the cigarette butts," and ran to catch the flight; otherwise, who knew when another plane might be headed in my direction. In Albuquerque I had to wait for a bus to take me to Las Vegas. It was nearly a four-day trip from Washington to Las Vegas, New Mexico. The only excuse—it was wartime, in addition to a big snow storm.

Las Vegas was and still is a small town. It reached its commercial peak in the 1890's when the Santa Fe Railroad decided to have its trains stop there. To eat at the railroad station's Harvey House Restaurant was a great treat, especially on Sundays. Las Vegas inhabitants frequently visited the station while the trains stopped for about twenty minutes. The Santa Fe *Super Chief* was the most exciting train to meet. This was the train that carried many of the Hollywood stars from East to West and vice-versa. When an actor allowed himself to be photographed by a local resident, the Las Vegan would be in seventh heaven.

The *Chief* was not quite as glamorous as *The Super Chief*, but still many important personalities were to be found on that train, too. *The El Capitan* was also a comfortable and attractive train for traveling, with a fine dining car, bar, and a spacious place to sit and reminisce—but it could not begin to compare with the other two trains.

The California Limited was the fourth of the Santa Fe line to travel from Chicago to Los Angeles and back. *The California Limited* was limited in everything—in food, in drink, and primarily, in comfort. The seats were hard benches, leading to the assumption that the cars were inherited from an earlier century; a coal stove provided warmth, and it took forever to get to your destination. At the end of a trip on *The California Limited*, one's bones were out of shape and you were a prime candidate for a session with a chiropractor. During the war *The California Limited* was packed with soldiers. It was the only train they could afford.

Why Las Vegas? Roberta. After spending the early years of her life in the upstate New York cities of Geneva and Rochester, she decided to move to the big metropolis of New York with her little boy. She had a degree in music, and WPA had just come into existence. She obtained a position teaching music to children. When I was first introduced to her she lived in the basement apartment at 67 Horatio Street, Greenwich Village. Later this became a popular street in the Village. Roberta, however, moved to the Columbia University area where she met a blonde, talkative woman who was full of ideas on how to make the world a better place to live—her name was Lini Fuhr.

Army Days

When the war broke out in Spain, a number of people in this country went there to fight Fascism. Lini volunteered to go to Spain as a nurse. It was on a rainy spring Saturday morning in the early thirties that several of us went to the pier to say farewell when she departed for Spain. Lini became a head nurse. Another head nurse was Freddie Martin. She was married to a doctor, yet she left him to go to Spain, possibly to sacrifice her life in the fight against Franco. Freddie was quite a personality. Tall, attractive, with a very clear mind, she weighed every word she said as every one listened to her. The third head nurse left her rich rancher-husband at home to join the armed forces in Spain and fight for a just country. Those three nurses were in charge of the front-line medical corps, and worked with a group of nurses from New York and other parts of the United States.

After the war, the rancher's wife returned to live at the ranch near Las Vegas, New Mexico, Freddie settled in Cuernavaca, Mexico. Lini went to Las Vegas, New Mexico to be a nurse in the villages close to Vegas and teach the poor women about birth control. Once a year, many of those who served in the Spanish Civil War met in New York or Mexico City to recall the war days they had spent fighting Franco in Spain.

After Lini had lived in New Mexico for a short time, she urged Roberta to migrate to Las Vegas. Upon her arrival it didn't take Roberta very long to obtain a position at Highlands University in the Music Department. In a short time she became a popular and successful piano teacher, as well as conductor of the university orchestra.

I was stuck fighting the war in Fort Belvoir, Virginia, and furloughs don't come easily in the service. It didn't take us very long to renew our friendship. After having known each other for nine years, Roberta and I finally decided to get married. We took a quick honeymoon trip to New Orleans before returning to Vegas so I could rush back to my army base and resume my duties for Uncle Sam.

I was supposed to board a Chicago-bound train and from there go to Washington. At the Las Vegas railroad station I was informed that my train would be about two hours late. The station master promised to call me when the train approached town. When I woke up it was after midnight. Upon inquiring about my train, lo and behold, I was informed that the train had said farewell for Chicago thirty minutes earlier. The station master was "sorry" but "plum forgot." What was I to do? "When I arrive at camp a day late they'll probably bust me from T-5[1] to plain private," I wailed.

"Oh hell," I said to the station master.

He said, "Don't you worry, I'll get you there on time."

"But how?"

A mail train was scheduled to go through within an hour or so and I would be put on that train. This time I didn't leave the station to wait to be called but stayed, glued to a bench. The mail train arrived about 3:00 a.m., I hurriedly jumped on the train and explained my plight, pleading that I didn't want to be AWOL. The conductor consented and, except for the mail personnel, I was the only passenger. The train traveled at full speed, like a devil running away from a fire—apparently trying to make up some lost time. The result was that I reported to camp a day ahead of time.

My army service became quite boring. It seemed that I would not be shipped overseas—although I wanted to go to the front very badly. Promotions continued to come swiftly. From private to T-5; from Mail Clerk to Company Clerk, then to sergeant, and staff sergeant, and finally supply sergeant.

---

[1] Equivalent to corporal.

The supply room won first prize several times on Saturday inspections. Quite a few soldiers wanted to be assigned "special duty" in the supply room, which would excuse them from heavier duty. The First Sergeant always provided me with all the help I needed, so keeping the area neat was no problem. The Colonel of Group III, which included my Company C-7, terrified everyone. The various stories about him were anything but complimentary. One Saturday morning he approached company headquarters to inspect the supply room. Everything was as neat and clean as can be. All he said was, "Very good Sergeant, keep it up." Little did he know there were several men hidden in one of the closets. When those men saw the Colonel coming, they took the fastest and easiest way out—hiding in the nearest closet instead of running out of the supply room. If the Colonel had opened the closet, that would have been the end of them, and me, I suppose. No one should have been there except me!

One man was so appreciative about working in the supply room that when he learned that I was going to Chicago, his hometown, for Christmas, he casually asked where I was to stay. Then he called his Chicago liquor store and ordered several bottles of liquor to be left at the door of my hotel room. That was the soldier's Christmas present to me.

One day the Company Commander approached me with a problem. After taking inventory in the supply room, he discovered twenty bayonets were missing. He would have to make good for them if they weren't found. We solved the problem of the missing bayonets: Take ten old bayonets and break them in half; then, take the twenty halves to supply headquarters and they would be obliged to exchange them for twenty new bayonets. Once that was done the CO was a happy man.

* * *

Peace!

Would the war ever be over? It seemed that the fighting would cease only after I was killed. But how could one get killed if he was not at the front?

1945 was a very eventful year. First, the Yalta Conference with Roosevelt, Churchill, and Stalin forecast the end of the war. Next, the sudden death of Roosevelt made Truman his successor. (I recall seeing people crying in the streets.) Finally, Nazi Germany surrendered.

Then came the Atomic Bomb. The army latrine was an important meeting place for soldiers. It was early on the morning of August 6th when I picked up a Washington newspaper and saw the large headline—the United States had dropped an Atomic Bomb on Hiroshima! I ran into the latrine to spread the news. Before long quite a few soldiers had gathered around me to read the headlines. Some of us didn't know what to say. Almost prophetically I uttered, "This is a sad day in the history of mankind."

Some of them nodded, "Yes, yes". About a week later, August 15, Japan surrendered.

I was scheduled to go to New York that same day. I went to Union Station in Washington, D.C. to take a train to my destination. It was V.J. Day. The mood in the capital was indescribable! Thousands and thousands of people crowded the streets, yelling, crying, laughing, embracing, and kissing each other. I finally made my way to the station. Actually the walking was rather easy—a mob just pushed me in that direction. At the station there wasn't an inch of free space, yet I finally managed to squeeze into a coffee shop.

A scene which I remember to this day took place in that coffee shop. A naval officer, in an immaculately white uniform, was waiting for a vacant stool at the counter. When his turn came, he was so intoxicated that he and the people near him didn't know if he could make the few steps to the counter. Yet he pulled himself erect and walked slowly, straight as could be, to the stool, sat down, and said with finality, "I made it." People observing this performance laughed. For some reason I never forgot that scene. Occasionally I related this incident to my acting students as an illustration that there are all kinds of drunks in the world.

Later in August, the army began discharging soldiers. My company commenced to dissolve. Captain Ramsey, the CO and a fine person with whom I got along well, said amiably but sincerely, "Sarge, let's reorganize this company. You will not be First Sergeant but Master Sergeant (the highest enlisted rank)."

I said, "No thank you."

When I was to be transferred to another army base for special duty, I insisted on being discharged from the service completely. Four years is enough!

One October day, dressed in my best uniform, several men and I reported to the army chapel where we received our discharge papers, also some medals for our service, and a few dollars for transportation. We walked out of the chapel as free men.

I didn't waste much time boarding a train for New York City. When I arrived in New York, my two dear friends, Kappy and Toby, were waiting on the platform to greet me. Kappy, who had enlisted in the service two or three months before I was drafted also beat me again and was discharged ahead of me. The three of us celebrated by drinking and eating all through the evening.

After a few days I realized that I better dispose of my uniform and get into civilian clothes.

When I visited Broadway, the casting agencies replied with their usual, "Nothing doing today, come back tomorrow."

I deliberated, "Should I stay here or go to greener pastures?" After all, twenty years of New York was enough. I decided to leave the big city and join Roberta and her young son David in New Mexico.

For some reason I became sick after arriving in Las Vegas. It took me about two weeks to get well. Perhaps I couldn't get accustomed to civilian life. After the New Year of 1946, I left Las Vegas for Los Angeles to see what Hollywood had to offer.

ACT II

Scene 3

THE FUTURE?

Hollywood is noted all over the world for its movie making, studios, and the creation of world-famous stars. Those studios may very well be called assembly lines where men and women of all ages, even children, come in search of a miracle—a director who might notice them and use them, even if only in a mob scene with hundreds of others. As a last resort they would polish a star's car, or scrub the floor of a producer's office, as long as it is in Hollywood.

Of course, film making has gone through many transitions since Hollywood emerged as the film capital in the first decade of the 1900s. To this day it remains a magnet to many star-struck people.

This was my second trip to Hollywood. In 1940, it was primarily a vacation and I had a great time—meeting interesting people and living in an apartment on Taft Avenue close to Hollywood Boulevard. Beautiful Griffith Park was nearby and I frequently went there to absorb the fresh air.

This time I had a small room between Los Angeles and Hollywood, close to the house where our friend Lini lived. She had left Las Vegas, New Mexico, and settled with her family in Los Angeles. Lini insisted on my having dinner with them. She even offered to do my laundry.

I became acquainted with a man who used to "hang" around the cafeterias in New York. He claimed to be an author. I never learned his name but met him strolling on Hollywood or Sunset Boulevard. We began chatting and, as long as I was in California we would meet daily in the middle of a street, leaning on a fence or telephone pole, or just strolling along on a sidewalk. We chatted about the state of the Hollywood scene, the theatre, the economy, and world affairs. He knew about everything, but he didn't know my name, nor did I know his. This continued until I left town. After I left he probably went on talking to himself.

On a clear day in Los Angeles, as I was strolling on the sidewalk along Sunset Boulevard, a man maneuvered his car out from the line of traffic and drove slowly alongside me. He asked me, "Are you looking for a job?" I was amazed. Even before I could say anything he told me to get into the car, which I did. He said, "Come to work tomorrow morning at this address," as he handed me a card. "You will not be sorry."

I thought to myself, "What could I lose?" and went the next morning to the given address.

There were about five or six people in the office. I was asked if I could type. I said, "Some." I was led to a typewriter and given several pages to copy. I became suspicious and asked to see the boss. The reply was, "He is in the next room in bed sick, you can't see him." The longer I sat there, the more mistrustful I became of the place. I was glad when the noon hour came and said, "I'm going to lunch."

Needless to say I was very relieved when I was outside and didn't return after lunch. However, within about ten days I received a check from that "firm." Figuring the little time I spent there, I was actually well paid. I never learned what kind of a place it was.

My main purpose in coming to Los Angeles was to find work in Hollywood as an actor. How does one go about it? My friend, Lini Fuhr, was a close friend of Albert Maltz and his family. Maltz was the author of a number of plays. Among them were *Peace on Earth* and *Black Pit*, both successfully produced on the professional stage. All of his plays depicted current social problems. Like other writers, the late Albert Maltz was drawn to Hollywood and engaged by Warner Brothers Studio.

I was first invited to dinner at the Maltz's, and he promised he would introduce me to some of the people at Warner Brothers. Before long I was asked to audition for Warner Brothers.

I prepared a monologue about a Polish farmer who came to this country and was soon met with the problems and complications of American family life. The twenty-minute scene was highly emotional and dramatic. Afterwards, the person for whom I auditioned was quite complimentary. He said I reminded him of a prominent actor by the name of Hersholt.

"Well," I asked, "what do I do now?"

"Now you will have to wait until there is a part fitted for you."

"How long will that take?", I asked.

"Who knows, it may take a week, a month or longer." That was the end of the interview.

I was warned not to put much trust in Hollywood people, and I needed to become busy with something specific—and soon.

* * *

Highlands University

In the back of my mind was the idea of working in educational theatre and perhaps this was the time. I took the first Greyhound bus to Las Vegas, New Mexico. I was late for the winter quarter and had to wait until March to commence college at Highlands University.

I must have talked about the Russian stage, because before long I was invited to present several lectures on the Russian theatre in a classroom at Highlands University. The drama program at Highlands was limited. Students interested in theatre were few. Most of the audience at my lectures consisted primarily of friends and faculty. One could not expect students who don't have an interest in theatre to be eager to listen to a talk about Stanislavski and Danchenko, Chekhov and Gorki, or learn about some of the prominent actors at the Moscow Art Theatre.

In March of 1946 I began my studies in earnest. Freshman as well as senior courses in the social sciences, literature, and Shakespeare, were all on my registration schedule. As for the students, I became friends with an older student, a Lutheran Minister, who also was working toward a degree. I was also friends with faculty members because, as the husband of a faculty member, it seemed they all wanted me to make good in their classes. It was soon after the war and the school was full of veterans. Like most returning veterans, I attended college on the G.I. Bill.

Once, in a speech class, we had a debate. The subject was the economy. I was assigned the liberal point of view and my opponent, a pretty young student from Texas, defended the conservative viewpoint. The debate reached such a crescendo that the supporters for each side almost came to fistfights. I was glad when the debate was over so I could become friendly with my opponent again.

I participated in a Moliere comedy directed by the Speech and Drama teacher. Her first name was Willian, but we called her William. She was a very excitable person, and at that time, the only person in the department. She happened to be in a backstage accident and I was asked to replace her as director of the upcoming summer production.

I chose Chekhov's *The Sea Gull*. I decided to produce it as a reading, and primarily chose faculty members to be in the play. I thought that would add a sense of maturity to the production. It was August 1946, my first Chekhov play. It was a dream come true to do *The Sea Gull*. I had seen the play for the first time during the thirties with Eva Le Galliene and Jacob Ben-Ami at the Civic Repertory Theatre in New York. The play made a strong impression on me. Directors and actors usually have their favorites. *The Sea Gull* is certainly mine, even to this very day. Through the years I directed this vehicle in different places. I also acted the writer, Boris Trigorin, and later demoted myself to Sorin, the oldest character in the drama.

The Sea Gull, like most of Chekhov's plays, deals with the futility and frustration of life. His characters are yearning for a more cosmopolitan life. There is the middle-aged actress, Irina, who finds it difficult to appear in older roles. Also, the author, Trigorin, complains that he has failed to achieve greatness, the very young Nina only becomes a common actress instead of the great actress she hoped to be, and the young melancholy poet, Kostya, kills himself, thus bringing the play to a sudden, tragic ending.

We took advantage of holidays to explore the surrounding country. During the Labor Day weekend we made a trip to see the Indian dances in the northwestern part of New Mexico, close to Gallup. They were colorful, theatrical, and worth seeing.

* * *

We went south to Juarez. Going through a small town at night, all I saw were the lights from a few houses—supposedly the residential section—and was told this town was called Las Cruces. Little did I know that within four years I would be teaching at the college there and that would be my home for many years to come. As for Juarez, I was not particularly impressed by the popular songs in either Spanish or English. They were uninteresting. We returned by the White Sands National Monument, which was all new to me, and continued to Las Vegas via Albuquerque and Santa Fe.

New York University

It was rather easy to become restless in Las Vegas, as well as at Highlands, and I went to New York and registered at New York University (NYU) for summer courses. The first was a course in Modern Drama, a class of about three hundred students, primarily candidates of law. Many law students took drama and speech classes to better prepare themselves for their courtroom presentations. I probably read more plays during those summer days than at any other time. This was followed by three courses in theatre during the second session. I particularly enjoyed the professor's lectures, and, if I may say, the professor enjoyed my presence in his classes. He seemed to enjoy my comments and we often had extended discussions. All my studying and reading of plays was done in a very small room at Waverly Place where I once had an apartment, and now I hardly had enough space to turn around. But outside of the classroom or my room there was Washington Square Park where I had spent many hours in the olden days, but this time I could afford only half an hour a day. Besides, there were more drunks and tramps in that park than during that earlier period.

The Future?

If you walked early in the morning you were bound to find Maurice Schwartz, head of the Yiddish Art Theatre, with a book of Shakespeare in his hands.

"Good morning Mr. Schwartz. What are you doing here so early in the morning? Reading Shakespeare?"

"Well", he hesitantly responded, "I am preparing various scenes from Shakespeare that I am scheduled to do before the Queen of England next Fall. What are you doing here? I heard you were in the Army?"

"The war is over, you know, and I am going to school here majoring in theatre."

"Majoring in theatre? That's nice, very nice, good luck."

Following our encounter, I began to reminisce about my experiences with Schwartz fifteen years earlier. Various plays came to mind—Leonid Andreyev's *The Seven Who Were Hanged*, *Green Fields* by Peretz Hirshbein, or I. Zhulavsky's *Shabtsai Zvi*. The latter play reminded me of Schwartz as the false Messiah, and an incident during one of those performances:

> *Schwartz was not only demanding of his actors, but of his audience as well. Once, at a performance of a revival of* Shabtsai Zvi, *during the thirties, in a highly dramatic and tense scene where the false Messiah is struggling to deprive himself from having any relations with his wife, the giggling of a young couple was audible throughout the theatre. Schwartz, in his white robe and face pale from fasting as the ascetic Messiah, jumped from the narrow cot on which he had been lying and walked down to the footlights. In a very loud, typical Schwartz voice, he yelled, "Get out of my theatre at once! Go to the other theatres on the avenue where they show 'khinke-pinke' (slang for a cheap play). That's where you belong. Curtain! Curtain!" The actors on stage were aghast. Schwartz then delivered a*

speech to the audience that his theatre was a temple of art and those who had no taste for fine drama had no right to come here. He then went back to the same scene and proceeded with the performance.[1]

University of Denver

I returned to Las Vegas and Highlands at the end of the summer and wrote papers on Greek drama instead of attending classes.

I couldn't wait to leave and register for the School of Theatre at the University of Denver.

There were three outstanding universities in the country during those days especially known for theatre programs: Iowa State, University of Denver, and Stanford University.

Dr. Campton Bell was the head of the Theatre Department at Denver. Very popular with his colleagues throughout the country, he was well versed in theatre, both professional and educational. He was also very successful in developing a theatre program at the University of Denver which attracted students from all over the world. Bell was a tremendous teacher. The first play he assigned me to direct was a Chekhov play. I asked, "Why Chekhov?"

"If you can direct Chekhov, you can direct anything!"

There were many students majoring in Drama at Denver; many showed promise and had a great interest in theatre. They seemed determined to make it their lives' career, whether it was in acting, directing, teaching, or other fields in drama. This was quite a change from my days at Highlands. Here, groups of students gathered for hours outside of class and discussed various plays and styles in theatre. A number of these students were gradually absorbed into the professional stage—some as actors, others as directors or teachers.

---

[1] Zohn, *The Story of the Yiddish Theatre*, p. 210.

Students even came from Europe to obtain degrees in theatre from Denver. One student with whom I became especially close friends was Gerhard Knoop from Oslo, Norway. I nicknamed him Max Reinhardt, and he, in turn, called me Konstantin Stanislavski. Gerhard even imported a bride from Norway and we all celebrated their wedding. In due time Gerhard became an important figure in the Norwegian theatre.

To this day I look back at that period of the late forties in Denver as an exciting and fruitful time where a group of about two hundred young people were all aiming towards a similar goal.

As busy as I was, I found time to become sick. One evening after I had returned from Las Vegas where I had spent a week between quarters, I experienced a night of extremely sharp abdominal pain. In the morning the pain subsided, and I attended the first classes of the new quarter. After my afternoon class I realized that I should pay a visit to the school infirmary and tell the doctor of the sharp pain of the night before. After a blood test, I was informed that it was appendicitis and I must have immediate surgery. An ambulance instantly appeared to take me to Fort Logan, an army hospital.

A doctor was waiting to take me to an operating room, but he also had to find a nurse and another doctor to stand by. The procedure began. Instead of putting me to sleep completely, I was given a "local" and it felt as if I had a shot of Scotch. I began to sing. Then I made a caustic remark about the nurse. She reminded me of the nurse in *Men in White* a popular contemporary play that was not too complimentary about the medical profession. She warned the doctors that she'd quit if I continued with such remarks.

I then began to recite Shakespeare: "Tomorrow and tomorrow and tomorrow creeps in this petty pace from day to day until the last syllable of recorded time."

One of the doctors followed. "And all our yesterdays have lighted fools the way to dusty death." I came in with a line, and the doctor followed with another and finished with, "It is a tale told by an idiot. Full of sound and fury, signifying nothing."

The doctor announced, "The surgery is finished. All done."

After I was taken to a ward, someone in a white uniform kept cursing because he had difficulty in finding my veins to feed me intravenously. All I wanted was to sleep, which I did. When I awoke it was morning. A man in a black suit was standing near my bed. He introduced himself, "I am the Rabbi from Denver." He picked up the card at the foot of my bed, read it and said, *"Vi vertes a Yid farvorfen in aza klein shtetel."* ("How does a Jew come to land in such a secluded little town?"), meaning Las Vegas.

I had arrived in Denver in January 1948 and received my B.A. in August 1948. Then I immediately began to work on my M.A., which I received in August 1949. It was summertime, and summers in Denver, as well as throughout the state of Colorado, are beautiful. It was a tradition with the School of Theatre to invite a guest director by the name of Norbert Silbiger to direct a play during the summer session. He chose to do a production at Red Rocks, an attractive, big, open-air theatre close to Denver. Red Rocks is surrounded by mountains, which can be seen miles away.

The play, *Distant Drums*, by Dan Thoteron, takes place during the California Gold Rush. The many characters come from the East and Midwest in search of gold. The people in the play are of different nationalities, including Indians and even Russians. The director insisted that I take a part in the play. No matter how much I argued that I needed to go on with my studies, the director won. Actually it was a good break for me. I looked like a Russian bear. Wearing a big fur coat (in the summer time), fur hat, and boots gave me the appearance of being that stereotyped Russian character, Ivan Ivanovich.

To create the proper mood there were covered wagons on stage. If I remember correctly there was one evening scene where the characters had a fire on stage to keep warm. (It was an extremely large stage.) Indians were located throughout the surrounding mountains to give the feeling of authenticity. *Distant Drums* was not an outstanding script, but its material was conducive to a spectacular production, especially for a theatre like the Red Rocks Amphitheater. I don't know why, but my name was the one favorably mentioned in Harry Lowery's review in the August 9, 1948 *Rocky Mountain News*. The headline read—"Zohn Well Liked."

I was not aware of any university in the United States commemorating the fiftieth anniversary of the Moscow Art Theatre. When I suggested the plan to Campton Bell, he thought it was a brilliant idea and instantly concurred. There is a saying in theatre circles, "If not for the Moscow Art Theatre, there never would have been a Chekhov," and *visa-vis*, "If not for Chekhov there never would have been a Moscow Art Theatre,"—reciprocal relationships.

We decided on two Chekhov one-acters: *The Swan Song* and *The Wedding*. *The Swan Song* is about an old actor, alone on stage at midnight after a performance given in his honor.

> OLD ACTOR: *The applause, the flowers, the embraces, the kisses, the praising of my acting—it is all a sham, a sham. Once they are outside of the theatre, they forget me. They wouldn't even invite me to their house, let alone to have me talk to their beautiful daughter.*

The prompter joins him. He seems to be the only person who understands him and sympathizes with him. The old actor reminisces about different characters he had portrayed and delivers passages from plays he did. He says to the prompter, "Nikitushka, do you remember my Othello?"

"Genius, genius," says the prompter.

"Never, Never, Never. Out of Moscow! I'll go there no more, outraged feelings at every turn! My coach, my coach!" The lights dim slowly to a blackout as he makes his exit followed by the prompter.

The Wedding is a farce based on a Russian wedding with a cast of twelve characters: Parents, bride and bridegroom and various friends. It is a supper or dowry dinner, with all actors sitting at a large table, eating and drinking as the audience laughed and enjoyed it immensely.

Then came my part, where the director had to present a talk about "Chekhov, the Man and the Playwright." But something else happened that evening before the curtain went up—a snow storm. It was a Sunday evening in November 1948. We had expected a good audience and the Russian consul was invited. However, for those who admire Chekhov and love theatre, a snow will not deter them from coming, and the theatre was full. The same program was repeated three months later for the Rocky Mountain Speech Conference. It was in a different theatre and presented for a different audience, but the reaction was still favorable.

The School of Theatre always had special programs taking place, like lectures by guest speakers or novel programs. I was asked to do a reading of *The Dybbuk*, and groups of high school students were invited to attend. It was scheduled at the main theatre for April 17, 1949 at 10:00 a.m. I awoke that morning with a high temperature, but I was determined to go through with the program. A friend said he would have a car ready to take me to the hospital as soon as I finished. I went on with the reading. Because of my temperature, I felt I was even more effective. The high school students seemed to be impressed by the strangeness of the plot and asked questions about *The Dybbuk*. My friend tried to get me out of the theatre by saying, "The cab is waiting for you."

I finally got into the vehicle and said, "To Fort Logan Hospital." I asked my friend to bring some of my books and papers so I could continue to labor on my research. I don't recall how long I was in the hospital, but it must have been a short time. All I remember was a desperate need to work on my thesis.

Then came the orals. Some students are nervous or uneasy; others don't give a damn. I felt confident, dressed properly and went to meet "my makers." Several "old men" were waiting to take me apart, I thought. But nothing of the kind. One member fell asleep. A discussion about Maxwell Anderson, the dramatist, did develop with one professor. He didn't care for him; I did. About my thesis, they knew little if anything about the Yiddish theatre and were careful not to touch the subject. They soon said, "That's it," and shook hands with me. I was disappointed that it was all over and so swiftly.

Campton Bell was very impressed by my thesis, "A Survey of the Yiddish Theatre" (he had read it before), and he wanted to see it published. He made an effort to raise funds, but had no luck. This subject had never been explored academically, and when word got around about the content of my thesis, a number of students became interested in making use of it for their own Master's theses or doctoral dissertations.

Graduation Day was on a Friday morning in August. It was sunny and warm. A special guest at the graduation ceremony was former President Herbert Hoover. The formalities were outside; the former president sat quietly until the warm sun put him to sleep.

* * *

In Search of Employment

Seeking a job, I sent letters of application to many universities. The reply was always the same: "We are impressed by your background, unfortunately there is no opening. However, we will keep your letter on file." Afterwards I appeared in person at various universities: University of Wyoming, Colorado State, Iowa, Michigan State, Syracuse, Cleveland, Chicago, a college in Long Island where the head of an Arts School came to the city to meet me. Fordham University in New York invited me to present a lecture on the Russian Theatre, and so on. But no job.

I returned to Las Vegas and began to offer classes in creative dramatics for children and also classes in acting for adults. Saturday mornings we gave cookies to children during recess. I said to one little girl: "Janie have a cookie," and she replied, "You are some cookie yourself."

I had a weekly radio program where I dramatized various selections from the Bible and Greek drama. Some people in Las Vegas objected to my dramatizing the Bible on the radio, but a group of nuns from Las Vegas came to my defense and I continued with the program.

However, I didn't care to continue with this work too long. I decided to resume studying toward my Ph.D., and in June I registered at Northwestern University. The university is close to Lake Michigan, and on days when the wind and the waves played havoc, even in my room one had a sense of being in the midst of the ocean.

Northwestern is considered a significant institution in the Midwest and so was its theatre program, but I found things were lacking in course offerings, as well as in its theatre productions. Still, there was something pleasing during the summer months. There was a nun who also majored in theatre and we would frequently sit near a tree on the campus and discuss theatre.

The Future?

I was living in student housing (for the first time) that summer. I shared a room with a fellow who seemed to enjoy relating stories about his "profession." He was studying to be a mortician.

Those were the turbulent days of the Korean War. Students discussed the rights and wrongs of that war. Suddenly I was interrupted when someone handed me a letter from New Mexico College of Agriculture and Mechanic Arts in Las Cruces. They offered me a position in drama for the fall semester of 1950.

I yelled, "Hey boys, I have a job." They applauded. I reread the letter several times and sat down to reply that I accepted the position. In my letter I also inquired about textbooks and plays to be done. As I was about to seal the envelope, another letter arrived from a college of Fine Arts in San Francisco, also offering me a job for next fall! I compared both positions and came to the conclusion that New Mexico A & M was the wiser choice.

I waited impatiently for the summer session to end. A fellow student offered me a ride as far as Denver. After about two hours of traveling I was asked to drive. Naturally I was willing to relieve the owner of the car and take my turn driving. After a short while we approached a bridge; I made a sharp turn, hit the iron railing of the bridge, and the car came to a stop. We opened the hood and found the engine looking pretty bad. The nearest station was called, and the mechanic who arrived advised us that it would take the rest of the day to repair it and perhaps by tomorrow noon we could be ready to continue our trip. Of course I felt terrible, but there was nothing I could do. The fellow, who was from the University of Oregon, was nice enough to tell me, "This could happen to anyone and the insurance will probably cover it." The next day we took off and by the end of the day we were in Denver. I stayed there about two days with some friends and then proceeded on to Las Vegas.

Naturally, Roberta was glad to learn that I had a job. She insisted on driving me to Las Cruces to help me find housing. Also, without having to say anything about it, we both knew our marriage was on the rocks. Within a short time we were divorced.

On our way to Las Cruces we stopped in Santa Fe for two days. I always thought Santa Fe was "a city different" and interesting. In earlier days I had made an attempt to have a theatre there but found it too difficult and gave up.

It was a Saturday afternoon in September when I arrived in Las Cruces. I found a little place near the college. As I had no car, it worked out well. Besides, I thought to myself, how long will I be with this college in any event—one year, two years at the most? Now it is 1992.

INTERLUDE

Hershel Zohn–Late 1940's.

INTERLUDE

Twenty-five years—a quarter of a century—normally, a third of a man's life. Forty-two years ago, September 1950, I arrived in Las Cruces. It was then New Mexico A & M (some called it a "cow college"). The theatre building was about fifty years old. The stage and all equipment left much to be desired, but it was a starting point.

During the 1950-51 season we introduced two plays which created quite a furor—*Antigone* by the French dramatist Jean Anouilh and *Candida* by Bernard Shaw. Anouilh's *Antigone* is an adaptation of Sophocles' drama of the same title.

The magic of theatre! I can still see the conflict scenes between Creon and Antigone as enacted by students Edmond Sironi and Dayne Hilford. Not only was the audience introduced to a meaningful piece of dramatic literature, but the students had the experience of portraying these two characters. An experience which will stay with them for a lifetime.

The same applies to Bernard Shaw's comedy *Candida*. Again, the students had the opportunity of portraying Shaw's characters—especially the middle-aged Candida (Kathryn Gibbs) and the eighteen-year old poet Marchbanks (Frank Richardson).

The aim of educational theatre is a multiple one: The student, the faculty, the community. The drama student, or the one who only takes a few theatre courses, both should learn the history of theatre and the various movements and styles that have emerged through the ages. The drama major must also acquire a knowledge of dramatic literature (gone are the days when an actor couldn't read or write), acting, make-up, costumes, etc. The student is expected to have a complete knowledge of the theatre. Like any other field—music, art, dance, literature—theatre is a wide field.

University faculty, too, may be interested in the theatre program and may even participate in productions. Since the college or university is usually near a community, the theatre offers community residents an opportunity to participate in and attend productions. "What's going on at the campus theatre?" "Do they have a musical or a comedy?" "What about Shakespeare?" As beneficial as the campus theatre is to the surrounding community and faculty, however, the theatre teacher's primary concern is with the students majoring in drama.

While theatre is one of the seven Fine Arts, it is also a synthesis of the arts—Art, Music, Dance, etc. But, at the same time, theatre can stand on its own as long as it has the dramatist, actor, and director.

Looking back on those years, there have been triumphs and failures, plus the joy of working with talented and enthusiastic students, faculty, and community members. It has been a time to see the campus theatre grow and mature to produce works by significant contemporary and classic playwrights. Hopefully, I have been able to impart a love of good drama to all who participated in productions throughout those twenty-five years.

ACT III

New Mexico A & M

The First Year
　　Mrs. June Sage was elderly, slender, and spoke in a high-pitched voice, especially when she became angry. "I wouldn't give you a penny," was her trademark. She would repeat the same phrase, "I wouldn't give you a penny," more than once to make sure you knew that she meant what she said. This expression was usually directed at a student who had come to ask her for a loan. She would gradually diminish the volume of her voice and ask the visitor, "What do you need the money for?" She normally could tell whether the young man was honest or not, and ordinarily would be moved by the story and ask the student to sit down. She would finally show sympathy and would

agree to let him have a loan, provided that he or she would wash the floors, at least two rooms every other day, until the loan was paid back. The friendlier she became, the less interest the borrower had to pay. If she became very friendly with the borrower, there could be no interest at all. At times she would become very concerned with the student's affairs—as a mother to a son or daughter.

Most of the time she conducted her business from a narrow couch where she liked to lie. She had about six or eight cabins she rented to students or faculty. The writer of these lines was one of her tenants. The very first evening she didn't ask, but demanded, that I play cards with her. I said that I was tired. She never forgave me. Yet one of our students, who was in charge of props, managed to become one of her favorites and she frequently loaned him props for our productions. For that we gave her complimentary tickets to the play.

Once she came to see a play without complimentary tickets and asked the price of tickets. She was told fifty cents. She began to bargain, "Why so much?" She then made a big production of raising several petticoats to search for the half dollar. The play she saw happened to be a comedy. Mrs. Sage must have enjoyed it because her attitude toward me changed, and me thinks, became more respectful. Yet when I once asked her, "How about contributing some funds towards a theatre?" she immediately yelled, in her high-pitched voice, "I wouldn't give you a penny."

To enter her house one had to ring a bell, and when that bell rang, at least a dozen other bells would ring at the same time. However, Mrs. Sage was a popular figure on the campus because of her willingness to aid students in need of cash. In return, some faculty members helped her to pass evenings away by playing cards with her.

* * *

Las Cruces was a small town in the fifties. When compared to the nineties, it is a metropolis today. The same changes apply to New Mexico A & M (it became New Mexico State University in 1959)—with the various colleges, the many departments, the variety of doctoral degrees offered. This could also be said for the arts, music, painting, and writing.

Since this chapter is about theatre, I must say that from the Greeks to Shakespeare, Ibsen to Chekhov, and other worthy dramatists of yesterday and today—all have been produced here during the past four decades. Outstanding guest actors, among them, James Earl Jones, Elizabeth Huddle, and Jacqueline Brookes, have come here to act with the students in plays like *Othello*, Brecht's *The Good Woman Of Setzuan*, *As You Like It*, and others.

True, there had been trickles of theatre in the early days of this institution. *London Assurance*, by Dion Boucicault, was directed by Professor Macarthur of the English Department as early as 1904, and two cuttings of Shakespearean plays were done at the turn of the century. Usually, an English professor volunteered to do Shakespeare. Professor Neff directed *As You Like It* for the Bard's 300th birthday in 1916.[1]

Student-formed dramatic clubs emerged—The Masque and The Yucca Players, leading up to The Coronado Playmakers established by Professor Breland, head of the English Department. Professor Alexander Chilton, also in the English Department, was quite active in directing as well as in acting through the years. This interest in acting also extended to Earl Beem who came here as head of the English Department (although it seemed Professor Beem was more interested in Speech and Drama than in English). Beem brought Joe Brown, who had directed some of the earlier plays, to the campus.[2]

---

[1] Simon F. Kropp, *That All May Learn*, New Mexico State Univ., 1972. p. 143.
[2] Earl Beem was killed in a car accident in early 1951.

The type of plays performed here during the thirties and forties were largely "The Boy Meets Girl" and "Daddy Long-Legs" type of plays.

When I arrived in September 1950, Edgar Garrett was already here. He was scheduled to teach speech and direct the first and last plays; I was to teach drama and direct the second and third plays of the year. Garrett's first play was *The Importance of Being Earnest*, by Oscar Wilde—a very good choice, especially for a college. My selection was *Antigone*—a modern version by Jean Anouilh. When people heard we had scheduled a Greek tragedy as the next play, they raised their eyebrows. "A Greek tragedy here? On this campus? He must be insane." A suggestion was even made that I should be sent to the state mental institution in Las Vegas. I explained that this play was based on a Greek tragedy by Sophocles and was written by a contemporary French dramatist. It was symbolic of the Second World War, where Antigone represented the French people and King Creon was Hitler. The author, Jean Anouilh, meant to give secret courage to the people of France through this version of *Antigone*.

"OK," they replied resignedly, still convinced it would be too 'highbrow.'

But, before we did *Antigone*, Henry Gustafson, then head of the Alumni Association and Director of Milton Hall Student Center, asked me to present a special Homecoming program at Hadley Hall.

We chose two Chekhov one-acters, *The Boor* and *The Marriage Proposal*. These two short plays are highly farcical, and we Americanized their names to Peters, Smith, Lester, Chandler, and Lumpkin. In addition, we added two short scenes—take-offs on *Romeo and Juliet* and *The Warrior's Husband*, a satire on Greek drama. I recall the mother of a student who participated in *The Warrior's Husband* thought the few lines her daughter had to deliver were not proper and she prevented her from being in the program. This necessitated a quick replacement.

Hadley Hall was packed to capacity and the students were in a very jolly mood. The following notice appeared in the program:

> *The audience is encouraged to laugh and applaud to their heart's content, but not to break our very old chairs. Please sing with us the Aggie song at the end of the program before going to the basketball game.*

Well, the audience enjoyed themselves immensely. Not, only the old seats and aged floor, but even the windows were shaking from the constant applauding and laughter. Needless to say the program was a big success. Subsequently, the two Chekhov one-acters became a part of our repertoire and we toured with them to public schools throughout the state, for a week each time, during the next two years.

Rehearsals for *Antigone* intensified. The cast consists of twelve characters. Most of the students were experienced in college productions and were serious about their work in the play. While *Antigone* is a modern version of the Greek tragedy, the set was similar to the conventional Greek settings. Several steps led to a platform above, in addition to a smaller platform on one side of the stage. A cyclorama hung at the back of the set. An archway on each side of the stage and a small table with two chairs downstage completed the set.

As for costumes, the leading male characters wore tuxedos, the guards wore trenchcoats, while the female characters had on evening gowns of varied colors.

The play opens with all the characters on stage in different positions, Antigone in the center. Chorus enters and says:

> *Well, here we are. These people that you see here are about to act out for you the story of Antigone.*

He analyzes each character, their relationship with each other, and their purpose in the play. About Antigone, Chorus says,

> *Antigone is thinking that she is going to die. Antigone is young. She would rather live than die. But there is no help for it. When you are on the side of the gods against the tyrant, of man against the state of purity against corruption—when in short your name is Antigone, there is only one part you can play; and she will have to play hers through to the end.*

Chorus speaks about the other characters, about the story, about the difference between tragedy and melodrama, and his purpose in the play, but he always comes back to Antigone. Then the highly dramatic scenes between Antigone and Creon set the tone of the play:

ANTIGONE: *I laugh at you Creon, with your platitudes about happiness.*
CREON: *It is your happiness too, Antigone.*
ANTIGONE: *I spit on your idea of happiness. I spit on your idea of life—that life that must go on come what may. You are all like dogs, that lick everything they smell.*
CREON: (Grasps her by her wrist) *Be quiet. If you could see how ugly you are shrieking those words.* (Yells) *Guard! Take her away* (and throws her on the edge of the floor as she starts rolling down the steps before a guard manages to get to her).

The audience in the house that night was tense as laughter was heard from the back row. I was standing behind the back row watching the performance when the laughter was heard. I momentarily looked down the back row and was sure the laughter came from a young fellow in my Speech class. I made a mental note to take him to account next time in class. However, he didn't show up for a week. When he finally came to class, I still hadn't forgotten his laughter at such a sensitive moment in the play and I questioned him. He replied innocently, "That is the way I always react in sad situations." Well, how could I argue with him when psychologists would testify to that.

The local newspaper reviewer seemed to be excited about that type of play, especially where all the actors were in their positions at the beginning of the performance and the identical mise-en-scene as they took their curtain call. "It is to be hoped that the Playmakers and their director continue to offer productions of such high standards as *Antigone*."[3]

President of the College John W. Branson came backstage after the first night of *Antigone* to congratulate the cast. He came over to me, shook hands and said, "I didn't understand it, but I liked it." I thought the modern version of *Antigone* did not have any hidden meaning and its theme was very obvious. But I didn't care to go into a discussion with a person who looked to be a fine gentleman, and I understood he always supported the theatre program. Before every play, President Branson came to get his own tickets, and always asked, "When is kick-off time?" He never missed a play.

Soon after New Year 1951, the Playmakers embarked on a tour. From Monday through Friday, we visited public schools in

---

[3] A complete listing of plays, readings, workshops, children's theatre, etc., produced at New Mexico A & M and New Mexico State University between 1950-1975 may be found in Addendum A.

the state presenting *The Boor* and *The Marriage Proposal*.

We performed at two to three schools a day. When we arrived in Española, we were told that the best place to perform would be in the gymnasium; however, there was no stage. We had to change our performance from conventional staging to theatre-in-the-round (without a rehearsal). Then came Taos, where we performed as planned. After we finished our program, we discovered we were snowbound and could not go any further. We were marooned in Taos for two days.

We finally took a chance and continued to Raton, stopping on the way at a school in Eagle Nest where we entertained the children with Chekhov's humor. Following that performance, we started out for Raton but our car rolled over. Fortunately there were some big trucks on the road, and the drivers came to our rescue. We eventually arrived in Raton in time to spend the night. The costumes were hung in the large theatre's dressing rooms and when the actors came the next morning, they discovered the costumes were frozen to the wall. This reminded me of how Russian theatre companies often found their costumes frozen during the winter days. We returned to Las Cruces on Friday evening, all in one piece. The main purpose of the trip was to attract students to the college.

Our next production was *Candida* by George Bernard Shaw. Like *Antigone* this play was also a first. Shaw had never been performed here before. Shaw had died only a few months earlier, but it wasn't chosen because of his death. I had always wanted to do *Candida*, and now was the time to do it, in memory of the late G. B. Shaw.

Candida has a cast of six characters and one set with no foreseeable problems; although once rehearsals begin, various complications could emerge. Marchbanks, an eighteen-year-old poet falls in love with the minister's wife, Candida, who is twice his age. Candida doesn't necessarily reject him, but she encourages his feelings towards her. However, when the situation becomes serious, Marchbanks realizes he must remove himself from the scene and leave Candida to her preacher. But Candida doesn't let him leave so easily. She tells him, "Whenever you think of me, repeat the following sentence: 'When I am thirty, she will be forty-five, when I am sixty, she will be seventy-five...'" and young Marchbanks interrupts her saying, "In a hundred years, we shall be the same age. Let me go now into the darkness of the night." Candida kisses him on his forehead and he runs out, never to see her again. She quickly goes over to her husband, embraces him, and says, "Ah, James." That's Shaw for you. One is not sure whether he is laughing at Candida, critical of her pastor husband, or laughingly sympathizing with the young poet, Marchbanks.

The acting was outstanding, with Frank Richardson as the young poet, Kathryn Gibbs as Candida, Edmond Sironi as the minister, and a newcomer by the name of Leo Comeau as Burgess. All were quite believable in their characterizations. The local reviewer said, "People that missed this show are to be pitied." That first season closed with *The Drunkard*, directed by Ed Garrett.

Hadley Hall Theatre
Master Pierre Patelin
author unknown

The 1951-52 season began with *Master Pierre Patelin*, a one-act play from the Middle Ages which we presented as a prologue to our year's program. The first full-length vehicle was *The Silver Whistle* by Robert McEnroe.

* * *

The Silver Whistle
by Robert McEnroe

It is about a group of elderly people living in a home for the aged. As far as the time period is concerned, our program states, "It doesn't make much difference. There are always old people in the world." A character by the name of Oliver Erwenter, a hobo, appears on the scene. He claims to be seventy-seven, but he is actually forty-seven. He wants to instill the idea among the older people that "one is as old as he feels."

To this very day I can still remember how these young students—Leo Comeau, La Noel Brazil, Doris Howe and all the others—turned into old characters. (It is easier for a young actor to play an old person than one closer to his own age.) A new actress, graduate student Bernice Beenhauwer (who was more mature than the other students), contributed greatly with her performance as the younger Miss Tripp. The cast enjoyed performing in this vehicle. For weeks after the play had closed they still longed for their roles, and would have liked to play them again.

* * *

Pygmalion
by George Bernard Shaw

"*Pygmalion*?—another Shaw play?" "It seems that new director is 'Shaw happy.'" "What are we, a Shavian theatre?" Those were some of the complaints when *Pygmalion* was announced as our next production. Actually, through the years, we didn't present Shaw any more than Chekhov or Miller, and much less than Shakespeare.

Pygmalion was a king and sculptor of Cyprus who made an ivory statue of a maiden called Galatea. *Pygmalion* was first produced in England in 1914 with Mrs. Patrick Campbell as Eliza Doolittle. The play was made into a film in 1938, and subsequently produced as the popular musical, *My Fair Lady*, in 1956. We presented the play in December 1951.

It is the story of a phonetics expert who wagers that he can transform a flower girl with a cockney accent into a lady. The main characters in the play are: Eliza Doolittle, her father, Alfred Doolittle, Henry Higgins and Colonel Pickering.

Bernice Beenhouwer portrayed Eliza, and she came through with flying colors—cockney accent and all. The same could not be said about Leo Comeau, who was a talented actor but not comfortable in the role of Henry Higgins. There were differences of opinion on how to end the play, which we managed to settle amicably. By the end, Eliza is strong and wise enough to talk back to Henry Higgins. When he orders her to buy him "a tie to match the new suit of mine," she says, "What are you to do without me I cannot imagine." (She sweeps out.) In other words, "Buy the tie yourself." Higgins is on stage and roars with laughter. But the audience knows that Eliza is now strong enough to tell him where to go, and she has the audience on her side.

Productions in those days ran for only three performances. Before an actor could find himself in the role he was portraying, it was all over.

After Christmas we took the two Chekhov one-act plays on another tour of various schools in the state.

* * *

The Girl From Wyoming
by John Van Antwerp

Soon after I settled in Las Cruces, students began to bombard me with requests to do a musical. "How come we don't do a musical? It's about time we do a musical." Musicals are highly expensive. The royalties alone would drive one bankrupt, not to mention the many costumes, scenery, large casts, and the problems of singers and dancers—all for just three performances. Well, there were a few musicals floating around which wouldn't be too expensive, like *The Fireman's Daughter* or *The Girl From Wyoming*. The titles alone turned one against them. But we finally decided on the latter.

Then there were problems with the Music Department. Usually musicals in those days were done together with the Music Department. They were afraid of some of the dialogue or action—that we might be arrested. I finally convinced Kenneth Bender of the Music Department to be in charge of the music.

Two friends, Charles Stubing, from Foreign Languages, and Bob Wichert, from the English Department (both now deceased), sat in at rehearsals. They were usually called the "kibitzers." Afterwards we would go for coffee and discuss the rehearsal.

A student playing one of the leading female roles continually disrupted rehearsals with her profanity. Finally, I had to speak to the Dean of Women, and asked her to tell the girl to behave herself. The second female lead was Pauline Plumbley. She played "Chiquori, a fiery vixen from South of the Border." It was her "task" to do the most "daring scene." When she first made her entrance, she slowly took off her bracelet. In a scene with her step-brother Pedro, who wanted to kiss her, she said, "Pedro, I am your seester," and Pedro replied "only half." That line tore the house down.

The college president was not too happy with this production. The campus newspaper, *The Round-Up*, ridiculed the musical as naive and the director was relieved when it was all over. No more musicals for some time to come.

* * *

The Mad-Woman of Chaillot
by Jean Giraudoux

The Mad-Woman Of Chaillot, presented here in October 1952, has a cast of thirty-nine characters and takes place in Paris—the first act in a cafe and the second in the Countess' cellar. The author is trying to prove that the Countess and her three friends, all called madwomen, are wiser than the people who live above the cellar.

I had to make a special trip to New York to order the many costumes needed by the thirty-nine characters.

Several of the more important characters are: Prospector, Doorman, Waiter, President, Baron, Flower Girl, Deaf Mute, Paulette, Irma, Four Mad Women, and the Ragpicker. The latter, a philosopher, has the most interesting lines in the play. One of these lines created a problem.

RAGPICKER: *These days every cabbage has its pimp. Little by little the pimps have taken over the world. They don't do anything, they just stand there and take their cut. Do you ever see one smiling at a customer any more, certainly not. The smiles are strictly for the pimps. That's why the cost of living keeps going up all the time.*

When we began rehearsals, I was reluctant to use the word "pimp" over and over again (let's not forget it was 1952!). I experimented with using another word instead. It didn't sound right. I consulted with people who knew French, and finally went to the college president. He said it was OK to use it. Some people probably did not like it, but there were no official complaints. The president wasn't too happy about this play, either.

* * *

The Hasty Heart
by John Patrick

This comedy takes place in a convalescent ward of a British General Hospital behind the Assam Burma front. Of the cast of nine, Pauline Plumbley played the only woman. I remember Leo Comeau getting a lot of laughs due to his Scottish costume. We also gave a special performance of *The Hasty Heart* at White Sands Proving Ground on a Monday evening.

* * *

Life With Father
by Howard Lindsey and Russel Crouse

I first directed the comedy *Life With Father* in 1953 at New Mexico A&M, and later in El Paso in the early seventies; and the audience still liked it. The actors liked to perform in this play but for a different reason. The play has three acts and each act has a breakfast scene. Thespians like to eat too.

One amusing recollection from this play centered around the youngest actor, a seven-year-old whose older sister played his stage mother. The cast was quite amused at my attempts to explain to him that his sister was now his mother and now he should react differently to her.

* * *

Death of a Salesman
by Arthur Miller

In *Death Of A Salesman*, Miller believes the common man is as apt a subject for tragedy as kings. This philosophy has been debated since it was first produced. Willy Loman was unable to accept the fact that his role in the world was a truly insignificant one, but instead, persisted in the belief that he is a man of great importance. That is Willy's "tragic flaw." The play became an enormous success from the day it opened. It has played in many countries and in many languages throughout the years. The last significant production was in the spring of 1983 in Beijing, where the play opened in Chinese under Miller's direction. *Death Of A Salesman* is an American classic.

It took our audiences a while to get used to some of the serious plays. For instance, before the opening of *Death Of A Salesman*, a group of students presented me with an enormous black handkerchief to wipe my tears, because they were afraid no one else would react properly to the play. Fortunately, the handkerchief was not needed.

* * *

There was a time when only one student majored in Drama. That poor student appeared in every play while he was here except one, *The Heiress*. But, even during that play, he stood by through performances in case a member of the cast should break a leg; such was his love for acting. His name is Leo

Comeau. He later served for four years as a member of the college Drama Department staff.

The theatre at Hadley Hall was built about the turn of the century. It had an orchestra and balcony and about five-hundred seats. Many of the seats were rickety and falling apart. We needed new seats very badly. There were even editorials written about the need for new seats and after much ado, seats were ordered. When samples of two chairs arrived, the college president himself came to examine them and tried to sit in one of them. He lovingly stroked the plush and pronounced them satisfactory. Those were the days.

* * *

The Male Animal
by James Thurber and Elliott Nugent

The Playmakers opened their 1953-54 season with a successful Broadway comedy, *The Male Animal*. Our program notes say, "In *The Male Animal* many autobiographical situations are present, very thinly veiled. Midwestern, our mythical college for tonight, is quite frankly Ohio State University, and indirectly it deals with free speech and the Sacco-Vanzetti Case." Dr. Paul Conklin, of the English Department, wrote a lengthy review in the *Round-Up*. The following is from that review.

> *The Playmakers gave a highly creditable rendition of* The Male Animal *to well-filled houses last week. This reviewer had the feeling that any performance on a higher level can hardly be expected from college players.*

* * *

The Heiress
by Ruth and Augustus Goetz

On another note, we moved from three performances to four performances per production. *The Heiress* by Ruth and Augustus Goetz, about a shy young girl, is based on a Henry James novel called *Washington Square*. First produced under the title *Washington Square*, it was not well received, but after it was rewritten by the Goetzes and reopened as *The Heiress*, it received praise from critics and audiences alike and ran for four hundred performances.

During the dress rehearsal, the lead actress became ill and it appeared we would need a replacement. There was a dance on campus that night and I hurried there and wandered among the dancers until I found Joy Miller. Joy agreed to help, and learned the part overnight. But, by five o'clock the next afternoon, the lead actress had recovered and returned. Joy's effort and sacrifice were not needed, but that was an example of student involvement and dedication.

* * *

An Enemy of the People
by Henrik Ibsen
adapted by Arthur Miller

Both Ibsen and Miller were realists, and depicted social topics in their plays. I identified them so strongly together, that I sometimes called them Arthur Ibsen and Henrik Miller.

Henrik Ibsen (1828-1906) was the founder of realism. His views, especially on women's rights, were considered too radical for his time, and he was forced to leave Norway and lived most of his life in other lands. When he did return, his people finally embraced him and recognized his talent. "Here lies the bricklayer of modern drama," is the epitaph on his tombstone. Ibsen is also noted for *A Doll's House*, *Ghosts*, and *Hedda Gabler*.

Because both were realists, it is no wonder that Miller adapted Ibsen's play. First produced in 1887 in Berlin, it opened in New York under Miller's pen in 1950. Sixty-three years later it was still a vital and timely play.

Dr. Stockman, a small-town Norwegian physician, discovers the water is poisoned. He feels it is his responsibility to warn the people not to drink the water. However, his brother, the mayor, does not want them to know because it might affect business in town. Speaking at a public meeting in town, the doctor is heckled by members of the audience (several actors are deliberately planted in the theatre, to break up the doctor's speech). So realistic was the scene that several members of the audience began to protest and demand the hoodlums be thrown out of the theatre. Dr. Stockman tries to help people but instead he is ridiculed and he and his family are forced to go into hiding. His last lines as they are huddled together:

> *Remember now, everybody. You are fighting for the truth, that's why we are alone. That makes you strong—we are the strongest people in the world.* (Crowd voices build.) *And the strongest must learn to be lonely.*

The male lead had great difficulty learning his lines, particularly for the mob scene. He claimed a girl in the mob reminded him of someone and that was his problem. Sometimes that happens.

It was an exciting production. The *Las Cruces Sun-News* of March 11, 1954, says, "Baldwin praises acting, direction, scenery." Dr. P. M. Baldwin, Professor of History, states, "the Miller-Ibsen play, *An Enemy of the People*, is excellent theatre."

"Fine As Snuff," says a cousin of author Henrik Ibsen at Playmakers presentation of *An Enemy of the People*, Friday, March 12, 1954.

Las Cruces Sun-News, Monday, March 15, 1954:

KINSWOMAN OF PLAYWRIGHT
PRAISES COLLEGIATE DRAMA

A standing-room-only house was the occasion last night of the visit of Henrik Ibsen's cousin, Marjorie, and of several members of the El Paso Players' group as the run of Ibsen's An Enemy of the People *closed in Hadley Hall at New Mexico A. and M. College.*

Marjorie Ibsen who is from Santa Rita, NM was interviewed following the performance. She declared that she first came to Santa Rita some years ago for a brief six-months rest and has remained ever since.

"This is the first time I've ever seen a complete performance of An Enemy of the People*," she said. "Of course, I had seen many scenes and short excerpts put on by amateur and college groups including one done over at Silver City at New Mexico Western College two years ago."*

Addressing the cast and its director, Hershel Zohn, she declared, "I think you're all to be congratulated for not only attempting this play, but for doing it so well." She remembered that years ago she had seen Walter Hampden in the role of the mayor in New York.

Miss Ibsen has been a nurse and school teacher and is a graduate of Drake University, Des Moines, Iowa. Her father was Ibsen's first cousin. Miss Ibsen visited her ancestral home in Norway in 1935, but was born in this country.

She remembers, she says, having read this play to her grandmother in Norwegian as a young girl, but she added sadly, "I've forgotten most of my Norwegian."

After she had congratulated each member of the cast and Director Zohn, she said there was a Norwegian expression which she thought adequately described the Coronado Playmaker production—"fin somm snuss" which she translated into "fine as snuff."

Director Hershel Zohn then told the group he hoped to do Hedda Gabler *next year, by the same playwright to which Miss Ibsen added that she wanted to be informed when it was performed so that she could return.*

Shortly after this, two members of the El Paso Players came on stage to congratulate Hershel Zohn and the cast for the Ibsen performance.

* * *

A Phoenix Too Frequent
by Christopher Fry
and
The Wedding
by Anton Chekhov

The final production of 1953-54 was a double bill: *A Phoenix Too Frequent* and *The Wedding*.

A Phoenix Too Frequent, a long one-acter, is a comedy by the British dramatist Christopher Fry. There are three characters, two women and one man. The action takes place in the tomb of Virilius where a pious widow and her maid mourn for the widow's recently deceased husband. They eventually get hungry for food and suddenly a corporal appears who happens to have food. Before long the mourning by the pious widow for her husband becomes less, while her interest in the corporal becomes more.

Anton Chekhov's *The Wedding* takes place in a second-class restaurant, during a wedding dinner where they eat and drink and have a good time—and so does the audience watching them.

Professor Stobie of the English Department liked Leo Comeau's acting in *The Wedding*, which he rightfully thought was plotless. He didn't like *A Phoenix Too Frequent*, which he thought was too heavily plotted, but he was enthusiastic about Joy Miller's portrayal of the servant.

The cast took this program to El Paso for one performance at Texas Western (later the University of Texas at El Paso).

* * *

The Country Girl
by Clifford Odets

Odets has been one of America's most successful dramatists. *The Country Girl* deals with theatre life, and the characters include a dramatist, producer, director, actor, his wife, a dresser, a stage manager, and an ingenue. The actor gets a major role but still can't stay away from alcohol. His wife does everything possible to enable the actor to go through with his role, but she fails. (I should like to add that Odets' *Awake and Sing*, about a family living in the Bronx after the First World War, is considered one of his finest plays.)

* * *

Twelfth Night or **What You Will**
by William Shakespeare

March 1955 was our very first attempt at Shakespeare. There was an elderly lady in town by the name of Mrs. Locke, who, I was told, was on the Board of Regents. When she learned we were going to do Shakespeare, she said, "I have two books on my little table near my bed; one is the Bible, the second is Shakespeare. I didn't think I was ever going to see Shakespeare at my college."

Faculty came from Texas Western to see it. Performances were very well attended. The play was done in period costumes. The scenery by Ray Veitch was also suited to the play, with the music arrangements by Oscar Butler. The actors were well cast with Edgar Garrett as Sir Toby Belch, Leo Comeau as Sir Andrew Aguecheek, John Bellamy as Malvolio, Judith Leslie as Viola, Shirley Mayfield as Olivia, Ken Guthrie as Sebastian, David Ivey as Orsino, and Jim Cole as Feste, a clown, Marjorie McCorkle as the Maid, and many others. In other words, it was an excellent cast. The success of *Twelfth Night* gave us the impetus to do more Shakespeare. Our policy was to do a Shakespearean play every other year and to alternate between comedy and tragedy.

* * *

The Winslow Boy
by Terrence Ratigan

The Winslow Boy, by this English playwright, deals with a prominent man who receives a letter informing him that his young son has been dismissed for forging a signature on a five-shilling money order. Based upon the Archer-Shee case, it was called the English "Dreyfuss Case." The boy was finally exonerated.

After Shakespeare, this piece was rather anti-climactic. This was the opinion of the actors as well as the director. Yet, I should mention Phil Mead as Sir Robert and Earnest Antonis as Ronnie Winslow, who stood out more than the rest of the cast.

* * *

We finally received four hundred nice seats. Then, we realized the chairs were too nice for the theatre. In other words, the theatre badly needed improvement. First we closed the balcony. We called in an advisor from the Home Economics Department about curtains for the windows and carpeting, at least, for the aisles. I wanted to get rid of the "Roxy Theatre curtain." The Hadley Hall theatre, had, at that time, a unique curtain. The joke was that the only other curtain like it was at the Roxy Theatre in New York. Therefore, we called it "The Roxy Theatre curtain." This curtain caused us indescribable trouble. Before each production, stage crews spent hours of labor to make sure the curtain would operate properly during performances; still the curtain got stuck. We frequently couldn't open it, or, when it did open, it would not close at the end of an act. At one time the student pulling the curtain was pulled into the gridiron[4] with the rope. The curtain was so thin, that when closed, the audience could see the actors through it. After an exhaustive search we finally obtained a draw curtain, a cyclorama, and other items. In other words, at last we had, more or less, a decent theatre.

During the same year we also presented *Down In The Valley* by Kurt Weill and *Brooklyn Baseball Cantata* by G. Kleinsinger—directed by Oscar Butler and Leo Comeau, respectively.

* * *

---

[4] An iron rod above the curtain.

The Crucible
by Arthur Miller

The Crucible is a highly significant work about witchcraft in Salem, Massachusetts, in 1692. It is historical, but also symbolic of the McCarthy days in this country in the early fifties. Miller said, "If it's interpreted this way, so be it," although that was not his intention.

About the principle character, John Proctor, Miller maintained, "Proctor is a man who fights against the loss of his identity, a loss which he believes would result if he joined the group. He believed in paradise but he didn't want to go there so quickly. Besides, if you confessed to being a fraud, you were someone who pretended to be decent who really was a liar."

It had a large cast with the leading characters being John Proctor and his wife, Elizabeth, and Abigail, the leader of the young girls who is largely responsible for the violence in the play.

The climax comes with John Proctor and several others being taken from the prison cell to be hanged, all because they refused to testify to a lie. Reverend Hale turns to Elizabeth Proctor, saying to her, *"Woman, plead with him! It is pride, it is vanity. Be his helper—what profit him to bleed? Shall the dust praise him? Shall the worms declare his truth? Go to him, take his shame away* (drum roll back stage). Elizabeth, (with bitter triumph) *"He has his goodness now. God forbid I take it from him."* (The drum roll heightens violently.)

An historical epilogue: Not long after the fever died, Reverend Paris, father of one of the girls, was voted out of office. He walked out on the high road and was never heard of again. Legend says that Abigail turned up later as a prostitute in Boston. Elizabeth Proctor married again four years after Proctor's death. In a solemn meeting, the congregation rescinded the excommunications—this in March 1712. But they did so on orders from the government. To all intents and purposes, the power of the theocracy in Massachusetts was broken.

The Crucible was first directed by Jed Harris with scenery by Boris Aronson. However, after several months of performances on Broadway, Miller stopped the performances and made changes in the script. He eliminated the scenery, directed the play himself, and reopened the production. He felt the original sets obstructed the message of the play. Since then, *The Crucible* has been performed either way.

When the play was produced here in October 1955, a few letters were received by the college president complaining about the "language." What they really meant was the plot. Professor Neuman Reed wrote to the president, stating we had a right to do the play as it was written. Years later, when I was in Mexico City auditioning a young actress for the role of Abigail, there was a scene where she cries. Suddenly there was a knock on the door of the audition room. "What are you doing to the young lady?" I had to explain that it was only a scene from a play and her crying was only an act.

Later that summer, when we opened *The Crucible* at the English-speaking theatre in Mexico City, it was also performed at the same time in Spanish at the Belles Artes and directed by Seki Sano, a popular director in Mexico at that time. Our English version took a little more than two hours, and the Spanish version was about twice as long. One reason for the longer time in the Spanish version is that the stage at Belles Artes is extremely large. It took more time for an actor to get from one place to another, and perhaps the translation had something to do with it.

July 1956, Mexico City

COLONYSCOPE
by Mary Martinez

Over coffee with Hershel Zohn yesterday morning I got an inkling of what Players and their guest director are going through. Russian-born Mr. Zohn, long a U.S. citizen, Broadway actor and for six years head of the Drama Department at New Mexico State College, looks forward to opening Arthur Miller's The Crucible *Tuesday night with enthusiasm and trepidation. First there were such casting difficulties (not enough men) that, after a week of readings, the play was abandoned for Shaw's* Candida. *Then actors presented themselves and the big work of rehearsing twenty people got underway. At one point Mr. Zohn in desperation cut out four roles. Then he put them in again. He rehearsed four different women in the key part of Abigail before he found the personality he needed. During rehearsal the other night a leading woman fainted. She now has an understudy. The small stage at Players has presented further problems. Belles Artes, currently playing* The Crucible *in Spanish has helped out by lending some Puritan (the setting is New England in the seventeenth century) male costumes they didn't need but all the women's clothes must be made. Rehearsals are going on until well after midnight; on Sunday all day and night.*

It was refreshing to talk to Mr. Zohn, a man who has been through the New York mill of commercial theater and has come to be an important leader in the non-commercial theater, which, through community playhouses and college drama departments, is a rapidly growing thing in the United States. So worthwhile have a number of university productions been in recent years that such stars as Raymond Massey, Paul Muni and Charles Laughton have volunteered to take part in them. At New Mexico State College, Mr. Zohn produces six plays a year. When he leaves Mexico at the end of next month he goes into rehearsal of The Inspector General *of Gogol and follows with Shaw's* Arms and the Man, Macbeth, *and* The Diary of Anne Frank. *A dream of his is to come back to Mexico to direct the last-named play in Spanish. Mr. Zohn feels that* The Crucible, *apart from its interesting thematic content, is, above all, good theater. The kind of play, he says, that "hits you in the face."*

We performed *The Crucible* here again in 1972 with a guest actor Clinton Kimbrough as John Proctor. I also did the play for the Classic Theatre in Albuquerque at the Popejoy Hall in 1976.

* * *

Gigi
by Colette
dramatized by Anita Loos

That same season we also performed *Gigi*. Judith Leslie played Gigi, Joy Miller was Mme. Alvarez, Ann Armstrong was Andree, with David Ivey, and David Travis as Gaston and Victor, respectively. The play centers around a family of French courtesans. This created some problems in the community. The pastor of a local church publicly objected to the play and complained to the college president. The students wanted to picket the church in protest. The protest was averted and the whole incident died peacefully.

* * *

The Imaginary Invalid
by Moliere

What Shakespeare is to England, Moliere is to France. Unfortunately, the adaptation of *The Imaginary Invalid* did not do justice to the classic comic writer Moliere. All I can say is that Jim Cole and Lou Wiseman did justice in their respective roles.

Oh yes, something happened at this time which eventually became a part of my life. A young lady appeared at my office one day and we got into a discussion about literature. She seemed intelligent, but kind of shy. Directors are always on the lookout for people—not only for actors, but also for others to work in the theatre. Since she was an artist, I asked her whether she would like to do a drawing of Moliere for the program. She immediately consented. When I returned from lunch the next day there was a nice drawing for the Moliere program on my desk with a note, "I hope it meets with your approval." I thanked her for the nice job and asked if she would like to do the program for the next play, *The Skin Of Our Teeth*. She said yes. Then I asked her about doing the posters. (I had a lot of nerve in those days.) She hesitated and then agreed. She did a very interesting, creative program cover and poster in harmony with the plot. She made one mistake however; on the poster she left out one letter, the first 'n' in Thornton's name.

* * *

The Skin of Our Teeth
by Thornton Wilder

The final play for the 1955-1956 season was Wilder's *The Skin Of Our Teeth*. This, along with *Our Town* and *The Matchmaker*, are his three most famous plays. When I saw *The Skin Of Our Teeth* in New York, I made a mental note that we should do this work. It is an interesting allegorical play, but difficult to do. (Since when did this stop us?) It required quite a large cast and posed many technical problems.

It is a comedy about George Antrobus, his wife, two children, and their utility maid, Sabina. The Antrobuses have survived a fire, flood, pestilence, the seven-year locusts, the Ice Age, the black pox, the double feature, a dozen wars, and many depressions. They are the true offspring of Adam and Eve. They have survived a thousand calamities by the skin of their teeth. It is a tribute to their indestructibility.

There are thirty characters, two sets, many props, and complex lighting—but we got through "by the skin of our teeth." Sheila Livingston was fine, but after the play I never saw her again. Patricia Pierce was OK. She was experienced but she was too busy with her job to continue performing. Terryl Neville was also OK, but he fell asleep before performance time and we had to hold the curtain for thirty minutes while I went to his apartment to wake him up. But we survived.

Earthquake

The production of *The Crucible* the previous summer in Mexico City had been well received. The relationship between the administration of Players, Inc. and myself couldn't be better. Before I left Mexico City, we agreed to produce another play the following summer, 1957. After some deliberation *The Sea Gull* by Anton Chekhov was chosen. Since I had done the play before as a reading at Highlands in Las Vegas, New Mexico, I was pretty well acquainted with the play. I did have problems in casting *The Sea Gull*. However, once the casting was finished we decided on performance dates and began rehearsals.

My hotel in Mexico City was the Emporio. I found this hotel quite comfortable and convenient; right on the Reforma and close to the theatre. Through the years I always liked to stay there. The lobby had an attractive, solid, good-sized table with a telephone for guests to use, or one could just sit around the table and chat. That's the way it was on a late Saturday evening in July when I returned from rehearsal. I didn't feel like going up to my room. Three or four guests of the hotel and I entered into a discussion on philosophy. We spent about an hour and came to no conclusion.

It was 1:00 a.m. when I went to my room, undressed, went to bed and quickly fell asleep. It wasn't long before I was awakened by the shaking of windows and the noise of people screaming and running in the hallway. I grabbed a pair of trousers so I could open the door to find out what was happening. Although I had never experienced an earthquake before, I knew that it was an earthquake. Windows were shaking and breaking. People were crying and running in the hallway. Luckily I was on the second floor. Originally I was on the fourth floor, but guests who had come in that afternoon wanted fourth floor rooms, so I offered to take their rooms on the second floor and they could take mine. During the earthquake, windows on the fourth floor broke, but mine were not disturbed at all.

I got quickly into a shirt and shoes and went downstairs; there was no electricity, so candles were lit. People were embracing each other without knowing who they were. One guest was yelling on the telephone, "Mom, I am OK, don't worry," and hung up. In general there was chaos and confusion. Outside young boys went into stores and walked off with whatever they could carry. It must have been about 4:00 a.m. when I finally went back to my room. Usually after an earthquake there are minor shakes and this was the case here, too.

When morning came, I was up and dressed because I couldn't sleep—one could not shave either because there was no water. Later in the morning coffee was finally made. It was Sunday morning and it's usually quiet and peaceful on the streets, but not this morning. The traffic was at its peak with people running around trying to find out what had happened to their friends and loved ones. They were especially concerned about their beloved "Angel," the famous statue at the Reforma.

Our rehearsal was scheduled for ten o'clock. I didn't expect anyone to be there. When I entered the theatre, I was surprised to see the entire cast ready to rehearse. I said, "I am sorry I can't rehearse now. I must go and see how my friends are. If you want to rehearse, do it without me."

On Monday morning we learned we could not use the theatre. The government had closed all public places until further notice, "Because of the earthquake, it is not safe to use public edifices."

Whether it was due to the earthquake or not, I became sick. The pharmacist and his wife (the drug store was next door to the hotel) supplied me with all sorts of medications and even chicken soup. It took two weeks or longer before the Mexican government finally gave permission for people to use some of the public buildings. Our theatre was only slightly damaged, but after some pleading with government representatives and ... we were permitted to use the building.

It has been thirty-four years since this happened, but I can still hear the voices crying and screaming, and imagine that I see people running. It's like it happened just yesterday. While it was not as big or serious as the most recent earthquake, quite a few buildings in the center of the city were demolished, in addition to a number of casualties. It took a long time before things were back in order.

People who reside in Mexico City know very well that the city is earthquake prone, yet it doesn't stop them from living there.

* * *

The Inspector General
by Nikolai Gogol

Gogol (1809-1852) was Russia's first significant novelist and short story writer. My program notes tell me he also occupied an honorable position in the theatre, chiefly on the strength of his broad satire in *The Inspector General*. Gogol's masterpiece, known in Russian as *Revizor*, was first produced in 1836 with the consent of Emperor Nicholas I, who attended the premiere—but later regretted his tolerance. It proved to be a devastating satire on bureaucratic corruption in provincial Russia. Gogol saw the theatre as an institution capable of influencing the spiritual needs of the audiences, of educating them toward a higher morality and ethic.

Vsevolod Meyerhold, called the "Mad Genius" of the Russian theatre, directed *The Inspector General* with a semi-circle of doors. The doors represented the maze of Russian bureaucracy. The play is a combination of constructivism, expressionism, and naturalism, and is called a highly theatrical and sparkling satire. Wherever men study theatre, scholars say, directors usually direct the play "as Meyerhold did it." In our own small way we also attempted to do it "as Meyerhold did it." Looking back, I doubt if our audience appreciated it.

The Communist government became dissatisfied with his style of production. They wanted Meyerhold to change his style; he refused. First, his theatre was taken from him; then he was put in jail, and afterwards shot. This was the tragic end of a great man of the theatre.

* * *

Hedda Gabler
by Henrik Ibsen

As previously mentioned, Norwegian dramatist Henrik Ibsen is considered the innovator of modern drama. About *Hedda Gabler* he wrote, "My intention in giving it this name was to indicate that Hedda, as a personality, is to be regarded rather as her father's daughter than as her husband's wife."

Casting plays is not easy. A director usually has a certain person in mind for a given character. The more complicated the character, the more difficult it is to cast. That was the case with Hedda Gabler. One Saturday afternoon a lady appeared at the door of my office. I said, "What can I do for you." At first I thought she was lost.

Then she replied, "I am interested in acting." I instantly thought of Hedda for her. As I got to know her better, I realized that Martha Gold was Hedda in life, as well as on stage. It turned out to be a fairly good production. Subsequently, Gold was in a number of plays, but nothing like *Hedda Gabler*.

Hedda is a case for a psychiatrist. She is afraid to face life. That's why she commits suicide. The play ends very suddenly. On stage are her husband, Tesman, Judge Brack, and Hedda, who is in the inner room starting to play the piano. (A shot is heard.) Tesman runs in to see what happened and soon returns shrieking to Judge Brack. *"Shot herself! Shot herself in the temple! Fancy that!"* Brack: *"Good God—people don't do such things."* This is how the play ends. Sometimes, people laugh at this line—it all depends on how the last two lines are delivered. However, this is definitely Hedda's play. No wonder actresses like Elanora Duse, Alla Nazimova, and Eva Le Gallienne appeared in this work time and time again.

* * *

The Rainmaker
by N. Richard Nash

The Rainmaker is an "easy" show to do. Set in the Southwest, it has seven characters and only one set. In the midst of casting I received a long distance telephone call; my father had passed away. There was a big snowstorm that day and planes could not take off from El Paso. I canceled rehearsals, closed the door to my office, put out the lights and visualized. I saw my father lying on the floor, like I remembered my grandfather when he died. As I was thinking about my father, my visualizing was disturbed by someone knocking at the door.

The only female character in *The Rainmaker* is greatly worried that she may never meet the right man to marry. The role was portrayed by Patsy McRee. She must have been very convincing, because the college president was so moved by her acting that he sent her a letter telling her not to worry, "You will find a man before too long." Little did he know that Patsy was married and about to have a child.

The Playmakers dedicated *The Rainmaker* to International Theatre month of March 1957. Our program quotes were in honor of International Theatre Month:

> *It is not the bright lights or the so-called female glamour that makes the theatre so exciting for the actor—it is the audience.*—Helen Hayes

> *Of all the Arts, that of the theatre is the most universal.*
> —Sir Laurence Olivier

* * *

Arms and the Man
by George Bernard Shaw

This was our first of several renditions of Shaw's clever comedy, which takes place in Bulgaria in 1885-86. There is an operetta based on this comedy called *The Chocolate Soldier*.

Poet John Masefield wrote a fitting tribute to George Bernard Shaw.

> *A happy task, to praise the mental prince*
> *Whose spirit began life a century since.*
> *Let those, who knew him better, better tell;*
> *Small knowledge mine, much urge to praise him well,*
> *Because, from all I either heard or saw,*
> *I think a marvel lived in Bernard Shaw.*

The Air Mechanics Building

It had been only two years since we put new seats into Hadley Hall theatre, added a new curtain, plus smaller curtains, carpets on the floors, and other improvements. Suddenly, as I was in Mexico City directing *The Sea Gull*, I received a special delivery letter from Dr. Neuman Reed, head of the English Department. A woman had fallen down the stairs in Hadley Hall and complained to the administration that the building was a fire trap; the whole structure was condemned. All kinds of alternatives were proposed as to what should be done with our scenery and all the costumes and props accumulated through the years. Two suggested alternatives were placing them in a classroom or storing everything in one of the old army barracks. But the immediate problem was where to present the plays for the fall of 1957. Overnight I had become a director without a theatre. I returned to Las Cruces soon afterwards and began a search for a place to present our plays. I looked at different places—student union and the cafeteria, among others.

Dean of Agriculture Robert A. Nichols, who in his student days had taken speech courses, said, "I have a suggestion. There are two barracks where pigs are kept for laboratory work. In the afternoon I can put all the pigs in one barrack, we can fumigate the other barrack, and you can do your Shakespeare there."

I thought for a while and finally said, "No thank you. We have enough ham among the drama students and its director as it is. I'll go on looking." Dean William O'Donnell interceded and obtained the hangar in the Air Mechanics Building for our temporary theatre. It took him awhile to convince the Mechanical Engineering Department to let us have the hangar for one year only. After a year we would have a theatre, I was told. The hangar was freezing cold in the winter and unbearably hot in the summer. Once, after a winter's snow, members of the cast and the director had to go out and remove the snow from the door so the audience could enter.

* * *

The Lark
by Jean Anouilh
adapted by Lillian Hellman

We opened this so-called theatre with *The Lark*, which called for a cast of twenty-two and many different scenes. We moved two hundred twenty of the new seats from the theatre at Hadley Hall into the hangar, actually an empty hall. It was to be a theatre on three sides with an open stage, instead of a theatre-in-the-round. But we needed a stage—a platform. For that we had to thank Willie Preciado, who was the College's Buildings and Grounds superintendent. He brought in several platforms made from twelve-by-four panels. Time was short, so we just put them together, hoping it would work. We installed some lighting and our production of *The Lark* was on. There was a lot of action and excitement in the play—running, jumping, fighting. Within a short time the platforms moved apart and the actors found themselves on the floor. If I recall correctly, at intermission we put the platforms together again. Another problem was, when the actors walked on the platform, there was a lot of noise because there was nothing beneath the platform to absorb the noise.

The Lark is about Joan of Arc, and is a beautifully written drama by Jean Anouilh which, has been adapted by another talented dramatist, Lillian Hellman.

There are at least four different versions of *Joan of Arc*: Shaw, Schiller, Mark Twain, and Anouilh-Hellman.

Twenty-five years after Joan's death in 1456, her sentence was annulled. In 1909 she was beatified and in 1919 she was canonized. That was one reason for the popularity of any play about her. Another reason, wrote the American novelist John Steinbeck, was "the factor of universality." I should add that Pat Weiler was quite a convincing Joan. And who can forget the late Charles Stillwell as Charles the Dauphin—he was most memorable.

* * *

The Glass Menagerie
by Tennessee Williams

My notes tell me that "there was quite a drop of interest in our second production." I don't know why. Was it attendance, or what?

The Glass Menagerie is a most poetic piece and one of Williams' best. It is about a fragile girl and her mother's concern for her. Other characters include the son, The Gentleman Caller, and the Father, who, after an absence of two years, sends a postcard consisting of two words: Hello, Goodbye.

Arthur Miller and Tennessee Williams are considered the two most significant dramatists to emerge in the forties. Miller is noted for his social dramas: *Death Of A Salesman* and *The Crucible*. Williams' plays are about the individual—the mentally sick in *A Street Car Named Desire*, or the physically sick such as Laura in *The Glass Menagerie*.

* * *

Macbeth
by William Shakespeare

Macbeth is one of the Bard's four tragedies. The others are *King Lear*, *Hamlet*, and *Othello*, with *Macbeth* being last of the four. We began our Shakespeare with *Twelfth Night*; then came *Macbeth*, which was followed by *A Midsummer Night's Dream*. Producer, director, actors, costumer, musicians, etc., all learned a great deal by participating in Shakespearean productions—an experience which remains with one forever. The following is one of the most memorable passages in *Macbeth*.

> *Tomorrow, and tomorrow and tomorrow*
> *Creeps in this petty pace from day to day*
> *To the last syllable of recorded time*
> *And all our yesterdays have lighted fools*
> *The way to dusty death. Out, out brief candle!*
> *Life's but a walking shadow, a poor player*
> *That struts and frets his hour upon the stage*
> *And then is heard no more. It is a tale*
> *Told by an Idiot, full of sound and fury,*
> *Signifying nothing.*

We gave six performances of *Macbeth*, the most we had ever offered. I remember the theatre was full every night. Jack Soules, a physics professor, was Macbeth, Robert Jones was Macduff, and Oscar Butler the Porter. Maurcena Learned, Ray Veitch and others worked on the scenery and props.

* * *

The Sea Gull
by Anton Chekhov

We performed this play as a reading. Readings are not unusual. Some plays lend themselves to readings; *The Sea Gull* is one of them. This was my second presentation of this play as a reading. Half of the cast was faculty, the rest were students. Rehearsals were long and argumentative (that's the way faculty like it).

Chekhov appeared on the scene when Ibsen realism dominated the European stage. Chekhov's realism, however, is subtle. He was concerned with the internal conflicts within the characters. His characters speak irrelevantly, sometimes not at all. The futility and frustrations of life are the main themes in Chekhov's plays. His characters are yearning for a different life, and there is much drama in that yearning. They would like to break away from their environment, but they realize that it's futile, like a sign in red letters—No Exit! When Chekhov finished *The Sea Gull*, critics were bewildered and didn't know how to react to it, although everyone realized it was something new on the horizon of the stage.

Chekhov himself was very dissatisfied with the theatre of his day. Through the young poet Konstantin in *The Sea Gull*, he speaks of the stage saying, "We need new forms of expression, and if we can't have them, we had better have nothing." His characters are so real and subtle that he becomes the artist who conceals art. That is why his plays are so challenging to the actor. It is the mood, the poetry, the-between-the-lines that are so essential in a Chekhovian production. The people in his works are universal; under different names they can be found in any part of the world. His influence on modern drama is evident.

During the summer of 1958 I embarked on a trip to look at theatres in this country, as well as in Canada, which used theatre-in-the-round: The Stratford Theatre in Connecticut, some smaller summer theatres in New York State, the off-Broadway, the off-off-Broadway theatres, and the Stratford in Ontario, Canada. At the latter I spent several days. I was invited to examine everything backstage, in addition to observing rehearsals and attending the Shakespearean productions they had that summer. Oh, yes, the Queen of England was there to see the Shakespeare repertoire. I believe the Stratford in Canada was superior to the one in Connecticut and even to the Stratford-on-Avon. I departed from Canada determined to have our own make-shift campus theatre "fashioned" after the Stratford of Ontario.

We built a sturdy platform stage, put a lot of cotton insulation beneath the stage to eliminate noise, elevated the seats to six different levels, and added more lighting and a cyclorama above the platform stage. The dressing rooms were still makeshift and we had a makeshift box office and lobby. We called our theatre "The Stratford of Las Cruces," when we were in a good mood, and "The Dump" when in a bad mood. We had come in for one year, but were there for six creative years.

* * *

The Teahouse of the August Moon
by John Patrick

Our first production of the 1958-59 season was *The Teahouse Of The August Moon*. The author said, "People sometimes ask if this play is listed as a comedy, is it not in reality a serious piece. Then I hasten to point out that they should make 'Teahouse' what they wish, for it was meant to be that way. *The Teahouse* was aimed to make one think, or to make you forget if you wish to forget." *Teahouse* takes place in Tobiki Village, Okinawa, during the latter part of the Second World War.

Of course we had everything in this production, including a live goat and a jeep. Mike Milam, as the interpreter Sakini, was as charming as can be, as was Charles Stillwell, Sylvia Lydick as Lotus Blossom, Scotty Clark, and many others.

It had great appeal to everyone. People continually stood in line for tickets throughout the run, and once inside the theatre, immensely enjoyed watching the performance. What else could a producer ask for? No wonder *Teahouse* won so many prizes, including the Pulitzer Prize.

* * *

The Playboy of the Western World
by John Millington Synge

This play has had a stormy history. Opening night in Dublin, Saturday, January 16, 1907, proved to be the beginning of a week of audience rioting in the Abbey Theatre. Many Irish nationalists were already hostile to Synge because of two previous plays, *In the Shadow of the Glen* and *The Well of the Saints*. *Playboy* merely confirmed their belief that the author was dedicated to slandering the Irish peasantry, particularly its women.

Our program notes relate the demonstrations, disturbances, and rock throwing the Abbey Theatre had to withstand. Today, of course, *The Playboy of the Western World*, is an acceptable classic in Ireland and throughout the world. Needless to say, there were no riots in our production which featured some fine acting by Karen Gardner as Pegeen, Larry Manning as the son, and the late Charles Stillwell as the father, Old Mahon. The set was interesting, and praised by a noted Taos artist. He exclaimed, "what a wonderful place to have a theatre!" Unfortunately, this was said in the presence of President Roger Corbett, whom I had been desperately trying to convince of our need for a new theatre.

* * *

Medea
by Euripides
adapted by Robinson Jeffers

Euripides, one of the Greek triumvirate, is closer to this age than Aeschylus or Sophocles. Euripides' tragedies are easier for today's audiences to appreciate. One hears, "You can find a Medea in our midst today too."

Medea is the portrait of a proud woman scorned; a woman whose rejected and betrayed love turns to hatred. She is able at last to stand alone against her husband. To portray this character is a great challenge. It takes a lot of emotional and physical vigor to be and act Medea. It is Medea's play. The audience is outrageously tense when she chants those four words, "Children it is evening." She leaves with them. Soon you hear the children scream. Probably members of the audience would like to scream too. It is too late. She has done it. It is true, she hates Jason more than she loves her children. The audience hates Jason too, but to kill two innocent cherubs? How can you? One must be inhuman to commit such an act. According to some critics, she possesses this element.

Jackie Clark lived that character every moment she was on stage, and probably carried her character offstage. It was an extremely difficult task. It wasn't easy, but she came through it very well.

* * *

Don Juan in Hell
by George Bernard Shaw

Don Juan in Hell is part of a much longer Shaw play, *Man and Superman*. It's called a comedy and a philosophy—a treatise. Shaw was a wise man. In this play, more than in all his other works, he expressed his wisdom to the world, but the play is much too long to do in its entirety. Therefore, someone got the idea of taking the third act and naming it *Don Juan in Hell*, after one of the characters in that act.

Many of the speeches are long. Performing it as a reading might be better than to theatricalize it, especially when such a quartet as Charles Laughton, Charles Boyer, Sir Cedric Hardwicke, and Agnes Moorhead are not available.

Well, if they could do it, why couldn't we at least try? Actually, it was an addition to our regular program, but it was easier said than done.

We finally settled on Jack Soules as Don Juan, Betty Williams as Doña Ana, Oscar Butler as the Statue, and Ted Allen as the Devil. Each stood before a stand which held a script. How did the audience accept it? I don't remember.

We had four performances, plus an additional performance at White Sands on a Saturday afternoon. It was at the Post moviehouse. They had advertised the movie, but didn't advertise the fact that *Don Juan* would be there on Sunday afternoon instead of the regular feature. The result was that every few minutes children came in expecting to see a movie; instead they saw four people standing and talking, so they got scared and ran out. We were glad when it was over. We got our stuff together as quickly as possible, piled into our car, and to Las Cruces we ran. I hope G. B. Shaw was satisfied.

* * *

Tea and Sympathy
by Robert Anderson

Tea and Sympathy was the last play of the year. Anderson was considered a respectable dramatist—no trash, and the play had run for two years on Broadway. Why not attempt this piece here, especially after such a philosophical treatise as *Don Juan* and a tragedy like *Medea*? Well, when a play is good, the actors take the credit, when a play is bad, the director takes the blame. So I am taking the blame. But please, no sympathy. Just tea!

* * *

Inherit the Wind
by Jerome Lawrence

Inherit the Wind portrays the Scopes Case, also known as the "Monkey Trial." The trial was held in Dayton, Tennessee in the summer of 1925. It became sensational, nation-wide news because it dramatized the conflict between liberalism and fundamentalism that raged in America at that time. The famous attorney, Clarence Darrow, presided for the defense and the well-known William Jennings Bryan was the prosecutor. When the play was produced in New York it created almost as much excitement as the original trial. Paul Muni portrayed Clarence Darrow.

After the play opened here it became one of the most successful productions ever done by the Playmakers. Townspeople, faculty, and students came to see this play, including some who had never entered the theatre before. Clarence Darrow, called Henry Drummond in the play, was played here by Duane Klein.

Because I knew Paul Muni—his facial expressions, the use of his hands, his walk, his vocal intonations, and the theatrical tricks he used to manipulate in developing a character—I could illustrate all this to Klein, and Klein was a good study. From the first performance, he was reminiscent of Paul Muni. (That is, if one had known Paul Muni.) One might say this was imitation, but since Duane Klein didn't know Paul Muni, he could not copy.

Everybody loved Klein's portrayal of Henry Drummond. The other actors were also quite convincing in their characterizations: Leo Comeau as Brady-Jennings Bryan, Charles Stillwell as Hornbeck, Gordon Roederer as Reverend Brown, Bob Jones as the Judge, Hillary Maveety as Melinda, Susie Herring as Rachel, and many, many others.

Dr. Walter J. De Mordaunt of the English Department reviewed the performance for the *Round Up*.

> *I don't hesitate to write a rave notice for* Inherit the Wind, *a play about the trial of Darwin's theory of evolution. This is the best play I have ever seen the Playmakers present; its polish and professionalism must be made known. This kind of fun and excitement simply won't remain untalked about and unattended. One could say that it is so good because the play is perfect for these actors or that Mr. Zohn has cast it flawlessly right down to the live monkey.*

De Mordaunt continued to rave about the play and the actors:

> *Mr. Leo Comeau's bombast is pure artistry; commanding the stage and the audience, he does not steal the show, he is the show...Duane Klein, who plays Clarence Darrow, is as near perfect for the part as possible.... The other two stand-outers in the play are Gordon Roederer as the Rev. Jeremiah Brown and Charles Stillwell as the Reporter, E. K. Hornbeck, the play's version of the critic H. L. Menken.*

To sum it up, we hated to see the play close.

* * *

The Diary of Anne Frank
dramatized by Frances Goodrich and Albert Hackett

The play is a dramatization of the real diary of a real Anne Frank, a thirteen-year-old Jewish girl who, with her parents, sister and a few acquaintances, went into hiding in an attic in Amsterdam, Holland in 1942. The Gestapo learned the location of the little cluster of Jewish people, arrested them, and as told in the play, sent them to various concentration camps. Only the father, Otto Frank, survived to be liberated. Anne and the others died in concentration camps. After the war her father found Anne's diary on the floor of the attic when he returned to visit the hideout.

Susan Strasberg played the lead on Broadway. Brooks Atkinson in *The New York Times* wrote, "Strange how the shining spirit of a young girl now dead can filter down through the years and inspire a group of professionals in a foreign land." Mr. Kerr in the *New York Tribune* said, "The real life legacy left us by a spirited and straight forward Jewish girl...as bright and shining as a banner. The diary and the play are famous to this very day."

In our production, a high school girl by the name of Judy Pille portrayed Anne Frank. I recall the talks I had with her during the rehearsals. I found her an extremely interesting and intelligent young girl. She was full of dreams and plans for the future. Whether they ever came through—*Quien sabe?* Mr. Frank was played by Jack Soules, a professor in the Physics Department. Because of Soules' steady involvement with the theatre, there was gossip on the campus that the Physics Department was interested in taking over the theatre program, jokingly of course. The whole cast, I thought, was quite good. Others involved were: Leo Comeau, Jackie Clark, Karen Gardner, Elizabeth Keill, and Duane Klein.

There were times when we invited high school students to our plays. Also, teachers brought their classes to the performances. This same happened with *Anne Frank*. Suddenly I heard laughter during a serious scene. I was angry and upset, and during intermission I reprimanded the high school students for laughing during a serious scene. This was something which I had never done before.

This was our last production before the Christmas holidays. Ann and I left for a trip to California to see plays in San Diego, and other places and, in general, to find out how other people did theatre.

* * *

A Midsummer Night's Dream
by William Shakespeare

A Midsummer Night's Dream was our first play of the new decade—March 1960. It is one of Shakespeare's poetic comedies. As someone said, "It shines merrily." It had a large cast, music by Mendelsohn, choreography by Anne Bandwell, who also appeared as a dancer, and beautiful, expensive costumes which were sent from Los Angeles. To mention only some of the large cast: William Barney, Ken Guthrie, Gordon Roederer, Leo Comeau, Rock Campbell (a promising new addition to our theatre), Ann Sutherland, Judy Pille, Rudy Apodaca, and five children as Elves. Scenery was by Jeri Elan, Maurcena Learned and a newcomer by the name of Ann Zohn. We never had to be concerned about audience attendance when we were doing Shakespeare.

* * *

A Touch of the Poet
by Eugene O'Neill

    This drama takes place in Melody's tavern in a village near Boston in 1828. Melody has been discharged from the military and frequently takes out his military uniform to parade in it. People standing nearby pity his wife and daughter, who labor in the tavern in order to take care of him. He is of Irish background and gets into raging spells, until one day he gets a real beating from a friend who cannot bear his storming behavior. Only then does Mr. Melody realize that he is no different from anyone else and begins to behave like a normal human being.

    O'Neill was discovered by the Provincetown Players in Massachusetts. He was the son of an actor and did a considerable amount of traveling. In his youth, he spent a great deal of time on the sea. It was the ocean that inspired him to first write one-act plays. Then came a full-length play, *Beyond the Horizon*. This was followed by *The Emperor Jones*, *The Hairy Ape*, *The Great God Brown*, *Desire Under the Elms*, but he is especially noted for *Strange Interlude*, and *Mourning Becomes Electra*. He claimed to be influenced by Greek drama and later by August Strindberg. To see a play of his is a great experience. Whether his characters express their inner thoughts to the audience or the actors wear masks, it is all different and all original. O'Neill received the Pulitzer Prize several times, and won the Nobel Prize in 1936.

I recall once spending an evening with one of his former wives in Cuernavaca, Mexico. The stories she told about him were quite interesting.

I can still remember Rock Campbell's performance as Cornelius Melody and Jackie Clark's as his wife, Nora Melody. This was, no doubt, Jackie's best performance here. Clark created a character of flesh and blood. She made Nora Melody the most interesting part of the play.

This season ended the first ten years of theatre under my direction at New Mexico State University. It would be much better, and also more proper, if others pronounced the verdict. Luckily there are two people who did just that: David Rodwell from the News Department of New Mexico State issued a small brochure with pictures and art work by Judy Leslie, and Mrs. Louise Nusbaum, *Las Cruces Sun-News* Fine Arts Editor, wrote two articles with two photographs for the Fine Arts Page of the *Sun-News*, May 15, 1960. Thanks to both of you. (See Addendum B.)

* * *

The Second Decade

All the King's Men
by Robert Penn Warren

This is Warren's dramatization of a successful novel about Huey Long. The piece was a major off-Broadway event. For some reason it never reached Broadway. Is it possible that people lost interest in the character called Huey Long? Thirty years have passed since the play was produced here. I remember an interesting, expressionistic set by Ann Zohn. I can see one big mob scene and Willie Stark (Huey Long) making one speech after another. I also thought that Al Risien fit the part very nicely. The play was praised by the *Round Up*.

* * *

The Lady's Not For Burning
by Christopher Fry

This poetic comedy is centered around Thomas Mendip, a discharged soldier who wants to be hanged, and Jannet Jaurdemayne who is sentenced to be hanged. Mendip offers to be hanged instead of the pretty girl, but the play ends with neither being hanged. Jack Soules, Elizabeth Keill, and Charles Stillwell were quite nice to watch in their roles.

It seemed to me that the last two works were without much pretense, but came through as fine theatre. "*The Lady Is Not For Burning* was another piece in the impressive list of successes chalked up by the Playmakers," said Dr. Ann Jones of the English Department.

* * *

Julius Caesar
by William Shakespeare

Julius Caesar had one of the largest casts of all the Bard's plays—forty characters. *Julius Caesar* has been performed in black costumes, in modern dress, and in various styles and periods. Ours was a conventional version with period costumes. This was the first time that serious friction developed among cast members. I was relieved when the rehearsal period was over, and even more relieved when the performances were over. *Et Tu Brutus!* Yet, John Kuhn from the *Round Up* said, "Shakespeare survived. Hershel Zohn has shown again the necessity of rescuing the dramatist from the classroom and bookshelves for a breather at least." Who's to argue with a critic?

* * *

The Matchmaker
by Thornton Wilder

The Matchmaker is based on a comedy by Johann Nestroy, *Einen Jux will es sich Machen* (Vienna, 1842); which, in turn, was based upon an English original, *A Day Well Spent* (London, 1835) by John Oxenford. The title was later changed to *The Merchant of Yonkers* and produced by Herman Shumlin, directed by Max Reinhardt, and designed by Boris Aronson; Jane Cawl was included in the cast. It opened in Boston for two weeks and moved to the Guild Theatre in New York, December 28, 1938. It was in August 1954 when the play appeared again; this time as Wilder's comedy, *The Matchmaker*. It was directed by Tyrone Guthrie and designed by Tanya Moiseiwich.

It opened first in Edinburgh, then London, and later Philadelphia. In December 1955, the play opened in New York, presented by the Theatre Guild and staged by Tyrone Guthrie. The two leading characters, Horace Vandergelder and Dolly Levi, were portrayed by Sam Levene and Ruth Gordon. It finally reached The Playmakers for the first time on May 8, 1961.

I saw a professional production of *The Matchmaker* later that summer in Heidelberg, Germany. I didn't particularly enjoy it.

The Matchmaker takes place in Yonkers, New York and downtown Manhattan, in the early 1880's. Horace Vandergelder is a merchant, a widower, who decides to find himself a wife. Mrs. Dolly Levi, a widow, a matchmaker of sorts, eventually marries Vandergelder. Cornelius and Barnaby are two clerks who work in Vandergelder's store. Vandergelder gives a reason why he wants to get married again. *"I am a man of sense. In the first place, I like my house run with order, comfort and economy...."* (At the end of the play Mrs. Levi says to the audience) *"There isn't any more coffee, there isn't any more gingerbread and there isn't any more play."* Barnaby chimes in, *"Oh, I think the play is about adventure. Good night."*

Charles Stillwell and Mildred Hayner were superb in their leading roles, and Michael Myers as Barnaby was as charming as can be. I don't know where Myers accumulated all the life he brought into the stage. The actors included Cherie Summers, Kenneth Guthrie, Al Riesen, Kathryn Harry, Claire Lewis, and others.

One particular incident caused quite a furor among the Playmakers, and on the campus in general, and almost broke up a performance. This was the bucket of red paint incident. During the period of final rehearsals for Wilder's *The Matchmaker*, posters announcing the dates of performances for the play would disappear. As soon as they were replaced by new posters, the replacements would also disappear. But, the payoff came on the evening of the first performance. About fifteen minutes after the play started, while several actors were on stage doing a scene, suddenly, red paint began to come down from above, pouring onto the stage floor. The audience first thought this was part of the action.

Sitting in the back row, I couldn't believe what I was seeing and did not know what to make of it. The actors on stage, however, didn't lose themselves and went on with the scene. One actor even found a few rags and began to wipe the floor as a part of the action. I soon ran outside in search of the culprit, and the college police were immediately alerted. We discovered a hole had been drilled on the outside wall. Wires coming through the hole into the theatre and up to the ceiling were tied to a bucket of red paint. All one had to do was pull the wire outside and the paint splashed onto the stage floor.

About midnight, a young man was brought to my office for questioning. This questioning was continued by the Dean of Students for several days afterwards. The person in question finally confessed. His past records showed abnormal behavioral tendencies. I was told that he was sent to an institution. Perhaps some others were involved in it who were out to play a "prank," and used that individual as a tool. We never knew why.

The Matchmaker is our *Life With Father*, as far as the length of the run is concerned. Professor Harold Stobie wrote about *The Matchmaker*, "Strong cast makes the play." Scenery—remove your Stetsons and bow to Ann Zohn. Directing—ask the cast. A student critic by the name of Steve Durkovich wasn't as complimentary with his review. "*The Matchmaker* lacks enthusiasm." At the time of our performance, Broadway was planning to make *The Matchmaker* into a musical, calling it *Hello Dolly*. More about *The Matchmaker* later.

After a lengthy correspondence with the University's architect, James Miller, about the kind of theatre desirable for us, and after many letters to the University president about the need for a theatre, announcements appeared in the press that the administration would build a theatre for the fall of 1963. Dean Boston of Arts & Sciences and I looked at various theatres in New Mexico and Texas. The administration wanted a larger seating house than we wished. The smaller the house, the easier it is for non-professionals (students) to perform. A four-hundred seat theatre was preferable. Although the student enrollment had more than doubled since my arrival, a four-hundred seat house would be the most ideal. The new theatre was built with four hundred eighteen seats.

* * *

"*J. B.*"
by Archibald MacLeish

I heard upon his dry dung heap
That man cry out who cannot sleep;
"If God is God He is not good,
If God is good He is not God";
Take the even, take the odd,
I would not sleep here if I could
Except for the little green leaves in the wood
And the wind on the water.

This is a beautiful and meaningful poetic drama of yesterday, today, and tomorrow. It's a drama of great stature. To quote from our program notes, "The author was seeking a metaphor to express the banalities and degradations, the suffering of our generation, and it was perhaps inevitable that he should turn for his inspiration to the life of Job (J. B.), the prototype of all sufferers." Two or three years later, MacLeish came to this campus to present a lecture (I assume on literature.) The next day he came to my office and was eager to know about the production of his *J. B.* Naturally, I was greatly honored to talk with him about his work.

When *J. B.* was produced here, students held heated discussions outside of the classrooms which, of course, is what a teacher likes to see about every important work of art. The *Las*

Cruces Sun-News said, "First nighters thrill to Playmakers *J. B.* The audience was spellbound." Rock Campbell, William Barney, and Walter Tyszka played the main characters.

I usually attended most of the performances, moved around in the lobby and back stage, and occasionally watched a scene. However, during the run of *J. B.* I didn't feel well one night and asked Ann to go in my stead. But after an hour or so, I couldn't rest and went to the theatre, too. As I entered the theatre to watch a scene involving many people, whom do I see in the mob—my wife, crying and praying with all the other people! How do you like that?

* * *

The Cave Dwellers
by William Saroyan

Like all his plays, *The Cave Dwellers* has humor, charm, and warmth. There is not a single mean character in the play. Even the poodle, Robere, and Gorky the Bear, are both lovable. The play takes place in an abandoned theatre (it was once a Yiddish playhouse) on the lower East Side of New York. The two leading characters are the Queen, a former actress, and the King, who was once a celebrated clown. Some touching scenes in the play include one where the sick old actress refuses the milk because the baby needs it more than she does. Actors usually enjoy being in a Saroyan play because there are no villains in it.

The late Millie Hayner and Bill Alford were very moving in their respective roles. But the audience even enjoyed Kim Hayner as the bear, and Kim himself enjoyed being the bear, of course with the help of his costume. There was even a live dog in the cast and it was different and interesting choosing one from the twelve canine hopefuls who tried out.

The *Round Up* said, "Saroyan's play is filled with compassion.

* * *

The Bourgeois Gentleman
by Moliere

This play was written at the request of Louis XIV. Monsieur Jourdain, who is a bourgeois, is advised that a man in his class must know music, so he engages a music master to teach him music, a dancing master to dance, a fencing master to fence, and a philosophy master to become a wise and a learned man. But it is all in vain—once a fool, always a fool. It is a highly satirical piece.

The play lends itself to being produced as a spectacle, which was the way it was done here. There was dancing and singing, attractive scenery, and colorful costumes. The acting was fine with Leo Comeau as Jourdain, Jackie Clark as his wife, and Judy Pille as their daughter. Ray Veitch and Ann Zohn designed the set. John Glowacki and Oscar Butler arranged the music. All this contributed to a highly spectacular and amusing production. For once I was highly satisfied.

* * *

No Exit
by Jean-Paul Sartre
and
The Chairs
by Eugene Ionesco

After the extravagant production of *The Bourgeois Gentleman*, we decided to do something in a lower key for the final production. Perhaps some one-acters. What about *No Exit* and *The Chairs?* They required very small casts and offered no unforeseen technical problems. "Yes, let's do them." Little did I realize how significant these two one-acters would be to me, both philosophically and artistically. Jean-Paul Sartre, the French philosopher of Existentialism, emerged in the fifties. John Gassner, in his *A Treasury of the Theatre*, said, "There was fire in his negations, intensity in his WELTSCHMERZ."

In *No Exit*, two women and one man are locked up together for eternity in one hideous room in hell. The windows are bricked up, there are no mirrors, the electric light can never be turned off, and there is no exit. Period. "Here the soul is shorn of its secrecy. It is an eternal torment."

The acting in *No Exit*—so so. It seemed to me the plot was more important than the acting.

The Chairs, by Ionesco, was a product of the new avant garde movement that appeared in France after the Second World War. A tragic farce, the theme of *The Chairs* is "nothingness." It concerns two very old people, and all they are left with are empty chairs.

Even in Paris, no director wanted to come near this play. At first, the actors themselves rented an old, unused theatre to open *The Chairs* in April, 1952. In due time, *The Chairs* became universally popular. Bill Alford and Millie Hayner were outstanding.

In a letter to the editor, Ms. B. Andrews wrote of *No Exit* and *The Chairs*: "Again thanks to NMSU for a wonderful, enjoyable evening of intellectual entertainment. I only wish there were more such evenings." Let me add, I only wish there were more such intelligent letters.

* * *

Volpone
by Ben Jonson
adapted by Stefan Zweig

Zweig (1881-1942) freely adapted Jonson's *Volpone*. "Freely" means Stefan Zweig eliminated the entire subplot and eliminated some minor characters. The principal characters are: Volpone the fox, Mosca the fly, Voltore the vulture, Corbaccio the raven (an old usurer), and Corvino the crow; also Canina a courtesan.

The program notes said: "It is a tribute to Jonson that he can violently attack covetousness, making it distasteful, while presenting a rollicking comedy." *The Round Up* said, "Kudos go to Playmakers director Hershel Zohn and to Leo Comeau, technical director, for a masterful presentation of *Volpone*."

The program also announced, "This is the year the new theatre building will be completed, and this is the year the Playmakers will travel to the South Pacific to perform for the Armed Forces!"

* * *

Ghosts
by Henrik Ibsen

Ghosts was our third Ibsen production. According to critics, *Ghosts* recalls the great Greek tragedies. "The very title of the play is symbolic and its story carries beyond the manifest drama of hereditary disease."

When written, the play was subject to violent attacks from all over Norway. Theatres refused to produce it; publishers refused to publish it. However, Bernard Shaw, Emile Zola, and Danish critic Georg Brandes (three giants of the written word) came to Ibsen's defense.

In brief, Oswald returns from Paris, where he studied art. That was Mrs. Alving's doing. She didn't want her only son to be close to his father, whom she knew suffered from a hereditary disease. Now that his father had died, she wanted her son back home. In addition, this is also an important day for Mrs. Alving, who was celebrating the opening of the orphanage she built with the money her husband left. However, before the day is over, the orphanage is destroyed by fire.

Oswald confides to his mother that he is a sick man. His frequent attacks can be relieved only by opium pills, which he carries with him. Due to all the excitement of the day, Oswald gets one of these attacks and begs his mother to let him have one of these pills. Mrs. Alving is now faced with a quandary—to give her son the opium, or see him suffer until he dies. The sun begins to rise slowly as Oswald mumbles, "The Zone, the Zone" ("The sun, the sun"). The spectator or reader is not sure what will happen to Oswald. Apparently, Ibsen wanted to leave it this way and left it up to the individual director. The director, in turn, may choose to leave it up to the audience.

I saw *Ghosts* many years ago with two famous actors, the German, Alexander Moissi, and the Russian, Alla Nazimova in the main roles. I still remember them. Strangely enough, *Ghosts* had its first production in America in 1881 as the first Ibsen play ever produced here. Rock Campbell, Jackie Clark and Robert Spitz portrayed the leading characters in our production.

* * *

Rhinoceros
by Eugene Ionesco

Ionesco, along with Samuel Beckett and Jean Genet were the three avant garde dramatists who emerged in France after the Second World War. They have also been called dramatists of "The Theatre of the Absurd." I find Ionesco's work the most intriguing.

The play opens in a square in a small French provincial town. It is Sunday morning. Different people come and go: a grocer's wife, a housewife, a waitress, an old gentleman, a logician, and a fireman. Berenger and his girlfriend Daisy, who together with his friend Jean, are the principal characters in the play. There is also the usual sidewalk cafe.

The actors engage in cafe chit chat and activities, when suddenly a rhinoceros appears and runs through the square. People begin to argue whether it was an Asian or African rhinoceros. If it had one horn it must be Asian, and if it had two horns it would have been African. Later, another rhinoceros runs by and it now becomes the main topic of conversation in town throughout the day.

It's been two days now since Jean has been seen. His friend Berenger finally goes to see him. He notices something wrong with him. Jean talks and behaves very strangely. His forehead is swollen; there is a bump. His skin is yellow, and after a while it turns green. His speech, slowly and surely, becomes abnormal. The scene ends with Berenger realizing his best friend has turned into a rhinoceros. Slowly, more and more people become rhinoceroses. Within a few days practically all the townspeople are trampling through the trees as rhinoceroses, except for Berenger and his girl Daisy, whom he loves dearly. However, before long Daisy begins to lean in the direction of the rhinoceroses.

DAISY: *They are all like gods.*
BERENGER: *I can see our opinions are directly opposed.*
DAISY: *You mustn't be jealous my dear.*
BERENGER: *You go too far Daisy, take a good look at them.*
DAISY: *Now you mustn't be nasty.*
BERENGER: *Then don't you be stupid.*

DAISY: *It's no longer possible for us to live together. He isn't very nice, really, he isn't very nice.* (She goes out and before long she too has turned into a rhinoceros.)
BERENGER: (has a long monologue, and ends it this way.) *I am the last man left, and I am staying that way until the end. I am not capitulating.*

Berenger and Daisy were played by Bill Alford and Kathryn Harry. Martha Gold, in a lengthy article in the *Sun-News* summed it up: "Zohn's *Rhinoceros* is 'tremendous.'"

ACT IV

Scene 1

The Far East Tour

The American Educational Theatre Association, AETA for short, must have originated soon after the Second World War. Every year they selected students from ten American universities to entertain the United States armed forces throughout the world.

We had applied twice before without success. On the third application our department was chosen to go overseas. We submitted a list of several plays, *The Matchmaker* being one. The AETA Overseas Touring Committee notified us in March 1962 that we had been selected to go to the Far East with *The Matchmaker* in mid-summer of 1963.

The maximum number of students they allowed for a straight play was fourteen, plus a faculty member. Although the cast of *The Matchmaker* consisted of seventeen, we easily adapted it to eight men, six women, and myself. I was told to include women in the cast because the men in the armed forces were lonely.

Preparations

When the announcement was made about our pending trip to the Far East, students registered in mass for drama courses. Also, participation in our production program became quite popular. Students anxiously prepared to read for various parts, and looked forward to that date for many months. At personal interviews held prior to the actual reading, each candidate received a mimeographed list of instructions. The information stressed that during the tour the play must be considered above everything else, and good behavior must be observed during the tour. Students active in drama and those majoring in drama received preference. Naturally, it was unavoidable that those not chosen were disappointed. One mother even called her congressman to complain because her daughter was not chosen to go on the tour. Only four members of the original 1961 cast were asked to go on the trip.

After a five-week rehearsal period, the play was presented on the campus for five performances. In order to keep the play in shape, we had at least one rehearsal and one public performance each week until departure time. During that period we gave six performances at military installations. Each cast member, in addition to his acting, had one or more other production responsibilities—setting up and striking the set, making and keeping the costumes clean, ironed, and ready to wear. Designing and building a compact, travel-worthy set which would also be versatile enough to fit into every theatre we might encounter, was a challenge. These same requirements also applied to props, lighting, and costumes.

Those fortunate fourteen and their roles were:

THE MATCHMAKER
by
Thornton Wilder
Directed by Hershel Zohn

Cast in order of appearance.

HORACE VANDERGELDER	Phil Wedding
AMBROSE KEMPER	Kenneth Golightly
JOE SCANLON	John Godley
GERTRUDE	Cherie Summers
CORNELIUS HACKL	John Taylor
ERMENGARDE	Jann Arrington
MALACHI STACK	David Kos
MRS. DOLLY LEVI	Claire Lewis
BARNABY TUCKER	Michael Myers
MRS. IRENE MOLLOY	Kathryn Harry
MINNIE FAY	Cherie Summers
A CABMAN	Phil Bruner
RUDOLF	Duane Wilson
A MUSICIAN	John Godley
MISS FLORA VAN HUYSEN	Lynnette Mawson
HER COOK	Mary Ella Mayfield

PRODUCTION STAFF

Assistant to the Director	Phil Wedding
Stage Manager	Mike Myers
Secretary	Jann Arrington

Dr. Frank Whiting of the University of Minnesota, and a member of the AETA Overseas Touring Committee came to brief us after one of these early performances. I remember the wonderful evening we had at our house with Dr. Whiting after the performance. Colonel Coray, from the USO office in New

York, came to instruct us about the trip. Also, something the students didn't know about at that time, but that I may now divulge, Senator Clinton Anderson had a bright idea which he thought would be nice for New Mexico as well as the University. He suggested that President Kennedy stop here on his way to California and say farewell to the *The Matchmaker* cast. It didn't materialize. Kennedy either canceled his trip or decided on a different route.

Two courses were offered in conjunction with the tour which cast members were required to take. Drama 305, Theatre Practice—each member of the cast earned two credits for participating in the production (a total of eighteen weeks was spent on the play); and Drama 290, Theatre in the Far East—a course aimed at familiarizing the students with the history of theatre in the countries to be toured. Four books were essential reading for each student in the course: *Kabuki Drama*, by Syutaro Miyake; *Highlights of the Japanese Theatre* (Pictures); *An Introduction to the Chinese Theatre*, by A. C. Scott; and *Japanese Theatre*, a very good and detailed work on the subject by Faubion Bowers.

Since we expected our tour to take us to Korea, we invited a Korean dancer to present native dances at the school. True, this recital was open to the public, but it was aimed specifically for the students going on tour. A faculty member from Formosa, then teaching on the campus, delivered a talk about the culture of that country, and we had a lecture by a Japanese on present-day Japan. The two-hour weekly lecture schedule continued until the day of departure. A research paper on the course was required at the end of the tour. Content was based mostly on the reading material studied before leaving for the Far East.

Approximately the last two months prior to our departure, the Department of Defense—in the forms of a lieutenant, captain, or major—and I became quite friendly. They called frequently and asked all kinds of questions, and they continually changed departure dates for our tour. The final decision was Tuesday, July 2, 1963. A bus would be waiting for us at the Air Mechanics Building (The Theatre) at 6:30 a.m. to deliver us to the El Paso airport by 8:00 a.m.

As we arrived at the Air Mechanics Building early that morning, a chartered bus waited across the street for us. We noticed smoke coming out of The Theatre in the Air Mechanics Building. We hurriedly entered the building and saw smoke in different areas of the theatre, which, if not stopped, would have easily turned into a big fire. We called the Fire Department and all of us took seats in the bus for the trip to the airport. The driver immediately started the engine. We couldn't afford to be late.

Two pleasant surprises awaited us at the airport. First, the Army Band from Fort Bliss played as we came off the bus. The second was a red carpet leading into the plane. We hurriedly said farewell to wives, relatives, and friends—some of them with tears in their eyes—as we stepped on the red carpet and marched into the plane. It was a first-class jet to San Francisco, but what I didn't know before was that particular flight was a "champagne" flight. As soon as the plane took off the airline hostess' voice was heard, "Champagne?" During the weeks and months of our preparation for the trip we continually stressed, "No liquor, no drinking. We are Uncle Sam's ambassadors and must be on our best behavior." And now, at the very first minute of the trip—such a temptation! I was seated at the front of the cabin. When I turned around, the entire group looked at me, questioning me, "What shall we do?" I finally nodded in the affirmative. Each one had a glass of champagne as the airline hostess handed me a glass. I stood up and said loudly to the group, "Here's to a very good trip!" as the plane was on its way to San Francisco.

* * *

The Tour

The next morning we left Travis Air Force Base via Pan American jet to Yokota, Japan, with a two-hour stop in Anchorage, Alaska.[1] We did not travel by jet again until the tail end of our trip from Hawaii back home. All of the other times we flew by propeller plane. Our longest plane ride was from the Philippines to Hawaii—a twenty-five hour stretch. One of the most exciting and enjoyable rides was on a mail plane from Tokyo to Iwakuni when we sat on top of mailbags, singing and writing letters. At one time from Iwakuni to Itazuke, the aircraft was reserved solely for our group. True, we had to report to the airport two hours ahead of time and sometimes even longer, but the planes always arrived and departed on schedule. From luxurious first class to cargo aircraft, we were always comfortable and content. As for the buses, they, too, were comfortable and departed and arrived on time. At all times our fifteen footlockers and personal baggage were with us on the same plane, very often on the same bus. If a truck was provided, it followed us with the baggage. In other words, no problems or complications arose during the entire 22,500 miles.

As for living facilities, our first night away from home we spent in a commercial motel in Fairfield, California, near Travis Air Force Base. That was the only time the members of the group had to pay as much as four dollars for their lodging. Otherwise, we paid amounts ranging from fifty cents to a dollar and a half, with the exception of Hawaii. I had to pay two dollars extra since I preferred a private room. Sometimes we were not required to pay at all. In the Philippines we spent eight, very comfortable nights as guests of Navy Special Services. In general, the women's rooms were better than the men's, but even so, the men were never really uncomfortable. Most of the time only two shared a room.

---

[1] A complete itinerary of the trip is provided at the end of this chapter.

As for food, it was always plentiful and tasty. Prices were also quite reasonable, except for Hawaii. Our seven-dollar-per-diem was, on the average, more than enough for food and lodging. Naturally, if anyone wished to eat exotic foods the per diem was not sufficient.

The size of the audiences ranged from two hundred to fifteen hundred, with an average attendance of four hundred. The performances were always better received when the theatre was full, and since we played in a number of large movie houses, the reaction here was not always the kind we desired. Also we had to contend with the terrific heat and lack of air conditioning in many of the playhouses. Two performances were canceled during our tour. The first because one member of the group became ill, and as two performances had been scheduled for that day, we thought it would be wise to cancel the matinee to be sure that we would be able to appear in the evening. Also, the Special Services officer had asked two female members of our cast to participate in a beauty contest that afternoon. Another show was canceled in the Philippines because of a typhoon. In general, the theatres where we performed were much better than we had ever anticipated.

The performances in Korea were the best received of our entire tour. Our presentations were almost always in service clubs, and we had to adjust ourselves to the particular club. The audiences seemed to be most receptive, enthusiastic, and were appreciative of our coming to perform. It is logical for the men there to react so favorably, as they were isolated from everything and had little to occupy their spare time. Our largest audiences were in Okinawa, where we performed in big movie houses. On several occasions our performances were sandwiched between two movies. Our poorest shows were the first two given in the Philippines; one in a large gymnasium and the other in an enlisted men's club.

Although we had free lodging and meals in the Philippines, our stay at Sangley Point was the most tedious of the tour. This was due to the typhoon. I spent at least an hour in a telephone booth trying to get a plane. Finally, thanks to the sympathetic ear of a Navy officer at that base, we were provided with a flight to Cubi and were able to save two performances which would otherwise have been canceled. The flight took only twenty minutes, but it was impossible to get there by bus because the bridges had been washed out by heavy rains. True, we were late in arriving and performances had to be rescheduled, but our breaking out of Sangley Point and the welcome reception at San Miguel and Cubi were a great relief to the entire group. Several NMSU students, on a special project there, anticipated our coming and were greatly relieved and happy upon our safe arrival.

Three performances were the highlights of the tour: Chyung-ang University in Seoul, Korea—a people-to-people performance—where fifteen hundred students, faculty members, and invited guests thoroughly enjoyed Thornton Wilder's farcical situations. Probably many did not understand the English language, yet they were all eager to hear Americans talk and see them move about on stage. Some, who were unable to get into the theatre, tried to break through the door. Children stood on the hillside trying to look through the high windows to catch a glimpse of the performance. The introduction by the Dean of the Graduate School, the performance, the exchange of greetings between the Dean and myself, the Korean drama students helping backstage, the flowers presented to members of the cast; all will long be remembered by every one of the group.

What a small world! It so happens that the director of the theatre in Seoul and I had a similar background—in the Stanislavski philosophy of theatre. We even had a similar taste in our choice of plays.

The second memorable performance was at Camp Zama, Japan. Though held in a very small theatre, it was so well-equipped, so well-managed, and so charmingly decorated, that this theatre would be the pride of performing groups anywhere. It was the only place where the stage props were pieces in harmony with the period of the play. The audience that night in Camp Zama was the most sophisticated, and yet the most appreciative, we encountered. The third was a performance in Iwakuni where the "belly laughs of a thousand Marines were heard accompanying Thornton Wilder's dialogue."

To be sure, there were other exciting performances during our tour, including the people-to-people performance in Naha. Two guards were posted on each side of the stage to prevent any enthusiastic member of the audience from jumping on stage and joining the cast. I also remember the wonderful reaction at Camp Casey, Korea.

Military audiences were not easy to please. They were very restless; they often walked out and came back several times during a performance. Some probably had never seen a stage play before; others stood in line in the rain for an hour, eager to see a play. The bulk of the audiences consisted of enlisted men.

Publicity, posters, and programs originated in Japan. They were sent to the various places where we were scheduled to perform. They were very colorful and cleverly done. Most local newspapers had stories concerning the play. In the service clubs the play was announced over loud speakers. For some reason, staff members were determined to make the title of the play plural, in other words, *The Matchmakers*. In one club the staff member announced, "*The Matchmakers* will start in fifteen minutes; three hands for pinochle needed," all in one breath. Publicity in some places could have been more effective. In two clubs we performed opposite professional USO units. In other words, we competed against each other, with the result that attendance at both events suffered.

There was always the usual invitation to officer's clubs after the performances. These I felt were sometimes overdone and it got to the point that invitations were rejected. Drinking is prevalent among the military, and since college administrators and faculty do not look favorably on drinking, these invitations to the officer's clubs were a problem. At one time I decided that we would go directly to the billets after the performance. The Special Service officer approached me to have the group be his guest for drinks. I mentioned to him that our next day's plan called for travel, and our people, being college students, should not indulge in drinking; his suggested compromise wasn't too helpful, "Why don't we go over for one drink, and then let nature take its course."

The morale of the company was generally high throughout the tour. Of course, there were exceptions. Soon after our arrival in Japan, one member developed a throat infection and the illness seemed to spread to other members of the cast. If it had been up to the doctors, many of the performances would have been canceled.

Morale was especially good throughout Korea and Japan. There was a slight decline in Okinawa, partly due to the heat and the fact that water had to be rationed. There was another decline in the Philippines, where there was too much water. We were marooned for four days by the typhoon. Morale again peaked in Hawaii, an ideal vacation place. There was very little conflict, if any, between members of the cast during the tour.

That such a tour is of great educational value to the students goes without saying. Travel is always educational. Students who had traveled very little were given the opportunity to see a great part of the world. Naturally, it became an experience they will remember the rest of their lives. Highlights of our stay in Korea included a visit to the United Nations-North Korean Joint Security Area, the meeting of students and faculty at a luncheon in a Jesuit college in Seoul. There we performed *The Matchmaker*, and spent some time at the Seoul Drama Center where we chatted with the director and students, and inspected their theatre and workshops. In Japan, attending a Kabuki play, staying in Kyoto, observing Japanese traditions, exchanging views with Japanese students who sat through a rehearsal of our play, and learning about the customs of the different peoples of the countries visited, provided many worthwhile experiences.

Students taking such a tour are not only sightseeing but also are presenting a play. It seemed wherever we went it was stressed to us that the live college shows were preferred to any other type of entertainment. What other occasion would permit a college group to do thirty performances of a single play during eight weeks? Performances in different countries, in different theatres, under different conditions are educational in themselves. Frequently we heard comments from the audience that they could always see a movie, but a play was a rare thing.

August 24 was our fifty-fourth day on tour and our final day in Hawaii. Departing at 2:00 p.m. from our billets, we left the airport at 4:30 for Travis Air Force Base. (This was the day I had looked forward to for eighteen months!) I thought, "If all goes well we shall be home tomorrow, August 25, the fifty-fifth day, Sunday." Everything went smoothly as we flew by jet from Hawaii to Travis, then on to San Francisco. It was cold! Several hours of waiting at the airport in San Francisco faced us. Then first-class TWA jet to Los Angeles, a good breakfast, and within fifty minutes we were in Los Angeles. After an hour wait we boarded a first-class Continental jet to El Paso. Another breakfast, this time steak and champagne. I didn't want the students to drink, at least on their last leg home. El Paso—Hurrah!

A bus from the Moore Bus Line awaited our arrival. We were held up because we were one piece of luggage short. Twenty-two thousand miles, and nothing lost until we returned to El Paso! We finally left El Paso, although we passed a red light and got off the main highway at one point. We arrived at the New Theatre on Sunday, August 25, 1963 at 1:00 p.m. Relatives and friends were there to greet us. Most of us had brought flowers from Hawaii for them.

Tour statistics: fifty-five days, twenty-nine performances, audience of 10, 569 people, and 22,500 miles traveled.

Marjorie Graham's column in the August 27, 1963 *El Paso Times* is a good summary of our tour.

IN THE SPOTLIGHT
By Marjorie Graham

DESPITE A TYPHOON that marooned them for six days in the Philippines, New Mexico State University Playmakers went on with the show in the theater's best tradition.

"It was high adventure," Director Hershel Zohn reported on his return to Las Cruces after a 55-day tour with this 14-member student troupe, presenting 29 performances of Thornton Wilder's comedy, "The Matchmaker," in the Far East.

Sponsored by the Department of Defense, American Educational Theater Association and the USO, they traveled 23,000 miles in all to entertain 11,000 people for an average audience of 400 at each performance.

"OUR LARGEST CROWDS were in Okinawa, but the soldiers' interest was most pronounced in Korea, perhaps because it is so remote," Zohn said. "They need such entertainment very much. We were right in the demilitarized zone on the United Nations line."

They were at Sangley Point in the Philippines when the typhoon struck, putting the whole island on an emergency status and marooning the college thespians after only two performances.

SCHEDULED TO RETURN to Cuyo by bus, they learned the bridges were all broken down and only a sympathetic Army officer with a special plane could get them out after four days' delay.

"When we flew in, some people from New Mexico were waiting for us and gave us a terrific welcome," Zohn said. "We had to take the bus from there to Clark Field and we just barely made it across the bridge there before it collapsed."

In Korea, although the 1,000 students at Chung-Ang University understood little English, they were delighted just to hear the Americans talking and see them moving on stage.

"The 1,000-seat theater in Seoul was full in that people-to-people performance and children were standing on top of the hill, trying to peek in the windows, while others tried to break through the door," he said.

THERE WERE TIMES when three or four USO units, which the government sends all over the world, would be arriving at the same time. They were professional and top educational theater groups as well as "the cream" like Danny Kaye.

"Uncle Sam is in show business," Zohn said. "I thought every day that the ax was going to fall on us, but, with the exception of the typhoon, it never did. We were treated royally and the military welcomed us with open arms. Lodging was excellent under the circumstances. It was all handled very smoothly."

IF THEY HAD LISTENED to the doctors, they would have canceled about 10 performances, but members of the cast, even if ill, went on with the show. Only two performances were not given. Thirty-one had been scheduled.

"The audiences liked 'Matchmaker' very much," Zohn said. "The last performances were in Hawaii, where we spent almost a week. The women brought us leis."

The Far East Tour

AFTER MONTHS WITH "The Matchmaker," which Playmakers first put into production last year and have since given 55 performances, do they plan a last curtain?

"There can be no more," Zohn said. "It has been sold to Broadway for a musical and taken out of production. That was done in early summer, but since those foreign countries in which we presented it were not a part of the Geneva Conference agreement on royalty rights, we could proceed."

WHAT NEXT FOR THE PLAYMAKERS?

They will open their new Fine Arts Center this fall and, in the meantime, director Zohn has left us. He's on vacation on the beach in California. It's a well deserved trip—more restful, we hope, than the one from which he just returned.

Tour Schedule - 1963

1	Osan AB, Korea	July 7
2	Chung-ang University, Korea	July 8
3	Seoul Area Command, Korea	July 9
4	Ascom, Korea	July 10
5	RC # Korea	July 12
6	Camp Red Cloud, Korea	July 13
7	Camp Casey, Korea	July 14
8	Camp Zama, Japan	July 17
9	Tachikawa, Japan	July 18
10	Tokota AB Japan	July 19
11	Iwakuni MCAS, Japan	July 21
12	Itazuke AB, Japan	July 22
13	Sasebo NS, Japan	July 23
14	Hakata AB, Japan	July 24
15	Nacha AB, Okinawa	Aug. 2
16	Camp Hansen, Okinawa	Aug. 3
17	Fort Buckner, Okinawa	Aug. 4
18	Camp Schwab, Okinawa	Aug. 5
19	Kadena AB, Okinawa	Aug. 6
20	Sukiran Area, Okinawa	Aug. 8
21	RBC Nall, Okinawa	Aug. 9
22	Sangley Point, N.S.P.I.	Aug. 11
23	Sangley Point, N.S.P.I.	Aug. 13
24	San Miguel, N.S.P.I.	Aug. 16
25	Cubi Nas, P.I.	Aug. 17
26	Barber's Point, NAS, Hawaii	Aug. 20
27	Kanohe MCAS, Hawaii	Aug. 21
28	Hickam AFB, Hawaii	Aug. 22
29	Fort Shafter, Hawaii	Aug. 23

ACT IV

Scene 2

The New Theatre

It was essential for me to have at least a short period of adjustment before beginning the new season. It hadn't been just an ordinary summer. It was a summer consisting of eight weeks of constant traveling from one country to another with a group of fourteen students and performing for audiences who were as foreign to us as we were to them.

And now a brand new theatre to perform in—an edifice for which we had pined for years. Therefore, the first production—and, also, all subsequent programs—must be different than anything previously presented. During the next few days I was busy checking and rechecking the new theatre building, time and again—it was inconceivable.

* * *

Ann and I decided it was time for a break, but ten days was the most we allowed ourselves. 'California here we come.' We were off to Pacific Beach, a place we had visited numerous times. It is near a part of San Diego where the Globe Theatre is located.

The Inaugural Production

First we must decide on the play with which to open the new theatre. Dozens of plays went through my mind, and then—Shakespeare. What could be more appropriate than Shakespeare? And it should be a comedy, a popular comedy. We had already performed *Twelfth Night*, *A Midsummer Night's Dream*, and a cutting of *The Taming of the Shrew*. What about *As You Like It*? *As You Like It*, it shall be. With a cast of about thirty-five and many different scenes, *As You Like It* would be a fitting way to open a new theatre. Also, who doesn't know this bit of philosophy?

> *All the world's a stage*
> *And all the men and women merely players*
> *They have their exits and their entrances*
> *And one man in his time plays many parts*
> *His acts being seven ages.*

How about romance? Of course:

> *O Rosalind! These trees shall be my books.*

This romantic comedy takes the audience into "a pastoral world of pleasant fancy; a world that offers escape from reality."

* * *

The schedule announced for that year also included, *The Miracle Worker* (the story of Helen Keller), the children's play *Hansel and Gretel*, *The Three Penny Opera* by Bertolt Brecht, and *Romeo and Juliet*, to celebrate Shakespeare's 400th Anniversary. The latter play was part of a New Mexico State University "Shakespeare Festival," which included musical concerts, poetry readings, and a Shakespearian comedy by the Las Cruces High School.

As You Like It
by William Shakespeare

I always planned to invite professional guest artists (stars if possible) to join our productions once we had a new theatre. That's where the Globe Theatre came in. As we attended a performance of *Anthony and Cleopatra*, I was especially drawn to the actress playing Cleopatra. Her name was Jacqueline Brookes. As soon as I returned to my hotel, I called Miss Brookes and asked if she would like to meet with me to discuss the possibilities of her coming to our university to appear as Rosalind in *As You Like It*. We agreed to meet the next day in the park adjacent to the theatre. It didn't take long for us to agree on her coming to New Mexico State for rehearsals and the performances of *As You Like It*.

Normally we had problems when casting a play, particularly finding the proper people for such a large cast. That was not the case at this time. We had a cast of twenty-five, plus twelve non-speaking characters, in only one or two days of try-outs. Soon rehearsals began. A week before performances, the actor playing Orlando had an accident and was replaced by Michael Coquat, an experienced actor. Jacqueline Brookes arrived in ample time for rehearsals. It was quite exciting for the students to perform with a Broadway star. The first performance went smoothly, especially on a new stage.

Opening night of the New Theatre! We had a full house with attendance by invitation only. Evening dress was required for the ladies, and tuxedos for the men. True, some of the men looked like "Charlie McCarthy" in their tuxedos—but that was OK. After the performance, I recall a few speeches, and then champagne and refreshments in the lobby. That was it. However, the stress of opening night was over, and the subsequent performances felt like a holiday. The theatre was full every night.

After the Sunday matinee performance, we had a party for Jacqueline Brookes. We took her to the railroad station, I said farewell to her, and then rushed home to sleep. And did I sleep! It was a wonderful climax after all those weeks of preparation. As for Miss Brookes, Ann and I remained friends with her for a long time afterwards and visited her whenever we went to New York.

* * *

The Miracle Worker
by William Gibson

The Miracle Worker is the story of Helen Keller and her relationship with Annie Sullivan during the 1880s. The play deals only with Helen Keller as a child, and doesn't show her as the important world figure she subsequently became and how she, in turn, helped the physically handicapped. The drama became quite successful in New York, and eventually spread to other major theatres in the country, as well as to regional and educational theatres.

Something very tragic happened during the rehearsal period of that play which caused us to cease working for several days.

It is true that theatre is of great significance to many of us, yet a world event may occur that stops everything, so our feelings and attention are occupied only with that particular occurrence. I am referring to the assassination of John F. Kennedy on November 22, 1963.

When Ann called me that Friday noon to inform me that she had just heard on the radio that President Kennedy was assassinated, I didn't believe it at first. When I, in turn, told Leo Comeau, who was working on stage, "There is a rumor that the president was assassinated," he didn't seem to react to it at first. I went home and didn't return to the theatre until Tuesday. All we did those four days was listen and talk about Kennedy's assassination. I was reminded of a passage in the prologue of the modern version of *Antigone*.

> *Since time began, men recoiled with horror from the desecration of the dead. It is this spirit which prompts us today to suspend battle in order to bury our dead.*

Another question comes to mind: How is it that a play—to be specific, a tragedy—has not yet been written about John F. Kennedy? Of course, there have been films and television programs, but a tragedy—none! Is it that the subject, J. F. Kennedy, is not worthy of a tragedy? Or do we have to wait a century before someone will write a tragedy with Kennedy as the protagonist?

* * *

The Three Penny Opera
by Bertolt Brecht (1898-1956)
music by Kurt Weill
adaptation by Marc Blitzstein

Musicals are an American product. Operettas, originating in Europe, certainly never became that popular or well-known here in the United States. *Oklahoma*, which emerged in the mid-forties, is considered the first musical. Since then, musical theatre has been the most popular form of entertainment on the American stage, and also in England. In musicals, the plot, acting, scenery, etc., are certainly superior to the operettas. Many people became rich in this enterprise. Straight drama is now secondary to the multi-million dollar business of musicals.

The Three Penny Opera, however, is a different kind of musical. It has to be, since Bertolt Brecht wrote it. Originally, the piece was written by John Gay (1685-1732) and called, *The Beggar's Opera*. In 1928, Bertolt Brecht, together with Kurt Weill, adapted *The Beggar's Opera* into German and named it, *Die Dreignoschenoper*. In 1954, a new adaptation appeared by an American composer, the late Marc Blitzstein, who called it *The Three Penny Opera*. Since then this work has been in circulation all over the world, and people continue to see it again and again. Many of the songs have become popular on their own because of their ability to stay in our minds: "The Ballad of Mack the Knife," "Pirate Jenny," and "The Solomon Song." The musical contains twenty-five songs.

It's about the poor and the downtrodden. If comparisons are necessary we say what Shakespeare was to his age, so was Brecht to the first half of this century. His plays are poetic. Enamored with the culture of China, his plays also have social significance, but are not necessarily realistic.

He called his style of theatre "Epic theatre." He was not interested in an audience becoming involved emotionally: for example, watching the play with a clear mind, and going out and doing something about the wrongs you observed. Brecht is the author of many plays, though some are more outstanding than others: *The Good Woman of Setzuan, The Caucasion Chalk Circle, Mother Courage, The Three Penny Opera*, and many other interesting works.

During the performances of this play, I received a call from President Corbett. He plaintively asked, "Why do you have a play about a brothel during Religious Emphasis Week?" He had received numerous calls from parents and community leaders.

Shakespeare Festival

There are all kinds of festivals, even Onion and Garlic Festivals. Naturally, the theatre profession decided to have a Shakespeare Festival to honor the Bard's four hundredth birthday. Our theatre group was no exception. *Webster's New Collegiate Dictionary* gives two definitions for 'Bard.' One is befitting Shakespeare, the other is a piece of armor. I'll take the first one.

It has been twenty-eight years since we celebrated the Bard's four hundreth birthday, and he is still the same beautiful and poetic dramatist. His *Othello* and *Macbeth*, his *King Lear* and *Hamlet*—you can't forget them once you've learned them.

A Message from the University President
Shakespeare Week - April 22-28, 1964

In the university theatre all of the talents on which academic premiums are placed find expression. Individuals of different talents find common cause and learn respect for talents other than their own.

The celebration of the four hundredth anniversary of Shakespeare's birth therefore is more than a bow to the playwright. It is a recognition also of the shorter but impressive history of the theatre at New Mexico State University and of the broader goals for which NMSU as a university of high quality stands....

PROCLAMATION

Shakespeare's plays were not only for his age and ours, not for one nation or language, but for humanity. He planted one leg of his compass in the Elizabethan era and then with the other swept the whole circumference of time.

I therefore declare April 22-28 as Shakespeare Week and urge everyone to participate in the various activities of the Shakespeare Festival such as drama, dance, poetry, and music on the New Mexico State University campus.

> R. B. Corbett
> President

Romeo and Juliet
by William Shakespeare

Romeo and Juliet was the major production during the Shakespeare Festival. The cast consisted of twenty-one major characters and a supporting cast of fourteen Ladies, Gentlemen, Pages, Watchmen and Maskers. Two actresses wanted to play Juliet. Since they were both good, we had two Juliets, a short one and a tall one. Each one appeared in three performances. (The cast had much fun with the short Juliet one day and the tall Juliet the next day.) Besides the Director, Technical Director, Choreographer, Fencing Master, etc., we had sixty-eight people involved in the presentation of *Romeo and Juliet*.

Elizabethan dances, choreographed by Judy Graese and performed by fifteen dancers, were performed for forty-five minutes before each performance.

In addition to *Romeo and Juliet* the festival program began on the first afternoon with a Shakespeare Panel consisting of six panelists: Phillip Birkinshaw, Edgar Garrett, Marion Hardman, Peter Hurd, Newman Reed, and Hershel Zohn.

The festival also included a concert of madrigal singers and Elizabethan music, both under the direction of Oscar Butler. Shakespeare's *The Comedy of Errors* was presented by the Las Cruces High School drama classes and their director Frances Rhome. Readings included Shakespeare's poetry, "The Phoenix and The Turtle" by Joan Quarm; sonnets read by Phillip Birkinshaw, Jackie Clark, Gordon Owen, and Joan Quarm. "Venus and Adonis" was adapted and presented by Joan Quarm, Phillip Birkinshaw, Jackie Clark, and Gordon Owen. After such a program, one may believe we did justice to the Bard, for at least another century.

* * *

An Experimental Program of Nine One-Act Plays

The plays were by Edward Albee, Lewis John Carlino, Tennessee Williams, Eugene Ionesco, Samuel Beckett, August Strindberg, Anton Chekhov, and John Millington Synge. Except for *The Zoo Story* and *Objective Case*, the other seven plays were chosen and directed by students. The student directors were members of Drama 415, Advanced Directing. After twenty-seven years, it would be difficult to express an opinion now on the directing. What I can comment on is their choice of plays—what a selection! For that itself, wherever you are, you all deserve an "A."

* * *

Come Blow Your Horn
by Neil Simon

This was the first summer production we undertook. Student enrollment was rather small during the summer. Our budget was even smaller. Also, this was our first attempt at producing Neil Simon. Up to that time, I was indifferent about doing his plays. This was also Simon's first play. Who could have foreseen that a quarter of a century later he would be one of the most successful playwrights on the American stage. About the play—it's a skillful piece about a father and his problems with his two sons. For July evenings, I assume, it was OK.

* * *

A Far Country
by Henry Denker

This drama is called a biography of Sigmund Freud. The prologue and epilogue are in Vienna, June, 1938, while the Nazis are playing havoc in Austria, Germany, and in other European countries. After the prologue, the play moves to the turn of the century, where Freud is engrossed with his theory of psychoanalysis. It then moves to the epilogue in Vienna, June 4, 1938. Freud is leaving Nazi Vienna where he had lived and worked for forty years.

I recall Michael Coquat portraying Sigmund Freud and Eva Holberg, whom I still remember from the *Three Penny Opera*, playing Dr. Freud's mother. It was an interesting play, yet something was lacking. One would expect a play about a personality like Sigmund Freud to have greater dramatic significance.

* * *

The Firebugs
by Max Frisch

Considered one of the most provocative plays of the sixties, it's basically a satire and an attack against complacency. Frisch, born in Zurich, Switzerland, was an architect by profession, and a writer by avocation. The actors were Bruce Shamel, Arlene Belkin, Bill Barney, Mike Myers, James Donohue, and Lee Miles.

* * *

The House of Bernarda Alba
by Frederico Garcia Lorca
translated by James Graham-Lujan
and Richard L. O'Connell

Lorca was known as a brilliant poet and dramatist when he was killed during the Spanish Civil War and his body thrown into an unmarked grave. Since then his life has become legendary and he is considered an important poetic playwright of our time. He is especially known for *Yerma*, *Blood Wedding*, *The Shoemaker's Prodigious Wife*, and *The House of Bernarda Alba*. The latter has an all-female cast. Too bad we didn't have a female director. Today the play would most likely be directed by a woman. Yet it was a good production, and the audience liked it. Arlene Belkin portrayed Bernarda—a difficult and highly dramatic role. I recall Arlene and the director had a "scene" on how to end the play.

Characters

Bernarda	Arlene Belkin
Maria Josefa, her mother	Robin Butler
Bernarda's daughters	
Angustias	Cheryl Hedrick
Magdalena	Judy Graese
Amelia	Susan Giombolini
Martirio	Judith Pattison
Adela	Dianne Haak
A Maid	Robin Hayner
La Poncia	Sharon Meier
Beggar Woman	Lois Reuth
Her Child	Robin Tanner
Prudencia	Lee Gemoets

Women in Mourning:

Judy Barbar	Kerri Kraft	Dianne Roether
Paula Barney	Ann Krentel	Mary Schwengel
Elizabeth Beckman	Shirley Richardson	Susan Scofield
Mary Cooper	Barbara McFall	Dorothy Shamel
Melody Dean	Karen McGinley	Jolly Smith
Eva Holberg	Laura Moore	Helen Sydow
Kathy Johnson	Dedie Myers	Valeria Want
Evelyn Kirby	Shirley Richardson	Nancy Ward

* * *

Oedipus Rex
by Sophocles
translated by William Butler Yeats

Oedipus Rex is still the most powerful tragedy in dramatic literature as well as on stage. In translation, however, it can be a different story. There are many translations, and some of the translators have taken much liberty. I believe Yeats' version is the best. We did the production in 1965, with a chorus of fifteen, plus fifteen characters.

However, something happened during the rehearsal period which was very upsetting to me and the cast, and unethical on the actor's part. I was in search of a professional actor for Oedipus. Actor's Equity recommended an actor to me, a so-called star who had performed Oedipus (although a modern version).[1] We came to terms. A New York daily newspaper announced our production, but about ten days before the opening I received a long distance telephone call telling me that he was in a car accident and was unable to make it. For several days afterwards I made many long distance calls to New York in search of another actor for Oedipus. I finally decided to have Mike Myers, a graduate student, play Oedipus. He came through with flying colors. Everyone who saw him was quite impressed by his Oedipus. That same "professional actor" who canceled out from our production "performed" the identical excuse at another university in New Mexico about a month later. Actor's Equity finally ceased recommending him to other theatres.

* * *

The Physicists
by Friedrich Durrenmatt

The Swiss dramatist is especially known for *The Visit* and *The Marriage of Mr. Mississippi*. The play's action takes place in a private sanatorium known as *"Les Cerisiers."* It's a madhouse. The attention is on three inmates. One thinks he is Newton, another Einstein, and another has visitations from Solomon. The play mixes bizarre comedy and, sometimes amusing, satire. The major characters were in good hands: Bill Frankfather, Mike Myers, Robin Hayner, and James Donohue.

---

[1] Jean Cocteau's *The Infernal Machine*, is a surrealistic version. It is completely different from Sophocles' *Oedipus Rex*. Although the actor was recommended by Actor's Equity, he might have felt this was not a part for him and, therefore, was reluctant to do it.

* * *

A View From the Bridge
by Arthur Miller

This piece creates a reverse Oedipus situation, in which a Brooklyn longshoreman called Eddie has 'desires' for his young orphaned niece, Catherine, stronger than he dares to admit. His passion warps her life, his own, and that of his wife, Beatrice. It leads to tragedy. The leading characters were portrayed by fine actors: Bill Frankfather as Eddie, Judy Pattison as Catherine, and Robin Hayner as Beatrice.

According to classic definition, a play about such an undistinguished, unheroic figure as a longshoreman, no matter how well-filled with shocks of pity and terror, cannot be a true tragedy. But Arthur Miller believes that "the common man is as apt a true subject for tragedy as kings ever were."

Joan Quarm of the *El Paso Herald Post* said,

> *I stand humbly, cap in hand before the first non-professional production of the entire season to approach perfection. I drove to Las Cruces, not expecting the beauty I found, but in complete confidence that whatever director Hershel Zohn did with Arthur Miller's* A View From the Bridge, *would be an intelligent interpretation of a good script.... The play moves strongly, scene after scene met with involuntary applause.... They all add to the final effect: Hershel Zohn's most poetic achievement to date.*

I'd like to say a few words about the person you have just met in these pages, and will continue to encounter. Lucky is the theatre group who has a dramatist or critic attached to it. Joan Quarm was professor of literature at University of Texas at El Paso (UTEP) for a number of years. Her major interest, in

The Three Penny Opera—1964. (Courtesy: RGHC/NMSU Library)

Oedipus Rex—1964. (Courtesy: RGHC/NMSU Library)

Romeo and Juliet—1964. (Courtesy: RGHC/NMSU Library)

The House of Bernarda Alba—1964. Arlene Belkin (center), as Bernarda. Her five daughters were played by Cheryl Hedrick, Judy Graese, Susan Giombolini, Judith Pattison, and Dianne Haak. (Courtesy: RGHC/NMSU Library)

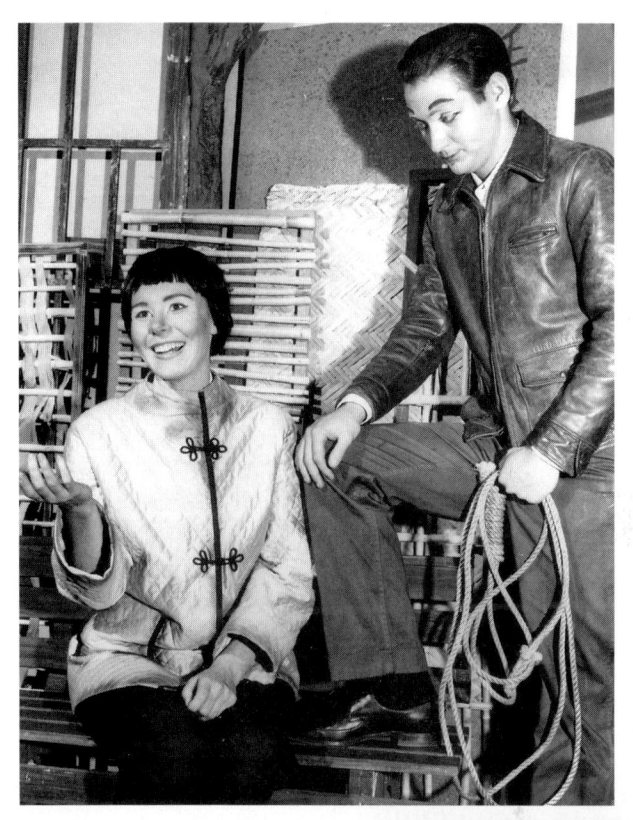

Elizabeth Huddle in *The Good Woman of Setzuan*—1967.

Rock Campbell as *J. B.*—1961
(Photos courtesy: RGHC/NMSU Library)

Maxim Gorki *l.* and Konstantin Stanislavski.

Marcia Riegel and Clinton Kimbrough in *The Crucible*—1972.
(Courtesy: RGHC/NMSU Library)

The Lower Depths—1972. (Courtesy: RGHC/NMSU Library)

Above: *Twelfth Night*—1955. *l. to r.*: John Bellamy, Ed Garrett, Marjorie McCorkle, and Leo Comeau.
Below: *As You Like It*—1963. Courtesy: RGH/NMSU Library)

Othello—1965. James Earl Jones *(upper)* and William Barney *(lower)*.
(Courtesy: RGHC/NMSU Library)

Left: Carolyn Johnson, William Barney and Ada Shook in *A Midsummer Night's Dream*—1960. (Courtesy: RGHC/NMSU Library) *(Below)*: Jack Soules as *Macbeth*.

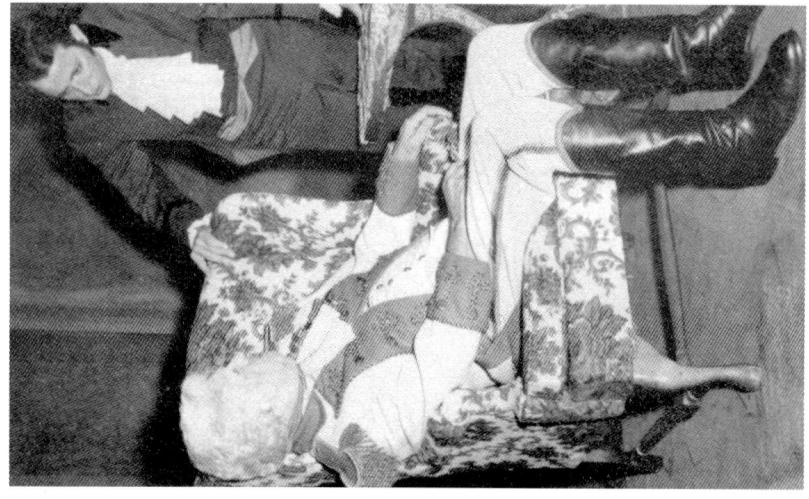

Zohn and Mark Medoff.

**War and Peace
1969**

Zohn and Judith Pattison.

War and Peace—1969. *l. to r.*: Hershel Zohn, Mark Medoff, Judy Pattison, Irene Oliver, Martha Fouse.

Fiddler on the Roof—1971

Hershel Zohn as Tevye in *Fiddler on the Roof*.
Cornelia Easterling as his wife - Golde,
and daughters *(clockwise from top left)*:
Diane Smith, Kay Brilliant, Corry Valdez,
Rose Schweiss, and Christine Brooks.

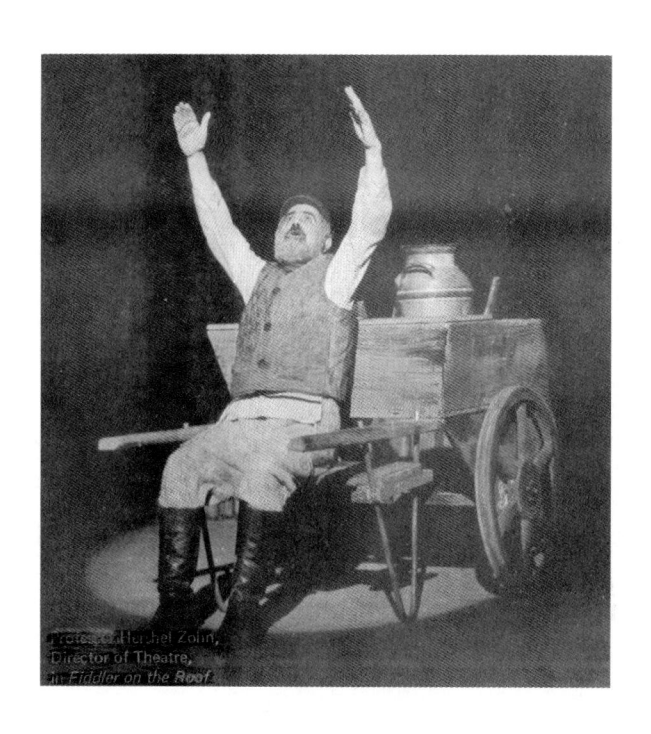

Hershel Zohn as Tevye in *Fiddler on the Roof*, 1971.

New Mexico State University President Gerald W. Thomas, Ann Zohn, and Professor Emeritus Hershel Zohn at the dedication of the Hershel Zohn Theatre, April 16, 1978.

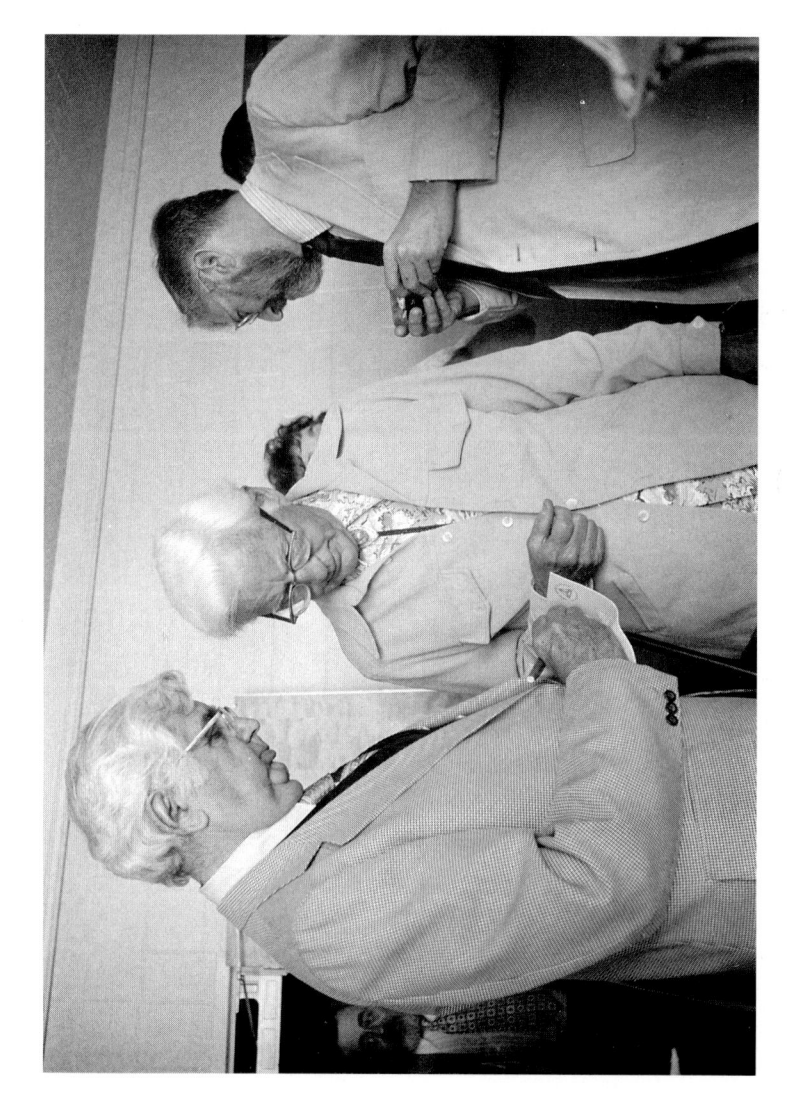

Zohn (l.), the late Professor Emeritus Charles H. Stubing, and Professor Jerome Brown at the theatre dedication, April 16, 1978.

The Matchmaker
1963

Above: Bert Seamans, Claire Lewis, Kathryn Harry, Michael Myers (under table) in 1961 production. *(Left)*: Mildred Hayner as Mrs. Dolly Levi in 1961 production. *(Below)*: Tour cast at final performance in Hawaii. Zohn far left, Claire Lewis and Phil Wedding in center. Seamans played Vandergelder in the 1963 on-campus productions. Wedding was Vandergelder on the tour. (All photos courtesy of RGHC/NMSU Library)

addition to teaching, was theatre. She participated as an actress in countless plays, and directed and wrote about the theater—primarily as a critic. She heard about our program at New Mexico State and did not rest until she made a trip to Las Cruces. Once she saw a production here, she became a zealous supporter of our work. She approached our productions, as a critic earnestly. Before she traveled to Las Cruces to see a play, she made a thorough study of the work she was to see—learned all she could concerning the author and the play. I was amazed at her knowledge of the theatre and the people in it. Above all, she loved the theatre! She lives in Portugal now. May she find happiness there, in and out of the theatre.[2]

* * *

Othello
by William Shakespeare.

Othello is the twenty-seventh of Shakespeare's thirty-seven plays, and was written at the peak of his powers.

> *This book,*
> *When brass and marble fade, shall make thee look*
> *Fresh to all ages,*
> *Now over four hundred years after Shakespeare was born, these superlatives have proved to be without exaggeration. Shakespeare is not merely a poet and playwright—he is simply The Bard, a figure in literature beyond compare.*
>
>   - from the play program

---

[2] Joan Quarm's "Tribute to Hershel Zohn," written when the new theatre was dedicated is included in Addendum C.

It was the summer of 1965, when, on my way to Russia to observe the theatre in Moscow, I stopped in New York to see several plays. One of the plays on my list was *Othello* with James Earl Jones. (By coincidence, it was at a theatre on Broadway and Twenty-eighth Street where I had performed three decades ago with Maurice Schwartz's Yiddish Art Theatre.) I was quite impressed by Jones' performance and, no sooner said than done, I went backstage after the show and introduced myself. We had a cup of tea and I invited him to come as a guest artist to do *Othello* at New Mexico State.

By the first of March, Jones was here ready to play *Othello*. We had a good cast waiting for him—especially Iago and Desdemona. The audience was greatly impressed by him. In general, he was so popular with our students that, when he was about to leave, some of the students (especially the females) were actually in tears. Not long after, he starred in a new play on Broadway, and then in another new play, and then on to the movies. In other words, James Earl Jones became a first-class star. Therefore we created a saying, "If you want to become famous on the professional stage, first come to NMSU."

* * *

The Thieves' Carnival
by Eugene Ionesco

Two plays comprised the Summer Theatre Program for 1966. *The Thieves' Carnival* by Eugene Ionesco, followed by *Uncle Vanya*. The former had a large cast, was loaded with humor, romance, and dances, and created an enjoyable midsummer evening. The acting was fine, and the choreography by Peggy Rogers was quite interesting.

* * *

Uncle Vanya
by Anton Chekhov

We all know Chekhov is famous for his four major plays: *The Sea Gull, Uncle Vanya, The Three Sisters*, and *The Cherry Orchard*. In all, he wrote seventeen plays. In addition to these four full-length plays, he wrote *Ivanov* and *The Wood Demon*. Chekhov revised *The Wood Demon* and called it *Uncle Vanya*, which contains most of the characters of the earlier play.

Jack Soules was Dr. Astrov; Bill Frankfather, Uncle Vanya; Oscar Butler, the retired professor; Robin Hayner, his twenty-seven year old wife; Sonya, his daughter by his first wife was played by Denise Chavez. Denise had a beautiful, moving scene at the end when she said: "Uncle Vanya, wait. We shall rest...we shall rest...we shall rest!"

* * *

The Queen and the Rebels
by Ugo Betti

Betti was born in 1892 at Camerino, Italy. The son of a doctor, he was educated in the classics and graduated in law. His career was interrupted by the First World War, during which he was taken prisoner and sent to Germany. He began to write poetry in 1917 as a prisoner in Germany, but, in later years, he was accepted as the leading Italian dramatist in the generation that followed Pirandello. According to program notes, *The Queen and the Rebels* was written in 1949 and produced in London in 1955. The principal character, Argia, finds her self-respect in her knowledge that she is "immensely important." It is a transformation that turns her whole life upside down, making a prostitute into a queen. Then, with a brilliant show of understanding and respect for the human person who is turning her, at last, she turns back into herself—no less a queen because she is still the woman she once was.

Joan Quarm wrote in the *El Paso Herald-Post*:

> The Queen and the Rebels *gives total involvement. Strong direction of course is the heart of any play, and this play is strongly directed, from leads to minor roles. Jackie Clark is a magnificent Argia. She combines the qualities of courage and desperation, earthiness and imagination, honesty and cynicism, into a convincing characterization of an extremely difficult role. Her voice and stage movement have variety and professional control. She is a pleasure to see!*

* * *

The School for Scandal
by Richard B. Sheridan

This is a period piece that lends itself to any manner or style of production the director chooses. First, it is comedy galore. The characters therein are amazingly funny, almost caricature-like. It's set in 1775 in London. Let's see what our critic Joan Quarm has to say:

> The School for Scandal *on the NMSU campus is worth driving to Las Cruces to see. It is beautifully dressed, well mounted and directed with the flair Zohn's audiences have come to expect. It interprets the play, rather than distorting it. It's one of style, done in style.*

* * *

After the Fall
by Arthur Miller.

To this very day the opening of a new play by Arthur Miller is a great event in town (New York). The play may receive poor reviews and close shortly afterwards, but the occasion is nevertheless a significant one in the "Theatre World." The New York opening of this play was especially important because Miller had not written a play in nine years. Also, this was the inauguration of a new theatre—the Repertory Theatre at Lincoln Center. The actual theatre at Lincoln Center was not yet finished so a temporary building for that occasion was erected at Washington Square, Greenwich Village.

The play opened in New York in 1964. "Rejoice that Arthur Miller is back with a play worthy of his mettle," cried one critic. The central character, Quentin, is an attorney who is not satisfied with his past or with his present. As one critic wrote, it's "a pain-wracked drama," yet beautifully written. Scenes showing Quentin's relationship with Maggie are sometimes even painful to watch. Incidentally, even to this day, you hear people criticizing Miller for drawing such a character as Maggie. Those who complained insisted that Maggie is Marilyn Monroe, who had committed suicide before the play was written, therefore Miller is severely criticized for having such an unpleasant character as Maggie in his play. In his biography, Miller writes, "As I was coming to the end of the writing of *After the Fall*, the horrifying news came that Marilyn had died, apparently of an overdose of sleeping pills."[3] In defense of Maggie and Marilyn, Miller said, "Indeed, if Maggie was any reflection of Marilyn, who had many other dimensions, the character's agony was a tribute to her, for

---

[3] Arthur Miller, *Time Bends*, Grove Press, 1987. p. 531.

in life, as far as the public was concerned, Marilyn was practically barred from any conceivable connection with suffering; she was the 'golden girl,' the forever young goddess of sexuality."[4]

The play opened in New York in January 1964. Miller made peace with Elia Kazan, who had directed his plays before their break. Kazan now came back to do *After the Fall*. Jason Robards, Jr. portrayed Quentin, Barbara Loden was Maggie, and Salome Jens, Olga.

We did the play exactly three years later and the program notes state that "The action of the play takes place in the mind, thought and memory of Quentin, a contemporary man."

Allen Holley designed the set—various platforms on stage, and a bridge, the width of the center aisle in the theatre leading from the stage to the center of the house so Quentin could address the audience. I went to New York in search of a guest artist for Quentin and engaged James Congdon, who starred in our production. A few of the large cast of thirty-six were: Nancy Sparger, Arlene Belkin, Jeff Moore, Carroll Wood, Evelyn Kirby, James Donohue, David Orin Charles, Nancy Herring, and Pat Dinkins.

* * *

That summer we had Neil Simon's fine comedy, *Barefoot in the Park* with Bill Frankfather, Evelyn Kirby, James Donohue, Bill Coleman, Jeff Moore, and Kathryn Myers. The second summer production was the children's play *Tom Sawyer* by Shorah Spencer, and directed by Bruce Shamel.

* * *

---

[4] Miller, p. 537.

Southwest Theatre Conference

During the summer of 1967 I was occupied with the task of inviting many people, important in the theatre world, to be guests at the Southwest Theatre conference.

The Southwest Theatre Conference is comprised of the following five states: Arkansas, Louisiana, New Mexico, Oklahoma, and Texas. The board decided to hold the Twentieth Annual Meeting in New Mexico, at New Mexico State University's new theatre, October 26-28, 1967.

Our hopes to have personalities of the caliber of Arthur Miller and Anne Bancroft didn't materialize. The final schedule included many individuals who were influential in their sphere of the theatre. Harold Clurman, famous for his directing, lecturing and writing on threatre, has exerted a great influence on the American stage as a director, writer, and philosopher of the theatre. Maria Douglas was called the 'First Lady' of the Mexican Theatre. Joseph Papp, well-known in New York theatre as a producer, director, author and for his "Shakespeare in the Park," spoke on "Theatre in a Democratic Society."

William Saroyan was the most popular guest, although all the previous speakers were important and respected in their fields. We anxiously waited to hear him. He was the last on the program, and spoke on "The Playwright and Playwriting." A full schedule provided attendees with a wide selection of speakers, workshops and activities.

Conference Program

Thursday, October 26

3:00-6:00 PM	**Registration**	**Ramada Inn Lobby**
6:00-7:30 PM	**Reception**	**Ramada Lounge**
	Honoring past presidents of the Southwest Theatre Conference	

218   All The World's A Stage

11:00 PM   **SWTC**   **Ramada Inn, Room 267**
Repertory Company Committee
Chairman: KENNETH BARRY

Friday, October 27
(All events unless designated differently are in the Theatre Building on the New Mexico University Campus.)

8:00 AM   **Registration**   Upstairs
Continental Breakfast
9:45 AM   **Welcome to the Conference**   Theatre
Host: HERSHEL ZOHN, New Mexico State University
President of NMSU: ROGER B. CORBETT
President of Southwest Theatre Conference:
RICHARD O'CONNELL, New Mexico Highlands University
10:15 AM   **The Achievement of an Ideal**   Theatre
Children'sTheatre
Chairman: J. HENRY TUCKER, University of Texas at El Paso
NAT EEK, University of Oklahoma
JEAN MICULKA, UTEP
DOROTHY MILLER, Shreveport, Louisiana
11:15 AM   **American Playwright's Theatre**   Theatre
DAVID H. AYERS, Executive Director; Ohio State University
12:15 PM   **Luncheon**   **Milton Student Center Ballroom**
Greetings: JOHN M. GLOWACKI, Head of Fine Arts, NMSU
Contempory American and European Theatre
Keynote Speaker: HAROLD CLURMAN
2:00 PM   **The Mexican Theatre**   Theatre
MARIA DOUGLAS (If time permits she will also read poetry)
3:00 PM   **Recent Studies in American**   Upstairs
Theatre Research
Chairman: GRESDNA DOTY, Louisiana State Univ.
CLIFFORD ASHBY, Texas Technological College
GEORGE BOGUSCH, Louisiana State University
HAROLD TEDFORD, Wake Forest University
Scene Design Trends   Theatre
Chairman: ALBERT C. RONKE, UTEP
EDWARD HOUSER, UTEP
WILLIAM GAMBLE, Festival Theatre, El Paso
JAMES HULL MILLER, Shreveport, Louisiana

4:00 PM	**Acting in Brecht**	**Theatre**

ELIZABETH HUDDLE, Lincoln Center for the Performing Arts Guest Artist: *The Good Woman of Setzuan*

5:00 PM	**New Mexico Theatre Guild**	**Upstairs**

Business Meeting (All members of NMTG are urged to attend)

8:30 PM	*The Good Woman of Setzuam*	**Theatre**

(SWTC delegates are invited as the guests of the Playmakers)

11:30 PM	**Afterwords**	**Patio Room, Holiday Inn**

Saturday, October 28

8:00 AM	**Continental Breakfast**	**Upstairs**
9:00 AM	**High School Drama-Theatre:**	**Theatre**
	Improving Standards and Teaching Methods	

Chairman: LOREN WINSHIP, Chairman, Department of Drama, University of Texas
BILL FEGAN, Founding director, Kaleidoscope Players, Raton, New Mexico
DON IRWIN, Fine Arts Program director, Texas Education Agency, Austin, Texas
Consultant: HAROLD TAYLOR, educator and author

10:00 AM	**The Critic-Friend or Foe**	**Upstairs**

Moderator: JOAN QUARM, critic, *El Paso Herald Post* and UTEP
BURNETT HOBGOOD, SMU
JULES ROTHMAN, College of the Holy Name, Oakland
JACK SOULES, NMSU

10:00 AM	**New Ideas and Projects in**	**Theatre**
	Community Theatre	

Moderator: MARYLIN POOL, Amarillo Little Theatre
LEE EDWARDS, Baton Rouge Little Theatre
JOHN HADSELL, Las Cruces Community Theatre
BERNARD THOMAS, Albuquerque Little Theatre

11:00 AM	**Business Meeting,**	**Theatre**
	Southwest Theatre Conference	
12:15 PM	**Luncheon**	**Milton**

Greetings: RICHARD BARRETT, Dean of Arts and Sciences, NMSU
The Teacher and Theatre Art
HAROLD TAYLOR

2:00 PM	**The Theatre In Human Affairs.**	**Theatre**
	A Rhetorical Perspective	

Chairman: RALPH B. CULP, UTEP

	REGINALD V. HOLLAND, North Texas State Univ. PAUL REINHARDT, University of Texas GIFFORD WINGATE, UTEP	
2:00 PM	**The Director's Role In The** **University Theatre**	**Theatre**
	Chairman: EDWIN SNAPP, University of New Mexico JACK CLAY, Southern Methodist University PRESTON MAGRUDER, University of Arkansas CHARLES SUGGS, University of Oklahoma	
3:00 PM	**Theatre In A Democratic Society**	**Theatre**
	JOSEPH PAPP	
4:15	*Anybody and Anybody Else:* *Very Short Plays*	**Theatre**
	By William Saroyan Presented for the first time by the NMSU Playmakers	
6:00 PM	**Social Hour**	**Las Cruces Country Club**
7:00 PM	**Banquet**	**Las Cruces Country Club**
	The Playwright And Play Wrighting WILLIAM SAROYAN	
9:00 PM	**Marat/Sade**	**Old Mesilla**
	Las Cruces Community Theatre (seating is limited)	
11:30 PM	**Afterwords**	**El Patio, Old Mesilla**

Many people contributed to the success of this Twentieth Annual Conference. Credit is due to current and past officers of the organization, as well as hard-working local people.

OFFICERS OF SWTC

President	....	Richard O'Connell
	New Mexico Highlands University Las Vegas, New Mexico	
Vice President	....	Nat Eek
	University of Oklahoma Norman, Oklahoma	
Secy.-Treasurer	....	James D. Baines
	Arkansas Arts Center Little Rock, Arkansas	
Editor	....	Richard T. Wiles
	Dept. of Theatre New Mexico Highlands University Las Vegas, New Mexico	
Editorial Associate	....	Bill Knell
	Editor Field Services Publications New Mexico Highlands University Las Vegas, New Mexico	

BOARD MEMBERS

Marylin Pool .... 1-year term
    Amarillo, Texas

John Wray Young .... 1-year term
    Shreveport, Louisiana

William Crawford .... 2-year term
    Lawton, Oklahoma

Burnet M. Hobgood .... 2-year term
    Dallas, Texas

Ruth Denney .... 3-year term
    Houston, Texas

Bernard Thomas .... 3-year term
    Albuquerque, New Mexico

PAST PRESIDENTS OF SWTC

Rupel J. Jones	R. Lyle Hagan
Paul Baker	Joe Salek
Walter R. Volbach	Lee Edwards
John Wray Young	Frances Prinz
Virgil L. Baker	F. Donald Clark
Monroe Lippman	Angus Springer
John Rosenfield	Preston Magruder
Loren Winship	Art Cole
Theodore Viehman	Burnett Hobgood
Oma Link Rowley	

LOCAL PLANNING COMMITTES

Chairman of Committees	Mrs. Elizabeth McComas
Housing and Registration	Mrs. Jean Erhard
Food	Mrs. Fern Porter
Publicity	Mrs. Jackie Clark
Decorations	Mrs. Helen Duncan
Transportation	Mr. Bruce Shamel
Art Work	Mrs. Ann Zohn
Hospitality	Mrs. Michael Szczukowski

The Good Woman of Setzuan
by Bertold Brecht, translated by Eric Bentley
Setting by Clifford Fellage, Music by Wolpe and Folson

Brecht was born in Augsburg in 1899, and died in Berlin in August 1956. His theory of theatre is a German term called "*Verfremdungs* effect" (alienation effect), or "epic theatre."

Guest artist Elizabeth Huddle was supported by an outstanding cast: James Donohue, Bill Frankfather, Dave Allgeier, Bruce Shamel, Robin Hayner, Denise Chavez, Irene Oliver, Judy Pattison, John Schuldt, Vicki Medoff, Robin Daviet, Lloyd Watts, Monte Wright, Bob Porter, Janice Reid.

Three gods descend to Earth to find a good human. Shen-Te, a prostitute, is the only one who gives them lodging. In return, the gods richly reward her. When friends learn of this good fortune, they badger her for a portion. Shen-Te's plan is to borrow her brother's cap, jacket, and name—Shen-Tu—so she can be as mean as he and tell everyone where to go. She then keeps the fortune for her boyfriend.

* * *

The Odd Couple
by Neil Simon

By the mid-sixties, Neil Simon was recognized as the funniest man writing for the American stage. His first play was *Come Blow Your Horn*, in 1961. We produced this piece here in the summer of 1964. We also did his *Barefoot in the Park*, *The Odd Couple*, and later, *The Prisoner of Second Avenue*. All are comedies, of course, where people laugh to their heart's content.

* * *

Royal Gambit
by Herman Gressieker

The next play that summer was *Royal Gambit*. (Some people called it Royal Garbage). It deals with King Henry VIII and his six women and takes place in England in the sixteenth century. What more is there to say except that perhaps it was an escape from the heat.

* * *

The Marriage of Mr. Mississippi
by Friedrick Durrenmatt
translated by Michael Bullock.

Due to the strangeness of his plays, the European press labeled Durrenmatt "an uncomfortable citizen." In this country, he is especially known for *The Physicists* (performed here in October of 1965). *The Marriage of Mr. Mississippi* established Duarrenmatt's fame in Europe. It is a study of four men—a revolutionary, a public prosecutor, a politician, and a count—fighting for possession of the same woman. Some of the remaining twenty-six characters are divided into three assassins, a priest, a minister, a rabbi, eight psychiatrists, and two wardens. Why so many psychiatrists? If I remember correctly, the audience was more or less indifferent to this play; that doesn't mean we should not produce such a play. Ours is not a commercial theatre. Students should learn to be in, or see, all types of plays—period plays, serious drama, comedies, realistic pieces, and modern plays of all styles. Audiences, too, should be exposed to varied types of plays.

* * *

Anton Chekhov

One of the most significant dramatists in world drama, Chekhov's impact upon drama cannot be overestimated. All of his works have been translated into many languages. Different translations continue to appear, not only of his dramatic works, but also his short stories, and his correspondence to his relatives— his wife Olga Knipper, his friends, and his colleagues. His first play, *The Worthless Fellow Platonov*, probably written in the 1880s, was discovered in 1923. Since then there have been three translations of this play; the last one, called *Wild Honey*, was translated and adapted in 1984 by Michael Frayn. His other early plays were *Ivanov* and *The Wood Demon*. In addition, there are a number of one-acters such as: *The Boor*, *The Marriage Proposal*, *The Wedding*, *The Anniversary*, *The Swan Song*, *The Harmfulness of Tobacco*, and others.

In his biography *Chekhov*, French writer Henri Troyat writes:[5]

> *My father began my education or, to put it more simply, began to beat me before I reached the age of five, wrote Anton Chekhov of his earliest memories. Every morning as I awoke, my first thought was, 'Will I be beaten today?'" After a thrashing, his behind smarting, he was required by custom to kiss the hand that had punished him so harshly. Yet twenty years later Chekhov was becoming a physician and at the same time had experimented in writing humorous pieces to be published in various publications. Before long he began practicing his writing in the dramatic form: one-acters, and then came his four masterpieces. As a physician he must have had the feeling that his life was limited. His four major plays were frequently produced all over and especially remained standbys of the Moscow Art Theatre.*

---

[5] The following quotations are from Henri Troyat, *Chekhov,* E. P. Dutton, 1986.

I want to share with the reader Henri Troyat's description of the final minutes of Chekhov's life:

> *Chekhov and his wife, Olga, traveled from Moscow to Berlin and then to Badenweiler which was a spa in the Black Forest not far from Basel, Switzerland. Suddenly Badenweiler was hit by a heat wave which did not help Chekhov's condition. A local doctor eased his condition by giving him morphine and oxygen. On July first he seemed to feel better and insisted that Olga take a walk at least in the hotel grounds. To cheer her up he improvised some humorous stories which made her laugh. He finally fell asleep but not for long. He awakened and asked her to call a doctor. He ran a high fever which made Chekhov delirious. The windows were wide open but he can't stop panting. The doctor arrived and Chekhov told him in his poor German, "Ich sterbe" ["I am dying"]. He gave him an injection, but his heart failed to react. The doctor was about to send for oxygen but Chekhov insisted "What's the use? Before it arrives I'll be a corpse." So Dr. Schworer sent for a bottle of champagne. When it came, Chekhov took a glass and turning to Olga said with a smile, "It's been a long time since I have had champagne." He emptied the glass slowly and lay down on his left side. A few moments later he stopped breathing. He had passed from life to death with characteristic simplicity.*
>
> *It was July 2, 1904, three o'clock in the morning. A large black-winged moth had flown in through the window and was banging wildly against the lamp. The muffled sound grew maddeningly distracting. All at once there was a joyous explosion; the cork had popped out of the champagne bottle and foam was fizzing out after it. The moth found its way out of the window and disappeared into the sultry night. Silence returned. When day broke at last,*

Olga was still sitting and staring into her husband's face. It was peaceful smiling knowing. "There were no human voices, no everyday sounds," she wrote. "There was only beauty, peace and the grandeur of death."

Before leaving Badenweiler, Olga arranged for the remains to be transported to Moscow, where the burial was to take place on July 9. That day a group of friends gathered at the station to meet the train carrying his body. They were flabbergasted to learn that his coffin had traveled in a dirty green van with the words, FOR OYSTERS, written in large letters on the door.

Gorki was furious. "I feel like screaming, weeping, bawling with indignation and wrath. He knew that Chekhov would not have cared whether his body traveled in a basket of dirty laundry. What he found unforgivable was that Russia could have treated him so shoddily, and he later called the oyster van an enormous smirk of triumphant vulgarity. Yet was the absurdity of it all so very far from the absurdity of life as depicted many times over in Chekhov's stories and plays?

"Chekhov is an incomparable artist. An artist of life. And the worth of his creation consists of this—he is understood and accepted not only by every Russian, but by all humanity."—Leo Tolstoy.

Tolstoy, as great as he was, contradicted himself, especially when it came to Chekhov. He said he didn't like Chekhov's plays, but was crazy about his short stories.

In Ernest J. Simmons' biography of Chekhov, he writes:[6]

---

[6] Ernest J. Simmons, *Chekhov: A Biography*, Little, Brown & Co., 1962.

> *On one of his rare visits to the theatre at this time, to see* Uncle Vanya, *Tolstoy occupied the governor's box and received an ovation from the audience. Like* The Sea Gull, *which he had only read, he condemned* Uncle Vanya. *"Where is the drama? In what does it consist?" he stormed to actor A. A. Sanin. "Uncle Vanya and Astrov were simply good for nothing idlers escaping from real life into the country as a place of salvation."*

Nemirovich Danchenko reported to Chekhov that Tolstoy just didn't understand the play. Tolstoy objected, saying there was no tragic situation, and anyway there was no point in trying to discover it in guitars and crickets. Far from being offended, Chekhov was vastly amused. He said to a friend, "You know Tolstoy does not like my plays. He swears that I am not a dramatist. There is only one thing that comforts me," he added.

"What's that?"

"Tolstoy said to me, 'You know, I cannot abide Shakespeare, but your plays are even worse.'" And the restrained, calm Anton Pavlovich threw back his head and roared so loudly that his pince-nez fell from his nose.

In his *Tolstoy* biography, Henry Troyat[7] wrote what Tolstoy said about Chekhov. "He [Chekhov] has so much talent, his stories and talks were admirable, but he could not stomach his plays, which the Russian public devoured so eagerly. *The Sea Gull* is nothing but rubbish. He had not been able to force himself to read *The Three Sisters*, he was revolted by *Uncle Vanya*. One evening he put his arm around Chekhov's shoulders and said with brutal frankness: 'Shakespeare's plays are bad enough, but yours are even worse.' And on another occasion, somewhat more gently, 'My dear friend, I beg of you, do stop writing plays.' Chekhov bowed his head, smiled and choked back a dry little cough, but kept his temper."

---

[7] Henri Troyat, *Tolstoy,* Doubleday & Co., Inc., 1967.

The Cherry Orchard

Bernard Shaw said: "Every time I see a play by Chekhov, I want to chuck my own stuff into the fire." *The Cherry Orchard* concerns the doom of a family and, by extension, the doom of the landed gentry class of pre-revolutionary Russia. Yet, in spite of the seriousness of the play, Chekhov injected a very thin line of humor into the play. That humor was the reason for the constant arguments between Chekhov and the two producers of the Moscow Art Theatre—Stanislavski and Nemirovich Danchenko. "Why is it that in the playbills and advertisements of my play it is so tenaciously called *drama*? Danchenko and Stanislavski see in my writing positively not what I write; and I am prepared to pledge my word that they both haven't read my play attentively even once."

Of all of Chekhov's writing, *The Cherry Orchard* is considered his masterpiece. In the very last scene; after Lyubov Andreyevna says, *"We are coming,"* and exits, Feers, a servant and an old man of eighty-seven appears (tries the knob).

> *"Locked. They have gone. They forgot about me. No matter. I'll sit here a while. Leonid Anreyevich didn't put on his fur coat* (sighing). *And I didn't see to it. These young people. Life has gone by, as if I hadn't lived at all. I'll lie down a while. You haven't got any strength, nothing is left, nothing—you good for nothing."* (He lies motionless. All is still, there is heard nothing but the strokes of the axe far away in the orchard.)

Chekhov worked on *The Cherry Orchard* for three years. He saw it as a comedy. Heated arguments resulted between Stanislavski and Chekhov. The director reasoned with the author that he must consider the audience.

The Cherry Orchard was finally performed by the Moscow Art Theatre on January 17, 1904 on Chekhov's forty-fourth birthday. Chekhov died almost six months later on July 2, 1904. The success of *The Cherry Orchard* established Chekhov, beyond doubt, as his country's foremost playwright.

Doing *The Cherry Orchard* also took me back several decades to that audition with Eva Le Gallienne in New York City's Civic Repertory Theatre.

Guest artist for the New Mexico State presentation of *The Cherry Orchard* was the late Martha Schlamme, who played Madam Ranevskaya. Other actors were: Vicki Medoff, Charles Lewis, Denise Chavez, David Allgeier, Irene Oliver, Monte Wright, Dan Case, John Schuldt, Chris Hepburn, Herb Hall, the late Chrales Webb, and Lloyd Watts as Lopahin.

* * *

Arms and the Man
by George Bernard Shaw

This Shaw piece was on its second time around, and as a summer play it was just fine. In it were Vicki Medoff, Linda Lynch, Charles Lewis, Monte Wright, Bill McGonigle and David Allgeier as Bluntschli.

* * *

War and Peace
by Leo Tolstoy
adapted for the stage by
Erwin Piscator, Alfrred Neumann, Guntram Prufer
English version by Robert David MacDonald

The following article I wrote after our production of *War and Peace* at New Mexico State.

Once I had finished reading the dramatization of War and Peace *I decided this was a play I would definitely like to produce.*

One reason I wanted to do the play was because of its timeliness—we were already in the grips of war in Vietnam and as War and Peace *is historic, it is also universal. Another reason was its theatricalism—Erwin Piscator's adaptation of this gigantic novel made it quite an intriguing play.*

However, one was full of doubts. How could such a vast play be staged? Yet I was determined to pursue it.

Obtaining the rights to War and Peace *became complicated. The play had been done in numerous European countries, but in the United States only at the Repertory Theatre in New York City, Second Avenue and Twelfth Street (formerly the Yiddish Art Theatre). It was difficult to find out who really had the rights to David McDonald's English translation. It took three years to trace the agent and then convince him to give us the rights for* War and Peace.

Then came the problems of casting this significant play, as well as all the scenery, costumes, and film which are a part of the production. To be sure, Piscator adapted War and Peace *in the Brechtian style. The final cast was comprised of students, faculty, and townspeople. For the role of Pierre we had guest artist Bill Frankfather. The Alley Theatre in Houston, which had recently presented* War and Peace, *rented us a huge trunk of dolls—they were the soldiers and officers which served as the French and Russian armies during the battle scenes. We also made use of the Alley Theatre's music tapes for the stage adaptation.*

After months of planning, and intensive rehearsals in

all departments, War and Peace *began. The play was too long for a campus audience and cuts were made. People frequently cornered us with the question—"How can you do* War and Peace *on stage?" One could see the skepticism on their faces. While we were deeply engrossed in the play, we were also full of doubts as to the audiences' reaction.*

But when the first night came, it was a great surprise to all associated with the production. The audience was riveted to their seats and the final curtain was accompanied by a standing ovation. The audience enthusiasm was repeated at every performance. Letters poured into the theatre office full of praise about the production. Four performances were added to the original schedule of eight. Every night people came back stage to congratulate the actors. The people in this area talked about War and Peace *for some time after the play had closed.*

We all felt a great sense of satisfaction and accomplishment that, not only were we the first university in the country to produce War and Peace, *but above everything else, we had contributed our share toward the struggle for peace.*

The name of Erwin Piscator, as one of the adaptors of *War and Peace* and director of the original production, should be reassuring to any doubter. Piscator was one of the most brilliant young directors in Berlin in the twenties, and the greatest of his successes was a theatrical version of Jaroslav Hasek's novel, *The Good Soldier Schweik*—again, both adapted and directed by Piscator himself. He left Germany when the Nazis came to power, spent the war in America, and afterwards returned to Berlin with his version of *War and Peace*. (I met Piscator in the late thirties in New York and we had a lengthy discussion on the American theatre.)

The translator, Robert David MacDonald, worked in England and Germany as a theatrical producer and was the guest director of *War and Peace* at the Alley Theatre in Houston the previous spring. The NMSU Playmakers was the first (and probably the only) educational theatre in this country to present *War and Peace*.

Leo Tolstoy began work on his voluminous novel in 1863 and completed it six years later in 1869. After the novel was published he was not satisfied with it and made several revisions. As a novel, *War and Peace* has been translated into practically every language.

So much has been written and said about Tolstoy's work that it would be futile to begin an analysis of *War and Peace* here. However, one cannot refrain from adding these quotations:

William Lyon Phelps, "It is a dictionary of life, where one may look up any passion, any ambition and find its meaning."

One of Tolstoy's English translators, Aylmer Maude, quoted a Tolstoy fan: "I should like to live my life over again, in order to have again the pleasure of reading *War and Peace* for the first time."

The complete play program is reproduced here to acknowledge those who were a part of the cast and production staff of this epic production.

The New Theatre

THE DRAMA DIVISION OF FINE ARTS
Presents
THE PLAYMAKERS
In

WAR AND PEACE

from the novel by LEO TOLSTOY
adapted for the stage by
ERWIN PISCATOR, ALFRED NEUMANN, GUNTRAM PRUFER
English Version by
ROBERT DAVID MACDONALD
Directed by HERSHEL ZOHN
Set Design and Technical Direction by JAMES GILBERT

CHARACTERS

Narrator	**Frank Pinnock**
Pierre	**William Frankfather** *
Andrie	**Mark Medoff**
Prince Bolkonski, Andrei's Father	**Hershel Zohn**
Lisa, Andrei's Wife	**Vicki Medoff**
Maria, Andrei's Sister	**Irene Oliver**
Natasha	**Judi Pattison**
Countess Rostova, Natasha's Mother	**Martha Fouse**
Nicolai Rostov, Natasha's Brother	**Dan Chase**
Dolokhov	**Jim Post**
Anatol Kuragin	**Charles Lewis**
Alpatich	**Bob Baker**
Karatayev	**John Hadsell**
Kusmich	**Jerry Mattys**
Napoleon Bonaparte	**Forrest Westmoreland**
Tzar Alexander I	**Bill McGonigle**
Kutusov, Commander-in-Chief of the Russian Army	**Monte Wright**
French Officer	**Joe Cabarrus**
Standard Bearer	**Michael Rudfin**
Prisoner	**Dan Chase**
Narrator's Attendants	**Patrick Alexander**

Angus Crawford, Robert Spaulding
Officers, Soldiers, Medical Orderlies.................. **Patrick Alexander**
**Angus Crawford, D. A. Evans, Charles Lewis,
Bill McGonigle, Jim Post, Michael Rudfin,
Mike Sizby, Robert Spaulding, Joe Speer**

* * *

The action takes place in Europe between the Rhine and Mitischi.
Time: 1805-1812

* Mr. William Frankfather received his BA and MA at New Mexico State University. During his time here, he appeared in numerous plays, among them in the title roles of BECKET and UNCLE VANYA. Lately, he has been with Stanford University and has also acted in the California Shakespeare Festival. He obtained special permission from Stanford when he was invited to come here to portray the role of Pierre.

* * *

ACT I

Scene I   INTRODUCTIONS

II   FAMILY QUARRELS

III   LEAVE-TAKING

IV   WAR

V   HOME AND HOMECOMING

VI   ANDREI BOLKONSKI

VII   OTRODNOYE

ACT II

Scene I   THE YEAR OF PROBATION

II   THE RACE WITH TIME

III   ACCOUNTS

IV   THE DEATH OF THE OLD PRINCE

V   BORODINO

VI   MOSCOW

VII   EPILOGUE

* * *

There will be one intermission after Act I.

Costumes Designed and Executed by.................................. **Elma Schmidt**
    Assisting: Yvonne Baca, Ruthie Bowden, Marilynn Gay,
    Susie Manning, Tenya Price, Tessie Shannon
Lighting and Sound Designed by.. **Joe Sievert**
    Assisting: Pierre Brunet, Paul Sievert, Dwayne Wilson,
    Phyllis Wright.
Make-Up.. **Charles Lewis**
Stage Managers .... **Cathy LeClair, Linda Lynch**
Scene Construction .... **John George**
    Assisting: Ruth Bowden, Joe Castillo, Frances Greenwood,
    Harry Holguin, Penny Hobbs, Bill McGonigle, Julie Murdoch
    Grant Price, Harry Sontag, Monte Wright, Phyllis Wright.
Properties... **Monte Wright**
    Assisting: Darlene Couchman.
Posters and Program Cover... **Ann Zohn**
Box Office ....**Denise Chavez,**
                                                                      Dianna Miller, Janus Olive
House Manager .... **Bonnie Hosie, Cathy Williams**
Doorman.................................. **Herb Hall, Larry Marr, Larry Wadsworth**
Ushers .... **SPURS**

* * *

Music, sound effects and marionette soldiers are from the Alley Theatre, Houston.

* * *

The Playmakers is a chapter of Alpha Psi Omega, National Honorary Dramatic Fraternity, American Educational Theatre Association, American National Theatre and Academy and Southwest Theatre Conference.

DRAMA STAFF

Hershel Zohn .... **Producer-Director**
James Gilbert.. **Designer-Technical Director**
Elma Schmidt...................................... **Costumes and Children's Theatre**
Janus Olive .... **Secretary**

* * *

Finally Try-Outs for SUMMERTREE
Tuesday, October 28 at 7 p.m.

TRY-OUTS for ALICE IN WONDERLAND
Wednesday & Thursday, October 29, 30 at 7 p.m.

* * *

The Tempest
by William Shakespeare

Written in 1611, *The Tempest* is one of Shakespeare's last plays. It takes place on an uninhabited island. Prospero, Duke of Milan, who is more interested in books and magic than in his dukedom, is expelled by his brother, Antonio, and put to sea in a damaged ship with his daughter, Miranda. They reach an island inhabited by Caliban, a savage creature, and Ariel, an imprisoned spirit. These two become Prospero's servants. There are plots and sub-plots, but these are the principal characters in the play.

Beginning with *Twelfth Night* in 1955 and ending with *The Tempest* in 1970, The Playmakers produced a total of nine Shakespearean plays.

* * *

Fiddler on the Roof
based on Sholom Aleichem stories
Book by Joseph Stein

Solomon Rabinowitz, who adopted Sholom Aleichem as his pen name, was born near Kiev, capital of the Ukraine, in 1859 and died in the Bronx in 1916. Sholom is a common daily greeting and means "Peace Be Unto You."

His short stories and plays were written in Yiddish almost a century ago. Even in translation, they are still popular today. Many of his sayings and anecdotes are "folksy" and have become a part of the Yiddish language. A story is told that when Sholom Aleichem arrived in the United States, he was introduced to Mark Twain. Twain said, "I am called 'the American Sholom Aleichem,'" and Sholom Aleichem replied, "I am called the 'Jewish Mark Twain.'" Through the years many of his stories have been adapted into plays in both Yiddish and English.

In the 1920s, a dramatization of one of his stories, *Tevye der Milchiger* (*Tevye the Dairyman*) was produced in New York by Maurice Schwartz at his Yiddish Art Theater. Later, a dramatization of another story, *Tevye and His Daughters*, appeared in English.

In September 1964, *Fiddler on the Roof* opened on Broadway as a musical. It is a dramatization of three short stories by Sholom Aleichem. Scholars and the "intelligentsia" are not satisfied with the dramatization of *Fiddler*—they are not true to the author's stories, they lament. Whatever, *Fiddler on the Roof* has been very popular since it first opened in New York in 1964. There are at least thirty countries where the play has been shown. A movie made several years ago of the musical can still be seen on late evening television. We were the first university to present *Fiddler* in our theatre, and it was extremely popular here. People came from El Paso and other places to see it. The Las Cruces Community Theatre also had a successful production many years later.

An elderly Las Crucen saw every performance at the university. He even came the first dark night asking for a ticket, unaware that *Fiddler* had closed.

Fiddler on the Roof is appealing to people regardless of nationality or religion. Stein wrote this about *Fiddler*.

> *Just as Marc Chagall expressed the lives, the dreams, the aspirations of his people in his art, Sholom Aleichem put them into his stories. [Incidentally, the figure of a fiddler standing on a roof which is on posters advertising the play is taken from a painting by Marc Chagall.*

Ironically, Chagall never saw the play.] Sholom Aleichem was the folk singer of the "shtetel," those small ramshackle poverty-stricken Jewish villages in Tsarist Russia.

A story is related that when the play opened in Tokyo, Japan, the author, Joseph Stein, went to Tokyo to see it.

At intermission a Japanese approached Stein and asked him, "Are you American?"

"Yes," said he.

"True, this play also big success in your country?"

"Yes, why not," replied Joseph Stein.

"Because it's so typical Japanese," replied the fellow.

During my travels, I was in different countries when they were presenting *Fiddler*. First Tel Aviv, but I didn't particularly care for that production; it was not much of a musical there. Then on to Paris with an opera singer as Tevye; I didn't find him convincing. The London production was much better; I saw it there twice. The New York production seemed to have lost all its enthusiasm. Perhaps that was to be expected after several years of daily performances. Then to El Paso with a road company version (where one didn't anticipate much); yet it was OK.

In New York, Zero Mostel was the first Tevye in the musical. As a person, Mostel was huge. Tevye, according to Sholom Aleichem's description, was not the Zero Mostel type. But Mostel was a very talented actor, and he became believable as Tevye. Of all the Tevyes I saw in this country, I preferred Hershel Bernardi.

At New Mexico State I cast myself as Tevye. As for the singing, I am not a trained singer, nor was Tevye. Actually it had been my ambition to do *Fiddler* here for some time. Cornelia Easterling was Golde, the three older daughters were Corry Valdez, Dianne Smith, and Kay Brilliant. Other cast members were Yente, Frances Williams; Motel, Charles Lewis; Perchik, Tom Odom; Lazar Wolfe, Monte Wright; and Herbert Seamans, Bruce Allen, Barthy Byrd, Juan Molinari, Mercedes Gilbert, Gordon Butler, plus many others; a total of forty people. The directors were Arlene Belkin and Hershel Zohn. The reason for my being co-director was because I had dreamed of doing that play for some time, and it is not a good idea to act and direct at the same time. Since I had done so much research, I didn't want to let it out of my hands completely. James Gilbert was the set designer and technical director; Oscar Butler, music director; and Juan Molinari choreographed the production.

The play is in two acts with ten scenes in each act. We scheduled it for eight performances and later added four additional performances; a total of twelve. Our production of *Fiddler* was also popular with the people in El Paso and other nearby towns.

> The Place: Anatevka, a small village in Russia.
> The Time: 1905, on the eve of the revolutionary period.

Critic Joan Quarm wrote in the Saturday, March 6, 1971 *El Paso Herald Post*:

> Fiddler on the Roof *must have been written with Hershel Zohn in mind, for Tevye is the part of a lifetime which every actor dreams of, and Hershel is Tevye as the Sholom Aleichem stories presented him. A brilliant and dedicated director, he transformed the New Mexico State University drama department into one of the best in the southwest. Professor Zohn is also a lifelong professional actor, who can teach both by precept and example.*

* * *

The Night Thoreau Spent in Jail
by Jerome Lawrence and Robert Lee

The authors of the play are both professional playwrights and professors—Lee at UCLA and Lawrence at NYU. Lawrence and Lee also wrote *Inherit the Wind*, which was immensely popular on this campus when we produced it in 1959.

> *According to the authors, Lawrence and Lee, the man imprisoned in this play belongs more in the 1970s than in the age in which he lived.*
>
> *For more than a century, Henry David Thoreau was dismissed as a gifted weirdo. Only a rebel like Emerson's handyman would dare to question the benefits of technology! Why, it is obvious to any educated mind that technological advancement and progress are synonymous. To create a better world, all we have to do is make things bigger, faster, stronger, or cheaper.*
>
> *But materialism is not the way. Thoreau knew that. He smelled the smog before we saw it. It smarted his soul before it smarted our eyes.*

Thoreau is a fascinating paradox:

> *A man who was and is. A self effacing giant. A wit who rarely laughed. A man who loved so deeply and completely that he seemed, sometimes, not to have loved at all.*
>
> - Program notes

On the recommendation of the authors we featured a guest actor by the name of Clinton Kimbrough for the leading role of Henry. The production had a very large cast of characters and production staff.

* * *

The Lower Depths
by Maxim Gorki

According to his biographies, Gorki the Bitter (Alexei Maximovich Peshkov, 1868-1936), lived from hand to mouth as a child. Even as a very young boy he supported himself by any labor he could find. Wandering over Russia, he learned the psychology of the lowest classes, and gradually cultivated the ability to tell what he knew. His stories depicted the bitter misery of the Russian working man and tramp. His stories drew the attention of Tolstoy and Chekhov. And it was Anton Chekhov who persuaded Gorki to experiment with plays and introduced him to Stanislavski of the Moscow Art Theatre. His first play, *Na Dnye* (*At the Bottom*), is also known as *A Night's Lodging*, but the most popular English title is *The Lower Depths*.

The play was a challenge for the Moscow Art Theatre actors, as well as for any group who undertakes to do it. The characters are "creatures who were once men." The actors from the Moscow Art Theatre went into areas where the real people of the lower depths could be studied.

The characters Gorki introduced in *The Lower Depths* are: The Baron (he was once a Baron), Kvashnya who peddles dumplings; Bubnov, a cap maker; Klesch, a locksmith; Nastya, a prostitute; Satin, a so-called philosopher; The Actor who lost his voice; Vaska, a young thief; Luka, an old man and a pilgrim; and Medvedev, a policeman. There are twenty characters in the play. The play takes place in Russia at the turn of the century in a place called "The Waste." This is where people who have absolutely nothing to look forward to gather. The Bowery in New York City in the twenties may be a good comparison, to a certain extent. A group of people, some of them "has beens," are now in that basement setting. It is hot in the summer and cold in the winter. When they can get the few *kopecks* to buy the cheap alcohol, they drink. The actor who lost his voice can only act in his mind; Nastya, can only offer her body for a slice of bread; they are all lost souls. *The Lower Depths* is a highly naturalistic drama and had a strong impact wherever it was performed. Gorki's compassion for mankind, his ultimate freedom, and his faith have been expressed in an essay where he wrote that the "true *Shekinah*"—the holy of holies—"is Man."

An example of the dialogue provides a feel for the play. Vaska the Thief says: *"Listen, old man, does God exist? Well does he? Answer me."*

Luka, a pilgrim (in a low voice), says, *"If you believe in him, he exists. If you don't, he doesn't. Whatever you believe in exists."*

When *The Lower Depths* was presented on the New Mexico State campus, after the end of the first performance, the student actors refused to leave the stage. They wanted to stay in their characters throughout the run of the play. I only wished the audience had felt that strongly about Gorki's *The Lower Depths*.

Gorki was also a short story writer and novelist. His novel, *Mother* is a very moving piece of literature. The book was turned into a movie of the same name, which had quite an impact on the public. Two of his plays, *Yegor Bulitchev* and *Dostigayev* were performed in Yiddish by the Artef Theatre in New York during the thirties.

* * *

The Crucible

Plays, like human beings, are fortunate—some are presented again and again. One such is Arthur Miller's *The Crucible*.

It was not long after it was first presented in New York, that we did it on the campus at New Mexico A&M, October 1955. In the summer of 1957 I directed it in Mexico City at Players, Inc., an English-speaking theatre. Plays usually run there for four weeks. Members of the organization do intensive work for each production. Many of the actors are experienced and have performed in Great Britain and the United States. In the case of *The Crucible*, it was also done at the same time in Spanish at the Belles Artes by a professional company under the direction of Seki Sano.

Our third Playmaker production of *The Crucible*, in October 1972, featured Clinton Kimbrough as John Proctor. Kimbrough was the professional actor who had also acted in *The Night Thoreau Spent in Jail*.

* * *

Antigone
by Sophocles
English version by Dudley Fitts & Robert Fitzgerald

This is a more traditional version of *Antigone* than Jean Anouilh's, which was the first play I directed after arriving at New Mexico A&M.

Our program notes provided these excerpts from his biography:

Sophocles was born in a small town near Athens in 495 B.C. He received his training in music and philosophy and was active in military and civil affairs. Sophocles was born into wealth and was known for his wit. He lived to be ninety. Of his more than one hundred plays, eighteen won first prize. Only seven are still in existence. These seven extant plays show a master of dramatic skill. "Though man is limited, he is still the noblest work of creation and only in the time of severe trial does he rise to the full height of his power."

It was actually the first play written in the cycle that Sophocles composed to dramatize the Theban story, but, logically, one begins with Oedipus, *followed by* Oedipus at Colonus, *and* Antigone *concludes the trilogy. The date is considered 445 B.C. Antigone was the daughter of the ill-fated Oedipus.*

Both of Antigone's brothers have died in battle–one as a patriot, the other a rebel. Although Creon has ordered the burial of only one brother, Antigone cannot accept his decree. Her moral imperative, as Antigone sees it, requires her to bury her brother Polyneices. She knows doing that will be at the cost of her life. It is the same problem which confronts man whenever he is faced with a choice between personal integrity and the duty he owes to the community.

Sophocles' four other plays are: *Ajax, The Women of Trachis, Electra,* and *Philoctetes.*

Set design and technical direction were by James Gilbert; costumes by Elizabeth Gaidry, with the electronic music provided by Warner Hutchison. The play has six primary characters: Antigone, Ismene, Creon, Haimon, Tiresia, and Euridice, with a chorus of nine men. Some of the actors were Marcia Riegel, Paula Gilbert, Dale Beatty, Larry Fiedler, Robie Haines, and Jim Carpenter.

* * *

Blood Wedding
by Garcia Lorca

It was in a Granada newspaper that Lorca first read of a double murder which had taken place in a village in the Almeria province. The murders were committed because a beautiful girl, on the eve of her wedding, eloped with her former lover. With the wedding veil still upon her head, she fled the marriage ceremony riding "on the back of his horse," to quote the newspaper report. Her bridegroom, provoked beyond reason, set out in pursuit of the couple, and in the ensuing fight, the lover and the bridegroom met their death. This story fired Lorca's imagination. He brooded on it. Some time later it inspired him to write one of the most poignant tragedies of our time, *Blood Wedding*.

Ray Veitch, Gordon Butler, and Larry Fiedler provided music for the production and Juan Molinari choreographed the dance. Monte Wright was stage manager. More than fifty people worked on properties, the scene construction and painting crew, lighting design and lighting control board and crew, costumes, make-up, program cover, house managers and ushers. The cast of twenty-six included: Jackie Clark, Mark Mandel, Cassandra Foley, Mercedes Gilbert, Richard Roman, Royalene Maynez, David Long, Lynn Butler, and many others.

Lament on the Death of a Bullfighter

At five in the afternoon
It was on the stroke of five in the afternoon
A boy brought the white sheet
At five in the afternoon.
A pail of quicklime already prepared
   at five in the afternoon
Nothing else was there but death and death alone
   at five in the afternoon.

— Garcia Lorca

* * *

The Sea Gull
by Anton Chekhov

Chekhov and his plays were frequent guests at the Playmakers. The October 1973 production was my fourth for *The Sea Gull*. This latter performance was in preparation for an American College Theatre Festival, presented by the John F. Kennedy Center for the Performing Arts and the Smithsonian Institution in association with The American National Theatre and Academy. It was produced by The American Theatre Association and sponsored by American Air Lines and The American Oil Company, and presented at the Scott Theatre, Forth Worth, Texas, January 16-19, 1974 as part of the Southwest Regional Festival. The following were members of that cast: Larry Fiedler, Star Hayner, Phillip Palmer, Mark Mandel, Larry Todd, Kathy Brown, David Long, Glorietta Thompson, John Hardman, Elizabeth Gaidry, James Post, John Gossett, Eileen Bennett, and Cassandra Carpenter.

* * *

The Prisoner of Second Avenue
by Neil Simon

Neil Simon has been the most record-breaking playwright ever to contribute to the American stage. The 1972 opening of *The Sunshine Boys* in New York marked an even dozen Simon plays that had been presented within a twelve-year span. At first we were reluctant to produce Simon's plays. Gradually, however, we realized he was an important American dramatist.

The first Simon play we undertook was *Come Blow Your Horn* in the summer of 1964. This was followed by *Barefoot in the Park*, *The Odd Couple*, and then, *The Prisoner of Second Avenue*. Like many of his plays, this work also takes place in

New York. It shows how difficult it may be to reside in New York. Although a comedy, the protagonist loses his job, has a nervous breakdown and encounters numerous other problems which may befall a New Yorker. The play ran in New York for seven hundrerd eighty performances.

With his *Brighton Beach* trilogy, Neil Simon's laughter became subdued—no more than two laughs per minute, and his plots and characters more believable. His latest play, *Lost in Yonkers*, now running in New York, won the 1991 Pulitzer Prize. Considering the present state of the Broadway theatre, that may not be saying much. Yet his characters have more depth and are more solid than they were in the past.

* * *

A Doll's House
by Henrik Ibsen

The play's first presentation was in Copenhagen in 1879 and within a year it was performed all over Europe. It was the most striking and influential call heard up to that time for the emancipation of women. It has changed our society. The closing of the door as Nora left her husband and children at the end of the play was a slamming sound heard around the world in the battle for women's rights that was just getting under way.

The play was first done in America in 1883, under the title of *The Child Wife*. This was in Louisville, Kentucky. It was not until six years later that the play stirred New York under the title of *A Doll's Home*, when its performance threw a number of people "into fits." One critic said, "The Ibsen cult is not likely to achieve popularity in this metropolis, if we may judge by the impression of *A Doll's Home*. It is a dose that will make even the Ibsen cranks quail." However, the play's message, that a woman must be regarded as a person instead of a plaything for her husband, aroused audience interest all over the country.

Even at our theatre classes, whenever *A Doll's House* came up for consideration, the discussions were extremely lively and heated, and we couldn't talk about any other subject during that period except *A Doll's House*. Sympathy was always more on Nora's side. Our program notes quoted Henrik Ibsen's "Notes From A Modern Tragedy," dated 19 October 1878.

> *THERE ARE TWO KINDS OF SPIRITUAL LAWS, TWO KINDS OF CONSCIENCE, ONE FOR MEN AND ONE QUITE DIFFERENT FOR WOMEN. THEY DON'T UNDERSTAND EACH OTHER. BUT IN PRACTICAL LIFE, WOMAN IS JUDGED BY MASCULINE LAW, AS THOUGH SHE WEREN'T A WOMAN BUT A MAN.*
>
> *A WOMAN CANNOT BE HERSELF IN MODERN SOCIETY. IT IS AN EXCLUSIVELY MALE SOCIETY, WITH LAWS MADE BY MEN AND WITH PROSECUTORS AND JUDGES WHO ASSESS FEMALE CONDUCT FROM A MALE STANDPOINT.*
>
> *A MOTHER IN MODERN SOCIETY, LIKE CERTAIN INSECTS, GOES AWAY AND DIES ONCE SHE HAS DONE HER DUTY BY PROPAGATING THE RACE.*[8]

* * *

This concludes a brief analysis of most of the plays I have directed during my years at New Mexico State University-beginning with Jean Anouilh's *Antigone* and concluding with Ibsen's *A Doll's House*. Ironically, both of these plays feature a woman, fighting for a cause, as the protagonist. These hundred plays we produced on the New Mexico State campus from

---

[8] The original English script had these notes from Ibsen in capital letters. The purpose being to stress women's rights, as Ibsen was one of the earliest to advocate a woman's right to be an individual in her own right, rather than an appendage of her husband or father.

October 1950 to March 1975—a quarter of a century. Of course, during this time, others also produced and directed plays here, such as children's plays, etc. In reviewing these plays, I have devoted the most space to Chekhov, Miller, Ibsen, and Shaw. Four different plays by each of these dramatists were performed here. Although we produced nine plays by Shakespeare, I made few comments on them, since it is assumed the public is well acquainted with them.

* * *

The university now has an enrollment of about fifteen thousand students and an abundance of distinguished professors in all areas of learning. It also has a significant Fine Arts Program which features noted painters, composers, authors, and playwrights.

One well-known playwright is Mark Medoff. His plays, with their unusual plots and racy dialogue, reach audiences all over the world. Medoff has his own method of developing a script. First, would be a try-out at his university, and then on to the Mark Taper Forum at Los Angeles—one of the finest theatres in the country. After that it may reach Broadway, as was the case with *Children of a Lesser God*, for which he received his Tony Award, and from there, to different cities in the country or to other parts of the world.

I recall in one of his earliest plays, *Miles Fife*, a character enters with a sack which he then puts down on the floor saying, "Those are the bones from the boys killed in Vietnam." That short line had a terrific impact upon the audience.

Medoff is the author of many plays. *The Red Ryder Trilogy*, *Children of a Lesser God, The Hands of Its Enemy*, and *The Homage That Follows* are a few of the more well-known.

One day while I was strolling on a London avenue, a theatre with bright lights attracted my attention. As I came closer, I saw the sign—*Children of a Lesser God*. No doubt such signs can be seen shining in other cities.

Medoff is now in the prime of his life and we may still expect from him worthy contributions to the stage and screen.

Since I left the department many changes have taken place. The current department head, Frank Pickard, was a student in our program here in the early seventies. A young man with many ideas, and enthusiasm towards his position.

Janeice Scarbrough majored in drama during the 1970s and is now teaching theatre courses and directing plays here. She is also a promising playwright.

In addition, other former university students are now involved in acting, directing, and teaching drama in colleges, high schools, or community theatres.

ACT V

WHAT'S IN A NAME?

This is a series of recollections. Beginning with the summer of 1961 until the summer of 1992, I made a number of journeys throughout Europe, the Middle East, and the Far East. There is no better way, I believe, to obtain knowledge of a people, country or special event than to visit those particular places in person. The experiences of travel are rich and most exciting when visiting a particular place or talking to a certain person.

The following material, excerpts from several articles I wrote for area newspapers and theatre publications, chronicles my travels and experiences.

In Search of Theatre: From Moscow to Prague

Traveling, whether it is in an organized tour or as an individual, is hectic most of the time, with every day and every city presenting different problems. This is contrary to the belief that traveling is a vacation. One thing, however, is sure: traveling can be exciting. It is also very interesting to look back upon the experience.

In my case, talking with people of the theatre profession and attending performances was the main purpose for the trip. When visiting the various capitals, one must also be aware of the political, social, and cultural aspects of the countries.

I counted about twenty-five theatres in Moscow during the month of October 1970. This included the Bolshoi, the Circus, a concert hall, and puppet and children's theatres. The Moscow Art Theatre and Malyi actually have two theatres each. All theatres give eight performances a week (two on Sunday). Most of the theatres present a different play each night—eight productions weekly. This requires a repertoire of about two-hundred different plays a week, which is very good as far as quantity for a city of seven and a half million people.

But when one begins to consider the quality, it is a different story. Let us take the Moscow Art Theatre (MXAT) and Vakhtangov Theatre as examples. MXAT has problems. The intelligentsia and students are full of criticism about the theatre; MXAT is too old and unexciting and has nothing new as far as their method of productions, they argue. Working class people say the theatre is too serious.

Therefore, the Moscow Art Theatre is going all out to present some of their plays in a new way. Chekhov's **The**

Sea Gull *is done almost like a movie. Each of the four acts is divided into several scenes, each with different scenery for each scene. This ruins the mood for which Chekhov's plays are so famous.*

The acting is probably the worst part of the Moscow Art Theatre productions. Perhaps one actor in a cast of twelve, O. A. Striezhnov—who portrayed the young poet Treplev—was satisfactory. Most of the time, they just rattled off their lines.

Chekhov was such a master of internal feeling. His unfinished phrases, his between the lines emotion that the actor is required to fill in, these Chekhov characteristics are certainly missing in these productions. After seeing such a production, one begins to muse that perhaps Chekhov should be done in English, where he is bound to fare much better.

In the case of Gorki's The Lower Depths *there was no improvement. For instance, the actor who was so unconvincing as Trigorin in* The Sea Gull, *was equally bad as Satan in* The Lower Depths. *The only difference in the portrayal of these two characters was the costumes.*

Admirers of Stanislavski, Chekhov, and Gorki must become greatly disillusioned when seeing how these plays are presented. The only consolation is to go to the little museums of these three great men and see how they worked and lived. It is still very thrilling to go through Stanislavski's home.

The Vakhtangov Theatre, which had such tradition for interesting theatrical works—such as Princess Turandot—*has now a tearjerker in its repertory called* The Warsaw Melody *by L. Zorin. It is a two-character play. A young lady in a concert hall listening to Chopin is seated next to a young man. At intermission they become acquainted and one can easily guess what happens—they fall in love, except that he is married and has a family. For ten years they pine for each other to no end. But since he also feels responsible for his children, they decide to go their own ways. Ten years later they meet again—by now she is a successful concert artist and he has gained his freedom. Alas, it is too late now to begin all over again. How sad! It is also sad that this play is very popular all over Russia.*

One night, the Bolshoi, which specializes in fine ballet and opera, presented Prokofiev's War and Peace. *(It was first presented there in 1959.) It was a very lavish production even for the Bolshoi, and good, too. The spectator often had the feeling that the real Moscow, from the walls outside of the Bolshoi to the Moscow scenes enacted on stage, had melted into one.*

Edward Albee and Neil Simon are the most popular American playwrights in the European countries, except for Russia. In Russia, the Mossoviet Theatre chose, of all American plays, John Patrick's The Curious Savage, *as an example of American drama. Was it because they do not know any better or because they wanted to prove how poor American drama can be?*

The playhouses in Budapest present Shakespeare and Pirandello, Albee and Simon, Chekhov and Gogol, and many others. Some of the finest actors in Europe are to be found in Budapest, with the result that the acting is far better than all other phases of production there.

One actor, especially, will remain in my memory for some time to come. Ivan Darvas was in a performance of The Diary of a Mad Man *by Gogol. It is a one-character play which is very seldom done. The actor is on stage, by himself, for two and a half hours. The nature of the play is such that he could easily become bombastic and melodramatic but here it was to the contrary—he kept a large audience spellbound throughout. He showed great depth and feeling for the character. It takes terrific emotional capacity to portray this character and at no time did the audience lose interest in him.*

A word should also be said about the attitude of the audience in Budapest. The people do not look wealthy but they come dressed in their best and seem to consider going to the theatre a great festive occasion.

The old city of Prague, with about a million population, has twenty-two theatres. Plays from different countries and periods are presented in different styles and forms. The theatre is bristling with experiments. In general, the theatre there seems to me to be of a higher intellectual level than in other places. Brecht, O'Casey, Schnitzler, Miller, Williams, Wilde, Capek, Chekhov, Gorki, Camus, Shakespeare, Goethe, Tolstoy, Arrabal and many other significant dramatists of all ages can be enjoyed in the theatres of Prague at any one time.

* * *

Back to New Mexico. After my retirement, it didn't take long before I was invited to direct *The Crucible* for the Classics Theatre in Albuquerque.

The Crucible - April 1976
Classics Theatre Company
Popejoy Hall, Albuquerque, NM

Since Albuquerque is much larger than Las Cruces, we had no problem in getting people, but the caliber of the talent was not as good as the students at New Mexico State. Another problem: The Classics Theatre Company obtained Popejoy

Hall for the performances. It's quite a large auditorium, with a mezzanine and a balcony; a total of more than two thousand seats. Large seating at a theatre always turns me away, especially when doing a straight play with non-professionals.

Ken Guthrie designed the set and was also technical director. Guthrie is quite an imaginative designer and a methodical technical director. Yet I was not really satisfied with the production. I felt the play and its important message was lost in such a big auditorium. Perhaps it was only my idea. It so happens *The Crucible* is one of my favorite plays.

As far as the reviews were concerned, they were not bad. One said, "*The Crucible*: Severe tests stunningly met." Another had this headline, "Presentation of *Crucible* is a delight in nearly all ways."

* * *

Death of a Salesman - March 1977
The Laguna Maulton Playhouse
Laguna Beach, California

It was a brand new, highly attractive theatre. Obviously the theatre had enough funds to undertake any kind of a production. Quite a few actors came all the way from Hollywood for the readings. Most actors will make every attempt to land a role in a Miller play. The actor chosen to do Willy bore a strong resemblance to Lee Cobb. That's all! The actor doing Willy had problems learning his lines. However, in the end, the production turned out to be OK. Of course, the local reviewers' notices were so full of praise that I am embarrassed to quote them here. That is, except for one headline, "From Russia with love." Why?

* * *

What's In A Name?

Twelfth Night - Summer 1977
The New Kaleidoscope Players
Armory for the Arts in Santa Fe

Whether it is New York, or New Hampshire, or this time, New Mexico, not a year goes by that a new theatre group emerges with the express purpose of producing plays of a more artistic quality. The New Kaleidoscope Players, with many new ideas and as many dreams, refurbished a building constructed by WPA in 1940 and turned it into a theatre. The group planned to do a half a dozen plays in the first year. Unfortunately, they did not succeed in meeting their goal.

Its first production was *Twelfth Night*. I was invited to be its director. Much planning went into it. What with complicated sets and lighting, costumes—some rented and others made—locally performed music and choreography, many new people, and two dozen actors—most of them experienced Shakespearian players—*Twelfth Night*, or *What You Will*, was ready. Although, in theatre, you are never ready until after the first night, and even after the first night the director may change scenes, cut scenes, etc., etc.

A reviewer for the *Santa Fe New Mexican* wrote: "The overall quality of the play is very high, and this includes the major actors, a terrific set, and technical backup, and original live music which effectively creates appropriate moods for each scene."

I would like to add a few words about its title: *Twelfth Night* seems to have been so named for no better reason that it was first performed before Queen Elizabeth I's court on the twelfth night after Christmas in 1601. The play's subtitle, *What You Will*, calls attention to the fact that there is something for everyone to enjoy.

* * *

An Evening with Hershel Zohn - November 1979
Las Cruces Community Theatre, Las Cruces, NM

The Las Cruces Community Theatre is always in need of one thing or another for their theatre—whether it is a curtain or enlarging a dressing room, installing a washroom, or what have you. This time they asked me to present "A One Man Show" or "An Evening in the Theatre with Hershel Zohn" as a fund raiser.

The program was varied and included:

    All the World—*As You Like It*, Shakespeare
    Shakespeare and Chekhov
    Sorin—Anton Chekhov—*The Sea Gull*
    The Magic of Theatre
    Vandergelder—*The Matchmaker*, Thornton Wilder
    The Dybbuk, S. Ansky
    "Tomorrow"—*Macbeth*, Shakespeare
    Life Is Like a River
    Storyteller, *The Caucasian Chalk Circle*,
        Bertolt Brecht
    The Chairs, Eugene Ionesco
    Tevye—*Fiddler on the Roof*, Sholom Aleichem

This was the beginning of many one-man shows I presented in Santa Fe, El Paso, Las Cruces, Los Alamos, and other communities. The programs were mostly for benefits.

* * *

A Telephone Call

It was Sunday morning, December 4, 1977. Ann was not well and in the hospital. Usually when the telephone rings on such occasions, there is a trembling in your heart. Is the hospital calling, or is it Ann herself calling? It was neither. Instead it was New Mexico State University President Gerald W. Thomas, informing me that "the Board of Regents decided yesterday [Saturday] to name the theatre for you—calling it 'The Hershel Zohn Theatre.' Congratulations. I'll be in touch with you about the official ceremony."

Later that morning I read in the local newspaper about the naming of the theatre. I went to the hospital to see Ann and informed her about the theatre. Naturally, she was elated, and the news made her feel so much better that she was discharged from the hospital before long.

Soon after New Year's we began to make plans for the naming of the theatre ceremony. It was finally scheduled for the University Theatre on Sunday, 3:00 p.m., April 16, 1978.

Before long, invitations were mailed to people from lists that I provided and I assume also that the university saw fit to invite. Barbara Glowacki, wife of the Chairman of the Music Department John Glowacki, was in charge of the entire program. From the design on the front cover, the photographs of the theatre on the back, the feature story, to the listing of the four participants in the program, it was a complete and attractive program. For my part, I volunteered to present scenes from three plays: Sorin, in Chekhov's *The Sea Gull*, Brecht's, *The Story Teller*, and Tevye from *Fiddler on the Roof* by Sholom Aleichem. Gayle Marie Treakle accompanied me on the piano for my *Fiddler* song. The four special guests on the program were the University President, Gerald W. Thomas; Joan Quarm, Associate Professor of English at University of Texas at El Paso and *El Paso Herald Post* Drama Critic; Dr. Thomas Gale, Dean of Arts & Sciences; and Rudy Apodaca, President of the Board of Regents.

Naturally, there were many students from the drama classes and also from other departments, and, of course, invited guests who greeted me in the theatre lobby during the refreshments. Again I should mention that this entire program was thoughtfully arranged and planned by Barbara Glowacki.

But this was not all; telegrams and letters came in from various parts of the country. I'll choose them at random:

Congratulations. Now you are immortalized in brick and stone and steel and glass. The brass you can supply yourself. Sorry we can't attend the ceremonies and especially your performance.
   Love, Shirley and Jack Soules — Cleveland, Ohio.

You two have enriched my life. It was a pleasure to read of the extraordinary honor that will be paid you on April 16. For New Mexico State University to name its theatre for you is indeed a kind of tribute and recognition seldom achieved, but indicative of the high regard in which you are held.
   Rabbi Joseph Klein.

What else should a theatre be named? We are thrilled and wish we could be there with you. Love. Congratulations.
Joyce & Norman Keifetz — New York, NY.

* * *

Filumena - October 1980
by Eduardo de Filippo
Albuquerque Little Theatre

One summer morning I received a telephone call from Mike Myers. Mike told me he had become the Producing Director of the Albuquerque Little Theatre. Would I like to direct plays at that theatre? Without any hesitation I replied, "Yes, I would." The Albuquerque Little Theatre had been in existence for many years. Under Mike's leadership, the old theatre took a new direction. I have known Mike for about twenty years, primarily as an actor. During that time he has done some good work, from *Oedipus* in the Greek tragedy, to the other extreme as Barnaby in *The Matchmaker*, where he was outstanding.

After considering a dozen or so plays and trying to avoid Neil Simon, at least for the first year, we picked *Filumena*. Scarcely known in this country, but popular in London, it was directed by Franco Zefferelli with Joan Plowright in the leading role. Joan Plowright also did the play briefly in New York under Lawrence Olivier's direction. It so happens Mike and I had seen the play in London, although at different times. The piece is written by the Italian dramatist Eduardo de Filippo. It's listed as a comedy.

Filumena had lived with Domenico for twenty-five years when he suddenly decides to leave her for a younger woman. Filumena doesn't give up so easily and confesses to a secret that she has kept from him for a long time: she has three sons, however, only one of them is his. She is not about to tell him which one is his, and Domenico consents to stay with her and the play ends happily for all concerned.

I recall we had problems in casting the two principle characters. However, after we gave the leading parts to Susan

Hafenfeld and Bill Hicks, rehearsals continued pretty smoothly till opening. Susan was quite convincing in her character and in general had some moving scenes. I believe we gave the production everything it needed—plus. Yet, looking back it was just an ordinary melodrama with laughs in between. Shall we blame the playwright? Yes! He may be popular in Italy, even in London, but not in the United States, and especially not in New Mexico.

* * *

One of the 'one-man' benefit programs took place at the Branigan Cultural Center. The program was called "Hershel Zohn in an Evening in the Theatre," with Cornelia Valach and Gayle Treakle. Setting and lighting, Ray Veitch, Al Eylar, Ann Zohn, and Stage Manager was David Weiselman. We'll let Mike Genovese, Entertainment Editor of the *Round Up*, do the talking:

"HERSHEL ZOHN: Alive and well. Hershel Zohn can be called the father of theatre in Las Cruces. Like old father time, he can recollect the unpleasant memories, along with the more frequent, pleasant times in his life involved around the theatre.

However last April 12, he made the evening pleasant for all that attended his performance in 'An Evening in the Theater' at the Branigan Cultural Center, Cornelia Valach and Gayle Treakle accompanied Mr. Zohn.

Mr. Zohn recited a gamut of theatrical pieces, ranging from William Shakespeare to scenes from Fiddler on the Roof. *The audience warmly applauded at the end of the show.*

* * *

A View From the Bridge - April 1981
by Arthur Miller
The Albuquerque Little Theatre

I always feel at home when I direct a Miller play. *A View From the Bridge* is powerful, dramatic, poetic drama, and yet so different from his previous two plays—*Death of a Salesman* and *The Crucible*. Critics point out that Miller comes closer here to the Greek tragedies of Aeschylus, Sophocles, and Euripides than ever before. Miller first wrote the *Bridge* as a one-acter and later turned the play into two acts. The character Alfieri, who is a lawyer, is reminiscent of the Chorus in Greek drama, summing up the play.

> ALFIERI: *Most of the time now we settle for half and I like it better. But the Truth is holy, and even as I know how wrong he was, and his death useless, I tremble—for I confess that something perversely pure calls to me from his memory—not purely good, but himself purely, for he allowed himself to be wholly known and for that I think I love him more than all my sensible clients. And yet, it is better to settle for half, it must be! And I mourn him—I admit it—with a certain ... —alarm.*

* * *

A Doll's House - February 1983
The Albuquerque Little Theatre

When the Little Theatre decided to produce *A Doll's House*, the role of Nora was especially difficult to cast. Gradually, all the characters were cast except for Nora. At last an actress came along for Nora. A director usually has his own conception of the characters he is casting. Sometimes, however, he must make allowances. This was the case with Nora. After a series of rehearsals it became evident that she was not my concept of Nora, but "the show must go on." As the director of the play I was not happy with it. This is not new; it often occurs in the theatre.

* * *

Santa Fe Festival Theatre

The Festival Theatre occupied the theatre at the Armory for the Arts for several summers during the eighties. Each summer they had a large company of professional actors, in addition to stars, for each production. During the summer of 1982, the Festival Theatre produced *Wild Oats*, by John O'Keeff, *Wings*, by Arthur Kopit, and *America*, a musical based on a novel by Franz Kafka. I was engaged that summer to do a role in *Wings*. It's a comparatively small cast with the principal character suffering a stroke. A therapist, two doctors, two nurses and three patients complete the cast. I was one of the patients.

The critic from the *Santa Fe New Mexican* said, "*Wings* is a play to be experienced," and praised actress Anne Pitoniak, who played the principle character, and also "John Procaccino and Hershel Zohn were memorable in their small roles."

In addition, Ann and I had a pleasant summer in Santa Fe.

* * *

Fiddler on the Roof - Summer 1984
Las Cruces Community Theatre

It was summer of 1984 that the Las Cruces Community Theatre decided to do *Fiddler on the Roof*, with me as Tevye and Cornelia Valach as Golde. The play was scheduled for twelve performances. It was quite different from the performance we did on the New Mexico State University campus in 1971. The university, of course, has a big stage, could accommodate more people, and had a larger budget. Yet, thirteen years later *Fiddler* was just as popular as it had been earlier. Every performance was sold out. Cornelia, who had also appeared as Golde in the first production, subsequently did many 'one-man' programs with me. As a result, I named her my stage wife. *Fiddler on the Roof* has a magnetism that draws audiences. Before the 1984 Community Theatre opening, the *El Paso Times* published a two page "spread" on *Fiddler*, and the actor doing Tevye.

* * *

Death of a Salesman - Fall 1985
The Las Cruces Community Theatre

In the Fall of 1985 The Las Cruces Community Theatre invited me to direct Arthur Miller's *Death of a Salesman*.

The most difficult part in directing this play is finding an actor who can interpret Willy Loman properly and rightfully. According to the author, Willy "never really knew who he was. He becomes a tragic figure when he finds that all the values he had lived by are false."

Joe Denk, who had appeared in many plays before, agreed to meet with me privately for a number of sessions to discuss, analyze, and read the role of Willy Loman. Yet when it came to the public tryouts, he hesitated to accept the role of Willy. However, once he accepted the part he gave it all he could. The audience was usually moved by his scenes. Willy Loman is the most difficult and yet challenging character in modern drama. The late Lee Cobb was the first actor to introduce Willy Loman to the American stage. Stories are told that during early rehearsals Cobb did not show any promise in developing the character of Willy Loman. Suddenly Cobb erupted like a volcano. The director, Elia Kazan, and Miller, were both stunned at the change in Cobb's acting.

It took much out of the actor, physically and mentally, and he discontinued playing Willy after a year. This is bound to happen in the theatre. A similar story is related about a Russian actor. The character he portrayed was called to go mad. After a series of performances he had to be taken to the hospital and could never appear in the play again. That's what we call "living" the part. However, this should not happen. The actor should always control the character he is portraying. It is not that easy. There is that very thin line between "reality" and "make believe," and the actor must be aware of it at all times.

* * *

One-Man Shows

The programs I presented for different organizations from 1978 to 1986 included a two-day performance at Los Alamos.

On a Friday evening in January 1982, I presented several scenes from a play titled *Zalmen or the Madness of God* by Elie Wiesel. The play was originally written in French and produced on the French radio, and then at the Arena Stage in Washington, DC. Afterwards it came to Broadway. Wiesel is greatly concerned with the victims of the Holocaust. The book, *The Testament*, deals with the twenty-four Yiddish writers executed by Stalin in 1952.

Zalmen or the Madness of God takes place on the eve of Yom Kippur. A group of Western actors visit a small Russian synagogue. The Jews in the community are surviving, but at great cost. They are warned by the authorities and their own leaders to avoid contact with the western actors. The cutting concentrates primarily on the two principal characters: the Old Rabbi and Zalmen the Beadle who had been nicknamed 'The Madman.'

Following the performance Rabbi Joseph Klein wrote me:

> *Your reading of the Wiesel play Friday night was truly masterful. The whole congregation was spellbound by your performance. It was a kind of an experience that we shall all remember for a long time. I can't thank you enough for giving us such a rich and rewarding evening. Listening to you was a Jewish religious experience in the highest degree. Your portrayal of both Zalmen and the Rabbi, with such sparse and limited props, was theatre art at its best.*

* * *

A Program by
HERSHEL ZOHN—DENISE CHAVEZ
in
CHEKHOV AND OTHER THINGS
Hershel Zohn Theatre
N.M.S.U. May 17, 1986

Proceeds of this program went to student scholarships. The program contained two folk songs—"A Robbery" and "A Letter to Mother;" the Vandergelder monologue from *The Matchmaker*, and "Seven Ages" by William Shakespeare. "Glimpses of Chekhov Characters" included Trigorin, Masha, and Dorn from *The Sea Gull*, plus the Sorin monologue and Arkadina— from the Trigorin Scene of Act III from *The Sea Gull*. I concluded the program with a talk on Chekhov's Moscow home, now a museum, that I visited in 1965 and 1970.

We have talked a great deal about Chekhov. We know he is the author of seventeen brilliant plays and many short stories. But Chekhov also had a voluminous correspondence with his immediate family, distant relatives, actors, directors, colleagues, but primarily with Olga, his wife. One of my 'one-man' shows consisted especially of letters from Chekhov to Olga and Olga to Chekhov.

October 27, 1899, Moscow

I ought not to write to you today, dear Anton Pavlovich. There is such gloom, such horror in my soul that I can't describe it. Yesterday we played Uncle Vanya. *The play was such a tremendous success, it captured the whole house, there can be no two opinions about that. I haven't closed my eyes all night and today I keep crying. I acted inconceivably badly—why? A great deal I understand, a great deal I don't. So many thoughts are racing through my head at this minute that I can hardly tell you clearly. They say I acted well at the dress rehearsal—now I don't believe that. My God, how wretched I am! Everything is shattered.*

Olga

November 1, 1899, Yalta

Dear Actress,

I understand your mood, sweet little actress, understand it perfectly well, but still in your place I wouldn't be in such a dither. You've got to cut out your worrying about successes and failures once and for all. They are not your affair. Your job is to jog along, day in, day out, like a quiet little creature, prepared for the mistakes that can't be avoided and for failures, in short, to do a job as an actress and let the others count the curtain calls. It is usual to write, or to act, and know all along that you are not doing the right thing—and for beginners this awareness is so useful.

Keep well. Write that you have already calmed down and that everything is going beautifully. I press your hand.

Your, Antonka

My Love,

I want to be with you. I abuse myself for not giving up the stage. I really don't know what is happening to me and this vexes me. It is unclear to me. It makes me ill to think that you are alone, distressed and lonely, while I'm concerned with some ephemeral business instead of surrendering to the feeling that is me. What prevents me?

You are dispirited, in a foul mood, and hate the theatre because of me. Yet it was the theatre that brought us together. Darling, banish your dejection, it is not worth it.

Love, Olga

Olga,

So you would soon become a famous actress, a Sarah Bernhardt. Would you dismiss me, or take me with you to keep your accounts? My darling, there is nothing better in the world than to sit on a green bank and fish or stroll about the fields.

I have nothing against your becoming famous and earning twenty-five to forty thousand a year.

Anton.

EPILOGUE

FROM KIEV TO SINYAVA

It was in the winter months of 1921 when my parents, sisters and I climbed into a wagon, with the driver and his horses waiting for my father's command to leave. That was the start of the journey from our hometown of Staraya Sinyava to the Polish border—the first part of our trip to America. All of us were so tense, not knowing what may await us, that my father remarked upon the atmosphere of gloom and shouldn't we change the mood with a song. This made one of my sisters begin the popular tune "*Prochai, prochai....* (farewell, farewell....)" Now, seven decades later, I am standing on the same soil where we sang that little hymn.

It was in the summer of 1965 when I first went to Moscow to do theatre research, that I expressed an interest in visiting the small town where I was born. But my wish to go visit was immediately thwarted by an official saying, "It's forbidden."

I repeated my request when I was in Kiev in 1970. At first they said, "*Da.*" But when it came to my actually going there, they again changed their minds, to "*Nyet.*"

However, with the drastic political changes recently occurring throughout Russia, one may go anywhere in the country, provided you have a sufficient package of American dollars. Dollars are the preferred means of exchange. One still needs a visa from the Ukrainian embassy, which may take two weeks or longer. In other words, there are still complications to traveling in that part of the world, complications which don't exist when traveling to other foreign countries.

Approaching the end of my book, I was haunted with the idea of completing it in the same setting as it started out—in the town of Sinyava.

I recall talking to a representative of Intourist in New York who said, "It's possible that Sinyava doesn't exist any longer." Yet, I was determined to travel to Kiev in search of it.

The night before we commenced our search for Sinyava was a night of unhappy and horrible illusions. After I retired for the night, I began to visualize one frightful situation after another; things which I feared would happen to me the next day upon arriving in Sinyava. Perhaps a hanging in the square, or that I would be led through town under a barrage of rocks. I finally dozed off about 4:00 a.m., only to be awakened two hours later to get ready to leave.

One cannot locate Staraya Sinyava on recent maps of the area. It doesn't seem to exist. The people in Kiev don't know about it, nor do they care to know. Yet the staff at the Intourist Hotel where we stayed recommended a young engineering student by the name of Slava, who was to go with us to locate the town. The three of us squeezed into the very small French-made automobile that Slava had borrowed from a friend.

Slava didn't know any English, but with my limited Russian, we made conversation. He told us that he was a Ukrainian patriot—this seems to be very popular among today's Ukrainian youth. We talked about Russian literature, the plays of Chekhov and Gorki. He was disgusted with Moscow and Leningrad.

Slava was an excellent driver and we rolled along from one city to another, cities which brought back memories—Zhitomir, Vinnitsa, Berditchev. When we reached Khmelnik, we knew that we must begin the search for Sinyava. Slava stopped every policeman on the road with the question, "Where is Sinyava?" We passed one beautiful field after another where men and women were at work. When asked about Sinyava, the reply was, "Go on, you'll find it."

We finally saw a sign "Stara Sinyava," with an arrow pointing to the left. (The Russian word *"Staraya"* meaning "old" becomes *"Stara"* in Ukrainian.)

Out of nowhere, we found ourselves in the yard of a school in Sinyava. All the children, from six to ten years old, came running out of the building and looked at us like we had come from Mars. A teacher named Maria took charge of us. Maria was a highly interesting and intelligent person.

"Do you remember this building?" she asked.

"No," said I.

"This one?"

"No."

"This one very solidly built?"

"Yes, I think I do."

My father's mill—no more. Four synagogues—no more. The river outside the town—yes, where I remember going swimming in the summer and skating in the winter.

According to records from 1897, Sinyava once had a Jewish population of 2,279.

"How about now?" I ask Maria.

"There is not even one Jewish person now," she says sadly, with her face down. Some of them were killed during the war when they served in the army. Many ran away to Tashkent,

Biro-Bidjan, Israel, or other parts of the world. In 1941, the Nazis gathered 357 people in Sinyava and killed them outright with machine guns. They are buried on a hill, facing the town. There is a monument with letters inscribed in Hebrew and Ukrainian. Some of the people are not too happy with the monument and plan to replace it with a more impressive one. Guests from different parts of the world will be invited to come to this location on the occasion of installing the new monument. Perhaps I, too, will be able to attend.

A children's doctor from the school claimed her father and mine knew each other and were friends.

We were invited to have lunch with them at the school, which we did. Now it was time to return to Kiev. The beautiful children, who continually observed us, waved as we left. Some of them were humming a tune very softly. Who knows? Perhaps it was *"Prochai, prochai."*

After our return to Kiev that night, I felt that a certain heaviness was beginning to leave me—a heaviness that had been with me a long time. I realized this had been one of the most interesting days I had had in recent times.

ADDENDUM

ADDENDUM - A

PLAYMAKERS' PRODUCTIONS
1950-1975

1950-1951
The Importance of Being Earnest - Oscar Wilde
Antigone - Jean Anouilh
The Boor & The Marriage Proposal - Anton Chekhov
Candida - George Bernard Shaw
Jack and the Beanstalk - Beatrice Lee
The Drunkard - William Smith

1951-1952
Master Pierre Patelin - anonymous
The Silver Whistle - Robert E. McEnroe
Pygmalion - George Bernard Shaw
The Boor & The Marriage Proposal - Anton Chekhov
The Girl From Wyoming - John Van Antwerp
Angel Street - Patrick Hamilton

1952-1953
The Madwoman of Chaillot - Jean Giraudoux
The Hasty Heart - John Patrick
Life With Father - Howard Lindsay and Russel Crouse
Death of a Salesman - Arthur Miller

1953-1954
The Male Animal - James Thurber and Elliott Nugent
The Heiress - Ruth and Augustus Goetz
An Enemy of the People - Henrik Ibsen
A Phoenix Too Frequent - Christopher Fry and
    The Wedding - Anton Chekhov

1954-1955
The Country Girl - Clifford Odets
My Three Angels - Sam and Bella Spewack
Down In The Valley - Kurt Weill and
    Brooklyn Baseball Cantata - George Kleinsinger
Twelfth Night - William Shakespeare
The Winslow Boy - Terrence Rattigan

1955-1956
The Crucible - Arthur Miller
Gigi - Colette and Anita Loos
The Imaginary Invalid - Moliere
The Skin of Our Teeth - Thornton Wilder

1956-1957
The Inspector General - Nikolai Gogol
Hedda Gabler - Henrik Ibsen
The Rainmaker - N. Richard Nash
Arms and the Man - George Bernard Shaw

1957-1958
The Lark - Jean Anouilh
The Glass Menagerie - Tennessee Williams
Macbeth - William Shakespeare
The Emperor's New Clothes - Charlotte Chorpenning
The Sea Gull - Anton Chekhov

1958-1959
The Teahouse of the August Moon - John Patrick
The Playboy of the Western World - John Millington Synge
Medea - Robinson Jeffers
Don Juan In Hell - George Bernard Shaw
Tea and Sympathy - Robert Anderson

1959-1960
Inherit the Wind - Jerome Lawrence and Robert E. Lee
The Diary of Anne Frank - Frances Goodrich and Albert Hackett

A Midsummer Night's Dream - William Shakespeare
A Touch of the Poet - Eugene O'Neill

1960-1961
All the King's Men - Robert Penn Warren
The Lady's Not for Burning - Christopher Fry
Julius Caesar - William Shakespeare
The Matchmaker - Thornton Wilder

1961-1962
J. B. - Archibald MacLeish
The Cave Dwellers - William Saroyan
The Bourgeois Gentleman - Moliere
No Exit - Jean-Paul Sarte and *The Chairs* - Eugene Ionesco

1962-1963
Volpone - Ben Johnson
Ghosts - Henrik Ibsen
The Red Shoes - Robin Short
Rhinoceros - Eugene Ionesco
The Matchmaker - Thornton Wilder

1963-1964
The Matchmaker - Thornton Wilder
    (Toured Far East for eight weeks)
As You Like It - William Shakespeare
The Miracle Worker - William Gibson
Hansel and Gretel - Charlotte Chorpenning
The Three Penny Opera - Bertolt Brecht
Romeo and Juliet - William Shakespeare
Drama Workshop
Come Blow Your Horn - Neil Simon
A Far Country - Henry Denker

1964-1965
The Firebugs - Max Frisch
The House of Bernarda Alba - Garcia Lorca
Aladdin and the Wonderful Lamp - Elizabeth Dooley

Oedipus Rex - Sophocles
Kiss Me Kate - Cole Porter
Drama Workshop
Take Her, She's Mine - Phoebe and Henry Ephron
The Waltz of the Toreadors - Jean Anouilh

1965-1966
The Physicists - Friedrich Durrenmatt
A View From the Bridge - Arthur Miller
The Wizard of Oz - Adele Thane
Othello - William Shakespeare
Carousel - Rodgers and Hammerstein
Drama Workshop
Thieves' Carnival - Jean Anouilh
Uncle Vanya - Anton Chekhov

1966-1967
The Queen and the Rebels - Ugo Betti
A School for Scandal - Richard Sheridan
The Clown Who Ran Away - Conrad Seiler
After the Fall - Arthur Miller
The Boyfriend - Sandy Wilson
Drama Workshop
Barefoot in the Park - Neil Simon
Tom Sawyer - Sarah Spenser

1967-1968
The Good Woman of Setzuan - Bertolt Brecht
Poor Bitos - Jean Anouilh
Pinocchio - George T. Latshaw
The Odd Couple - Neil Simon
Stop the World-I Want to Get Off - Leslie Bricusse
    and Anthony Newley
Drama Workshop
Royal Gambit - Herman Gressieker

1968-1969
The Marriage of Mr. Mississippi - Friedrich Durrenmatt

Peter Pan - J. M. Barrie
The Cherry Orchard - Anton Chekhov
Bye Bye Birdie - Michael Stewart and Charles Strouse
Drama Workshop
Arms and the Man - George Bernard Shaw

1969-1970
War and Peace - Leo Tolstoy and Erwin Piscator
Summertree - Ron Cowen
Alice in Wonderland - Lewis Carroll
The Tempest - William Shakespeare

1970-1971
A Funny Thing Happened on the Way to the Forum -
    Shevelove and Gelbart
Miles Fife - Mark Medoff
The Indian Wants the Bronx & It's Called a Sugar Plum -
    Israel Horovitz
Drama Workshop

1971-1972
Fiddler on the Roof - Sholom Aleichem
The Night Thoreau Spent in Jail - Jerome Lawrence & Robert Lee
The Lower Depths - Maxim Gorki

1972-1973
The Crucible - Arthur Miller
Antigone - Sophocles (traditional)
Blood Wedding - Garcia Lorca
The Sea Gull - Anton Chekhov

1973-1974
The Sea Gull - Anton Chekhov
The Prisoner of Second Avenue - Neil Simon

1975
A Doll's House - Henrik Ibsen

ADDENDUM - B

HERSHEL ZOHN'S TEN YEARS WITH PLAYMAKERS THEATRE
By David Rodwell, New Mexico State University

This must come as something of a surprise to Hershel Zohn. Modest as it is by the usual standards applied to commemorations, it is still vastly more ambitious than his proposal to "print up a list of the plays we've done in the past 10 years."

Certainly it is an impressive list—especially when one considers that any previous list of dramatic productions at New Mexico State University would heavily lean toward melodrama, not-quite-good farce, the ladies' aid sort of thing. "Good, clean, wholesome—and empty," muses one faculty member who endured.

Weigh that against the 1950-60 decade. One is impressed with the authors—Chekhov, Shaw, Ibsen, Shakespeare, Moliere, Arthur Miller, Tennessee Williams. There, too, are solid Broadway titles—*Life with Father, The Rainmaker, The Teahouse of the August Moon, The Diary of Anne Frank.*

As significant as any is the final play for 1960. O'Neill's *A Touch of the Poet* is given its first non-professional production by the State University Playmakers under Hershel Zohn's direction. It is O'Neill's last play—lengthy almost inhumanly demanding on actors, four hours of sustained tension. By its excesses it underscores Zohn's idea of what the educational theater must be.

In studying the list one thinks of the actors who have given their varying abilities to become the Playmakers. They have been townspeople, students, faculty, too numerous to list, generally too good to be slighted by an attempt to list the outstanding. Excellent and mediocre, sensitive and plodding, they have in common the experiences of being inspired, infuriated, complimented, berated, stimulated by the single constant factor of the University Playmakers—Hershel Zohn.

This matter of singleness—single-mindedness, single-purposed for instance—is essential to an appreciation of Zohn.

A faculty member who shared directing assignments during Zohn's first year recalls their different attitudes toward educational theater. "I felt that if students had a good time in presenting the plays they were accomplishing our purpose," he says. "Not so with Hershel. He will drive everyone—himself most of all—to seek professional competence in the play. If it is a good play, good theater, well done, he feels that is the ultimate reward and by the depth of the experience the student is that much better."

Another professor likes to muse about Zohn's moods when a play is in rehearsal. "He is always depressed about a production. You can almost anticipate how well a play will go by studying Zohn's moods before the play. If he is merely sad, the play will probably be mediocre. If he is terribly depressed and dreads a stinkeroo (his favorite term of ultimate failure), it will be good. The more depressed he is, the better the play will be. He probably works harder on those plays in which he's most interested. So he seems to fall far shorter of the goals he has set."

Another colleague points out that a merely dour look without restlessness means a rehearsal is going well. If he becomes restless and begins muttering to someone near him, things are going badly. Suddenly he will erupt from his seat and have the actors re-do the scene.

This colleague's favorite recollection of a Zohn eruption stems from rehearsal of a romantic scene from one play several years ago. A youthful male actor assigned a romantic lead would, between turns on the stage, sit in a darkened theater corner more than attentive to his lady-love of the moment. Yet on stage when he was to woo the female lead he would become self-conscious, freezing up. Zohn's roaring eruption down the aisle, demanding the actor at least "kiss the woman, kiss the woman!" is memorable.

Noting Zohn's moodiness in the throes of readying a play, a former English professor used to call the Russian-born director, "the melancholy Muscovite."

Zohn's family emigrated from Russia in the early 1920s when their son was 14. If New York to them epitomized all America promised, the discovery of Manhattan's theater district was for the young Zohn the ultimate in self-realization.

He set about finding work in New York, mixed night school with dogged haunting of theater balconies. As the depression deepened he worked his way into the Federal Theater Project. He recalls with excitement the surge of new talents, new ideas, new audiences, the talk about a "living" theater.

In 1937 he began to get bit parts and now likes to muse about moving down out of the balconies, on to the stage. It was all very promising, until 1941. The arts of the battlefields preempted all others. Zohn found himself transported from the beloved boundaries of New York to the totally strange America lying something west of the Hudson. He was horribly homesick in the early months of his four-year service career.

The GI Bill presented one of those turning-point opportunities. At Denver University he unloosed his zest on the academic world and earned his bachelor's and master's in theater in the time most undergraduates are entering their senior year. He found time to teach, act, direct. And here his education, New York work, federal theater experience melted together into the dedication for educational theatre that marks him today.

This and his work as professional play reader and senior research worker in the New York Library Theater Collection joined to give him an ideal background as top candidate for the teaching-directing opening he accepted at New Mexico State University in 1950.

The New Mexico thing was long on challenge, short on available talent, budget, facilities.

Yet almost immediately Zohn translated his convictions about educational theater into unbelievably good campus productions. His first program had two Chekhov one-acters, *The Boor* and *The Marriage Proposal*. There were *Antigone* and *Candida* that first year, *The Silver Whistle* and Arthur Miller and Shaw the next. The beloved list tells the rest—experimental plays, classical Greek, the best of Broadway, Shakespeare—

To all of it Zohn applies himself as educational theater personified.

"Because people are not paid in the educational theater is no reason to fall short of professional standards," he declares. "We need to do the best plays—not the most popular. We need to do classical theater, from the Greeks on, experimental plays the commercial theater would not touch, to present Ibsen, Chekhov, O'Neill. Time is our only limit, time for coaching and rehearsal and study when our actors must also be students and housewives and professional men."

The success of this approach at New Mexico State University reaffirms faith in the ultimate success of difficult but good things. For Zohn and the Playmakers have found that good theater draws at the campus box office. Most of a season's four or five productions run six evenings. They fill two-thirds of the university temporary theater's 240 seats the first night or two, then sell-out for the rest of the run, whether Shakespeare or *Teahouse* or *Medea*.

Not that there haven't been flops. Zohn recalls with a grimace the 1952 production of *The Girl From Wyoming*. Downtown critics charitably damned it with the faintest of praise, but student newspaper editorials, letters to the editor, and a cutting, quipping verse going the campus rounds still come readily to his mind.

There have been the defeats and reverses one expects in a story of this kind. They add their part to defining theater at State University and its director. Budget-cutting which sheared a technical director from the staff only led Zohn to learn about the field, develop student assistants who could help. He had finally replaced old wood seats in venerable Hadley Hall with modern, cushioned theater-type seats, only to have the whole of Hadley Hall torn down on condemnation. Into a make-do air mechanics building went the Playmakers. With no proscenium, theater-in-the-round became a technical necessity, introducing the trappings of avant-garde professional theater as ideally suited to the make-shift. The seats went, too, and eventually were elevated on risers. Air conditioning cajoled from somewhere has made it almost bearable.

Zohn's work load is crushing—teaching theater and drama in the Department of Fine Arts plus production of four to six plays a year—done with his demand for perfection stamped all over them. Many another drama professor is harried, in better-healed situations, with a one-a-semester play schedule.

Yet the load apparently stimulates Zohn. He can turn in a full day teaching and coaching, return to the theater after supper for four or five hours of rehearsal, still able to vigorously erupt from his seat if the occasion arises.

He sparkles when he informs you that in 10 years, the Playmakers have never postponed a production or, once in production, canceled.

There's also an intensity when you hear the teacher in him list the things good educational theater should do. It must teach drama students, he believes, not necessarily for professional acting but capable of teaching others in turn; provide an outlet for self-expression (as distinct from self-indulgent theater); provide a university and community theater which offers to a non-participating student the opportunity to experience 15 or 20 top-level plays in his four years at college.

The zest and drive which brings all this about promises some very tangible returns. University administrators, notably resistant to being swept off their feet, now plan a half-million dollar fine arts wing to be completed by Fall 1963 as the first part of a million-dollar plus Arts and Sciences Center. It will include a theater—incorporating many of the director's ideas but something short of lavish—plus rehearsal facilities and offices as part of the first wing. And for the 1960 fall semester a technical director will be added to the university faculty, freeing the director from a field he admires, operates in acceptably, but admittedly feels less than expert.

Perhaps because he operates on what Broadway types would define, perhaps in a fit of expansiveness, as a cultural frontier, Zohn's work is not so widely known as it might be in a more populous or prestigious atmosphere. Yet there are signs in this area, too—his selection for several summers as director for the Players of Mexico City, his frequent roles as judge in off-campus dramatic competitions, his contributions to theater journals.

All of this, though, is beyond the mainstream of his interest—the actual accomplishment of solid educational theater.

And all of this, of course, is quite beyond Hershel Zohn's suggestion for listing Playmaker productions of the past 10 years. You sometimes find yourself being angry with him, sometimes stimulated, sometimes depressed—and then turning around and doing more than he asked, hoping to surprise him, and perhaps, even to be pleasing. And that's a good attitude for a drama director to arouse in his players.

* * *

Las Cruces Sun News, May 16, 1960

TEN SUCCESSFUL YEARS OF THEATRE WITH ZOHN CELEBRATED AT UNIVERSITY
by Mrs. Louise Nusbaum

Hershel Zohn, now in his tenth year as director of dramatics at New Mexico State University, is also celebrating his 32nd year in the theater, and the most successful year for the Playmakers Theater.

No doubt the university is celebrating its good fortune in securing Zohn. For in 10 short years he has raised the standards of educational theater from mediocrity to top-flight, as witnessed by those who have attended Playmaker productions.

Brochure Commemorates

Those attending *A Touch of the Poet,* the year's final play presented this past week, received a brochure printed by the university commemorating Zohn's 10 years with the Playmakers.

The pamphlet came as a surprise to Hershel Zohn, who had asked only that there be compiled a list of the plays during his 10 years here.

Zohn's Philosophy

It is his philosophy to present "not run-of-the-mill plays, but those audiences would not see otherwise—plays that are not necessarily popular—plays of all periods, all styles, all countries, and plays of ideas, such as greed, fate of man, etc."

Educational theater in this area is conducted not only for students at New Mexico State, but for all those in the community interested in participating, since no other theater is offered here. "Also it is the duty of such a theater to educate an audience for better type of theater...."

ADDENDUM C

THE CRITIC – JOAN QUARM

A TRIBUTE TO HERSHEL ZOHN
El Paso Herald Post, April 16, 1978

Only in the theatre do we meet the naked face of humanity. Only the drama brings before us, human beings as they are with their defenses gone: stripped bare of pretense, vulnerable in all their folly and sweetness and pain. The laughter we share with them, the tears we weep for them, raise us above our own selfish concerns. No wonder that to those who love it, there is something holy about the play. Born out of the rituals of ancient worship, it continues to cleanse our spirits, strengthen our understanding, and enlarge our sympathies.

To Hershel Zohn, who gives his life to theatre, there can be no greater tribute than one bearing his name, particularly when it is the building he dreamed of, brought into being, and filled with love and joy. In it here today he is surrounded by applauding spirits: the characters of Shakespeare and Chekhov, Gogol, Lorca, Ionesco, O'Neill, Arthur Miller and a dozen more great playwrights of many times and places. All have come to life on this stage, by one director's art. A few wait in the wings, to recall their scenes of triumph. All remain with us permanently, in the effect they have had on our hearts.

It is wrong to call the drama an evanescent art. It is not bound by time. We may forget the dates of productions and the names of those who played in them, but the great moments stay with us all our lives. More than any other playgoer, a critic hungers for such moments, rare as they must be. Working with students, Hershel Zohn created enough of them, year after year, to bring this critic many a mile in eager anticipation. Our friendship grew out of a mutual love for the work, and my own respect for the artist.

Out of the bounty of Hershel Zohn's gifts to us, we all cherish memories. The high school one-act play contests are among my own, with Hershel scanning the stage like a lion hungry for young talent, and Ann waiting in the office to letter the names of the award-winners in her elegant beautiful script. Ann has always been there, designing posters and programs, ready when needed, smiling and gentle and patient. No tribute to her husband would be complete without her name, for she is part of the life we honor.

* * *

SHOWCASE
El Paso Herald Post, April 21, 1978

Hershel Zohn took the stage of his own theater on Sunday afternoon and filled it in a one-man show which brought three completely different characters alive. This was but one of the many small miracles he has worked there, which led New Mexico State University to honor him by a ceremony which gave the playhouse his name.

"It is," he said, in a short speech of thanks, "a pleasure to be given a theater. It is mine. Of course, I don't know what I shall do with it. It is too heavy to lift on my back and carry away to the hills, although that could be the subject for a cartoon."

Among the friends and ex-students present were many almost convinced that if he wanted to remove that theater from the campus, Hershel Zohn would find a way to do so. After all, he found a way to have it put there in 1963, found a way to turn students into polished Shakespearian and Chekhovian performers, found a way to bring bright stars such as Jacqueline Brookes and James Earl Jones to act with them; and found a way to tour the South Pacific with his student production of *The Matchmaker*. He also brought William Saroyan, Joseph Papp, and Harold Clurman to speak at the 1967 Southwest Theater Conference there.

During his tenure as chairman of the drama department, Hershel Zohn made New Mexico State University familiar to leading theater people across the country. Nothing has ever been too ambitious for him to try, and nothing too costly for his university administration to support. His experiments have succeeded, for he is a man who knows his art and accepts no short cuts or limitations.

Welcoming his guests, Dr. Gerald W. Thomas, president of NMSU, spoke warmly of Hershel Zohn's achievement. Dr. Thomas Gale, dean of Arts and Sciences, made introductions and expressed his pleasure in the occasion. Rudy S. Apodaca, president of the Board of Regents, recalled that once, as Prof. Zohn's student, he auditioned to play Puck in *A Midsummer Night's Dream* but was only cast as Mustardseed.

As a drama critic who has seen much of Hershel Zohn's work, I was invited to speak a tribute. Remembering years of his selfless perfectionism, I said, among other things. "It is a time to say thank you to a man who has held to the highest ideals of his profession; who has enriched his students' abilities and his audiences' awareness; who has struggled to do only what is valuable, and to do it well; who has, in short, removed the mask from us and let us look into the mirror of our own humanity. Long may he do so, and long may the Hershel Zohn Theater continue to follow his example."

ADDENDUM - D

SAROYAN
1969

William Saroyan, the noted playwright and author, was in Las Cruces a few years ago, arriving in a beaten-up old jalopy he had herded all the way from New York City.

"He couldn't drive well at all," Hershel Zohn, at whose invitation Saroyan came here, said of the man.

"He did not seem to have the feel of the mechanics involved with driving a car. They did not go well together, the car and Saroyan. When he was ready to leave Las Cruces, I followed him to the parking lot to see him off—and he nearly ran into our campus post office as he started driving away."

Professor Zohn, head of the Theatre Department at NMSU, was not issuing a professional critique on the driving ability of the famous dramatist, but was speaking in context to Saroyan's own references to the automobile in a recently published diary-journal kept over the years.

"Places where automobiles take over do not have it [beauty]," Saroyan has commented in *Days of Life and Death and Escape to the Moon*.[1] "But automobiles have something else. Space and race—a sense of going, not lingering."

He lingered in Las Cruces about 10 days, one of several top figures in the theatrical world who were in town in October, 1967, for the Southwest Theatre Conference.

* * *

---

[1] Published by Dial Press, 1970.

Saroyan arrived here several days ahead of schedule, and, not announcing his presence, had those several days to himself soaking up the atmosphere of life down near the border.[2]

"He enjoyed himself hugely," Zohn reports.

And while the Professor at NMSU isn't the one who tells us, from another source it is learned that on one night in particular did Saroyan—and Professor Zohn—enjoy themselves.

There had been a party...it was to progress to another home.... Zohn's wife, Ann, was driving, and with the Interstate construction going on, and the destination and address unfamiliar to her, she became lost and for all practical purposes was doing little but driving in circles....

Her husband and the great Saroyan were no help at all.

Seated in the back seat of the car, they were singing Ukrainian songs at the top of their voices and seemingly cared little whether Ann found the way to where they were going...or if they remained lost for the remainder of the evening.

They were having a fine time....

* * *

It is likely Professor Zohn and William Saroyan may continue their duets this fall.

Saroyan's permanent home [is] in Paris, France and Hershel Zohn, taking a one-semester sabbatical leave as of Labor Day, will spend a part of that leave in Europe, in Paris.

Studying and working with the theatre in European capitals and in New York City, he expects to visit the great dramatist in the French capital.

---

[2] Returning from lunch one afternoon, I saw a group of students in a circle in the lobby chatting with a man in their midst. To my surprise it was William Saroyan having a good time. He told me he had been here more than a week. (Hershel Zohn)

ADDENDUM - E

Letters

OFFICE OF THE PRESIDENT

Box 3Z/Las Cruces, New Mexico 88003
Telephone (505) 645-2035

December 5, 1977

Mr. Hershel Zohn
Professor Emeritus
Rt. 2, Box 940
Las Cruces, NM 88001

Dear Hershel:

My heartiest congratulations to you for being recognized in the recent Board of Regents meeting. Those of us in the university community and in the surrounding area are most pleased that the Board has named the university theater in your honor. This is a justly deserved recognition for your many years of service to the university and community.

I will be back in touch with you for the appropriate recogntion ceremony sometime soon.

Congratulations again, and my best personal regards.

Sincerely yours,

Gerald W. Thomas
President

GWT/ab

cc: Board of Regents

DEPARTMENT OF FINE ARTS

Box 3F/Las Cruces, New Mexico 88003
Telephone (505) 646-2421

February 7, 1975

Mr. Hershel Zohn
Rt. 2, Box 940
Las Cruces, NM 88001

Dear Hershel:

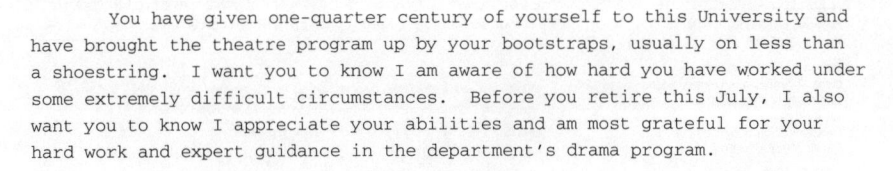

    You have given one-quarter century of yourself to this University and have brought the theatre program up by your bootstraps, usually on less than a shoestring. I want you to know I am aware of how hard you have worked under some extremely difficult circumstances. Before you retire this July, I also want you to know I appreciate your abilities and am most grateful for your hard work and expert guidance in the department's drama program.

    We have not always agreed on some policy matters, but somehow we worked out our differences to the best advantage of the program. We may not have always shared philosophical or practical opinions, but I have never doubted your professional capabilities or your knowledge of your field. You have given all of us some fine theatre experiences and we are grateful for that opportunity.

    Without your twenty-five years of capable, talented leadership, the drama program may never have gotten so well established. We can only hope that our leadership has provided a solid foundation for the departments new directions.

    To you and Anne always my best and all good wishes for many long, happy, productive years ahead.

Most sincerely,

John

John M. Glowacki, Head
Fine Arts Department

cc: Dean Gale

SOUTHWEST THEATRE CONFERENCE
Arkansas • Louisiana • New Mexico • Oklahoma • Texas

October 22, 1981

Dr. Hershel Zohn
205 McDowell Rd.
Las Cruces, NM 88001

Dear Dr. Zohn:

You have been nominated by the New Mexico State University Theater Department for a special honor at the Southwest Theater Conference. This award is for your outstanding theater work in the state of New Mexico.

A brief resume of your state theater work will be printd in the conference program and we would like very much to introduce you and present your certificate of excellence during the brunch on Saturday, October 31, 1981, between 10:30 a.m. and 12:30 p.m.

The New Mexico Theater Association is proud to present this award to you at this time. I hope you will be able to meet with us during the conference and to attend the brunch. I have enclosed an application form for you to register for the conference, or you can do so at the Regeant Hotel during the conference.
If you are unable to attend the conference, we hope you will at least be able to come to the brunch and accept the award.

Congratulations on having been active in theater development in New Mexico and in being nominated for special recognition.

I look forward to meeting you at the conference.

Sincerely,

J. Richard Waite

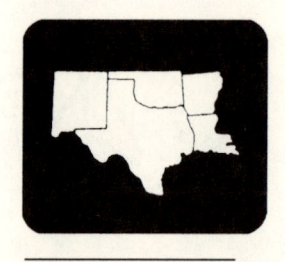

OFFICERS

J. RICHARD WAITE, President
P.O. Box 2043
Portales, New Mexico 88130
Res. (505) 762-9149
Off. (505) 562-2476

GREGORY D. KUNESH, Vice-President
School of Drama
University of Oklahoma
Norman, Oklahoma 73019
Phone (405) 325-4021

MONA BROOKS, Secretary
Dept. of Drama and Communications
University of New Orleans
Lake Front
New Orleans, Louisana 70122
Phone (504) 283-0317

COY SHARP, Treasurer
1412 Rosewood
Odessa, Texas 79761
Res. (915) 366-7466
Off. (915) 362-2329

DAVID RINEAR
Editor: Theatre/Southwest
University of Oklahoma
Norman, Oklahoma 73019

PAST PRESIDENTS

Rupel Jones, Paul Baker, Walter R. Volbach, John Wray Young, Virgil L. Baker, Monroe Lippman, John Rosenfield, F. Loren Winship, Theodore Viehman, Oma Link Rowley, R. Lyle Hagan, Joe Salek, Lee Edwards, Francis Prinz, F. Donald Clark, Angus Springer, Preston Magruder, Art Cole, Burnet Hobgood, Richard O'Connell, Claude L. Shaver, Stocker Fontelieu, James G. Barton, Ronald Schulz, Charles C. Suggs, August W. Staub, Nadene S. Blackburn, Enid Holm, Nancy Vunovich, Maurice Berger.

Dear Mr. Zohn,

Our congratulations to you, the Playmakers and the Drama Department!

Bill and I saw "War and Peace" Friday night and were so impressed with the excellent production of a very difficult play. Bill says he thinks it is the best thing we have seen at the University—and I agree. It is also very <u>much</u> better than many plays done by professionals.

The audience was held spellbound—and when you can do that, you have made a fine production from every standpoint.

Our congratulations to everyone involved and especially to "the old Prince."

Sincerely,

Florence D. Erwin
(Mrs. William S.)

Tuesday 1 a.m.

Dear Mr. Zohn,

Not having had the opportunity to tell you tonight in person how very much I enjoyed the play, I would like to do so now, and to congratulate you on an outstanding production and on the superb performance of your part.

It was an evening long to be remembered.

Sincerely,

Hanna Spier
El Paso, TX

INDEX
(See List of Illustrations for locations of photographs.)

acting techniques 63, 202, 222
Actor's Equity 209
After the Fall 215
Air Mechanics Theatre 155ff
Albee, Edward 205, 254
Albuq. Little Theatre 261, 263
Alford, Bill 175, 177, 181, *photo*
All the King's Men 169
Allen, Bruce 239; Ted 163
The Alley Theatre, Houston 230
Allgeier, David (Dave) 222, 229
American College Theatre Festival 246
American Educational Theatre Association (AETA) x, 182ff, 193
American Nat. Theatre & Academy 246
American Theatre Association 246
Anderson, Robert 164
Andreyev, Leonid 107
Anouilh, Jean 119, 124, 156
Antigone x, 119, 124, 243, *photos*
Antonis, Earnest 142
Apodaca, Rudy 168, 260
Arena Stage, Washington, DC 266
Armory for the Arts, Santa Fe 257
Arms and the Man 155, 229
Armstrong, Ann 147
Arrington, Jann 184
Artef Theatre 68, 242
As You Like It xi, 123, 199, *photo*
Asch, Sholem 67

Baldwin, Percy M. 138
Barbar, Judy 208
Barbusse, Henri 82
Barefood in the Park 216
Barney, Paula 208
Barney, William 168, 175, 207, *photos*
Beatty, Dale 244
Beckman, Elizabeth 208
Beem, Earl 123
Beenhouwer, Bernice 130, 131,*photo*
Beilis, Mendel 56
Belkin, Arlene 207, 216, 239, *photo*
Bell, Campton 108, 111
Bellamy, John 142, *photos*
Belles Artes Theatre 145, 243
Ben-Ami, Jacob 62, 67, 105
Bennett, Eileen 246
Bentley, Eric 222
Betti, Ugo 213
Birkinshaw, Phillip 205
Blitzstein, Marc 201
Blood Wedding 79, 244
The Bolshoi Ballet 254
The Boor 124
Boucicault, Dion 123

The Bourgeois Gentleman 176
Branigan Cultural Center 262
Branson, John W. 127, 133-4, 136
Brazil, La Noel 130
Brecht, Bertolt 123, 201, 222
Brilliant, Kay 238, *photo*
Bronx Art Theatre 66
Brookes, Jacqueline xi, 123, 199
Brooks, Christine *photo*
Brooklyn Baseball Cantata 143
Brown, Jerome *photo*
Brown, Joe 123
Brown, Kathy 246
Bruner, Phil 184
Budapest, theatres 254
Butler, Gordon 239, 245
Butler, Lynn 245
Butler, Oscar 142, 143, 159, 163, 176, 205, 213, 239
Butler, Robin 208
Byrd, Barthy 239

Cafe Crown 67; *Cafe Royal* 67
Campbell, Rock 168, 169, 175, 179, *photo*
Candida 119, 128, *photo*
Carlino, Lewis John 205
Carpenter, Cassandra 246
Carpenter, Jim 244
Case, Dan 229
Castle Garden 43
Catskill Mountains 58
The Cave Dwellers 175
Chagall, Marc 237
Chains 71
The Chairs 176
Chaliapin, Peodor 60
Charles, David Orin 216
Chavez, Denise 213, 222, 229, 267
Chayefsky, Paddy 69
Chekhov, Anton 62, 104, 108, 111, 124, 140, 149, 159, 204, 213, 223, 241, 246; correspondence 268; death 225; *photo*
Chekhov, Olga 225; correspondence 268
The Cherry Orchard 62, 228
Children of a Lesser God 249
Chilton, Alexander 123
Chyung-ang University, Seoul 189
Civic Rep. Theatre, NY 62, 105, 215
Clark, Jackie 163, 167, 169, 176, 179, 204, 214, 245, *photo*
Clark, Scotty 161
Classics Theatre Co., Alb. 147, 255
Clurman, Harold 217
Cobb, Lee 256, 266
Cole, Jim 142, 148
Coleman, Bill 216
Colette 147
Columbia University 78, 94
Come Blow Your Horn 206
Comeau, Leo 129, 130, 131, 134, 135,

300 Index

141, 142, 143, 165, 167, 168, 176, 178, 201, *photos*
Congdon, James 216
Conklin, Dr. Paul 136
Cooper, Mary 208
Coquat, Michael 199, 206
Corbett, Roger B. 162, 203, 204
Coronado Playmakers 123
Country Girl 141
Craft, Hy 67
The Crucible 144, 242, 255, *photo*
The Curious Savage 254

Danchenko, Nemirovich 104, 227, 228
Dassin, Jules 68
Daviet, Robin 222
De Mordaunt, Walter J. 165
Dean, Melody 208
Death of a Salesman 135, 256, 265, *photo*
Denk, Joe 265
Denker, Henry 206
Depression, life during 69ff
The Diary of a Mad Man 254
Diary of Anne Frank 166, *photo*
Distant Drums 110, *photo*
A Doll's House 138, 247, 263
Don Juan in Hell 163
Donohue, James 207, 209, 216, 222
Dos Shtetel *photo*
Douglas, Maria 217
Down In The Valley 143
Draiarsh, Velvel 63ff, *photo*
Dressell, David & Lee *photo*
The Drunkard 129
Durkovich, Steve 173
Durrenmatt, Friedrich 209, 223
Duse, Elanora 153
The Dybbuk 68, 112

Easterling, Cornelia (see also Valach) 238, *photo*
education, college 104ff
El Paso Herald-Post 210, 214, 260
Elan, Jeri 168
Electric Chair 67
Ellis Island 43
An Enemy of the People 137, *photo*
epic theatre 202, 222
Erwin, Florence D. 297
Euripides 162
Eylar, Al 262

A Far Country 206
Fascism 95
Federal Theatre Project 74, 76, 77
Fiddler on the Roof 236, 265ff, *photos*
Fiedler, Larry 244-6
Filippo, Eduardo de 261
Filumena 261
Finland, USS 42ff

The Firebugs 207
The Fixer 56fn
Flanagan, Hallie 74
Foley, Cassandra 245
Fort Belvoir, Virginia 87, 95
Fort Dix, New Jersey 83, 84ff
Fouse, Martha *photo*
Franco, Francisco 78, 95
Frankfather, William 209-10, 213, 216, 222, 230, *photo*
Freedley, George 75
Frisch, Max 207
Fry, Christopher 140, 170
Fuhr, Lini 80, 94, 102

Gaidry, Elizabeth 244, 246, *photo*
Gale, Dr. Thomas 260
Garcia Lorca, Frederico 79, 207, 244
Gardner, Karen 162, 167
Garrett, Edgar 124, 129, 142, 205, *photo*
Gemoets, Lee xi, 208
Genet, Jean 179
Genovese, mike 262
Ghosts 138, 178
G.I. Bill 104
Gibbs, Kathryn 119, 129, *photo*
Gibson, William 200
Gigi 147
Gilbert, James 239, 244
Gilbert, Mercedes 239, 245
Gilbert, Paula 244
Giombolino, Susan 208, *photo*
Giraudoux, Jean 133
The Girl From Wyoming 132
The Glass Menagerie 157, *photo*
Glowacki, Barbara 259ff
Glowacki, John 176, 259, 297
Godley, John 184
Goetz, Ruth and Augustus 137
Gogol, Nikolai 81, 152, 254
Gold, Martha 153, 181, *photo*
The Golden Bride 60
The Golden Peacock 64
Golightly, Kenneth 184
The Good Woman Of Setzuan 123, 222, *photo*
Goodrich, Frances 166
Gorki, Maxim 104, 241, 253, *photo*
Gossett, John 246
Graese, Judy 208, *photo*
Graham, Marjorie 193
Graham-Lujan, James 207
Green Fields 107
Greenwich Village 66, 72, 94, 215
Gustafson, Henry 124
Guthrie, Kenneth 142, 168, 172, 256

Haak, Dianne 208, *photo*
Habima Theatre 63
Hackett, Albert 166

Index

Hadley Hall Theatre x, 124, 129, 135, 155, 143
Hafenfeld, Susan 262
Haines, Robie 244
Hall, Herb 229
Hands of the Enemy 249, *photo*
Hardman, Marion 205
Hardman, John 246
Harry, Kathryn (Deedie) (see also Myers, Kathryn) 172, 181, 184, *photo*
The Hasty Heart 134, *photo*
Hayes, Helen 154
Hayner, Kim 175
Hayner, Mildred 172, 175, 177, *photos*
Hayner, Robin 208-10, *photo*
Hayner, Star 246, *photo*
Hedda Gabler 138, 153, *photo*
Hedrick, Cheryl 208, *photo*
The Heiress 137
Hellman, Lillian 156
Henderson-Zohn, Roberta 72, 80, 92, 95, 100, 116
Hepburn, Chris 229
Herring, Nancy 216
Herring, Susie 165
Hicks, Bill 262
Highlands Univ. 73, 92, 104, 108
Hilford, Dayne 119
Hirshbein, Peretz 107
Hodges, Sally *photo*
Holberg, Eva 206-208
Holley, Allen 216
The Homage That Follows 250
Hopkins, Harry 74
House of Bernarda Alba 79, 207, *photo*
Houseman, John 76
Howe, Doris 130
Huddle, Elizabeth 123, 222, *photo*
Hurd, Peter 205
Hutchison, Warner 244

Ibsen, Henrik 62, 137, 153, 178, 247
Ibsen, Marjorie 139
The Imaginary Invalid 148
immigration ix, 47ff; leaving Sinyava 33ff; family in New York 45ff; ocean trip 42ff; U.S. customs 43
Inherit the Wind 164, *photo*
The Inspector General 81, 152
International Theatre Month 154
Ionesco, Eugene 176, 179, 205, 212
Ivey, David 142, 147

Jeffers, Robinson 162
Jewish holidays, Bar-Mitzvah 27; New Year 90; Passover 14, *photo*; Succoth 15
Jewish Scientific Institute (YIVO) 10
Jews, persecution in Russia ix, 25ff
Johnson, Carolyn *photo*
Johnson, Kathy 208

Jones, Ann 170
Jones, James Earl xi, 123, 212, *photo*
Jones, Robert (Bob) 159, 154
Jonson, Ben 178
Julius Caesar 170
J. B. 174, *photo*

Kabtsen Vee Krikhstee 45
Kafka, Franz 264
Kapner, Irving (Kappy) 76, 81, 99
Kazan, Elia 216, 266
Keifetz, Joyce & Norman 260
Keill, Elizabeth 167, 170
Kennedy, Pres. John F. 185, 201
Kennedy (John F.) Center for the Performing Arts 246
Kiddish Hashem 61
Kimbrough, Clinton 147, 240, 243, *photo*
Kirby, Evelyn 208, 216
Klein, Duane 165, 167;
Klein, Rabbi Joseph 260
Kleinsinger, G. 143
Knoop, Gerhard 109
Kopit, Arthur 264
Kos, David 184
Kraft, Kerri 208
Krentel, Ann 208
Kropp, Simon F. 123
Kuhn, John 171

The Lady's Not For Burning 170
Laguna Maulton Playhouse 256
The Lark 156, *photo*
Las Cruces, NM x, 106, 115, 119,
Las Cruces Community Theatre 237, 258, 265
Las Cruces High School drama 205
Las Cruces Sun-News 78, 138, 169, 174, 181
Las Vegas, NM 73, 92, 104, 114
Lawrence, Jerome 164, 240
Le Feu 82
Le Gallienne, Eva 62, 153, 229
Leadwill, Bill 91
Learned, Maurcena 159, 168
Lee, Robert 240
Leivick, H. 71
Leslie, Judith 142, 147, 169
Lewis, Charles 229, 239
Lewis, Claire 172, 184, *photos*
Life With Father 134, *photo*
Lincoln Center, New York 76, 215
Lindsey, Howard 134
Livingston, Sheila 149
Long, David 245-6, *photo*
Loos, Anita 147
Lower Depths 241, 253, *photo*
Lowery, Harry 111
Lydick, Sylvia 161
Lynch, Linda 229

Macbeth 158, *photo*
MacDonald, Robert David 229
MacLeish, Archibald 174
The Mad-Woman Of Chaillot 133
Malamud, Bernard 56
The Male Animal 136
Maltz, Albert 103
Mandell, Mark 145-6, *photo*
Manning, Larry 162
Mark Taper Forum 249
Marriage of Mr. Mississippi 223
The Marriage Proposal 124
Martin, Freddie 95
Martin Beck Theatre 64
Martinez, Mary 146
The Masque 123
Master Pierre Patelin 129
The Matchmaker xi, 171, *photos*
The Matchmaker Far East tour, 187ff; schedule 196
Maveety, Hillary 165
Mawson, Lynnette 184
Mayfield, Mary Ella 184
Maynez, Royalene 245
Mazel Tov 64
McCorkle, Marjorie 142, *photo*
McEnroe, Robert 130
McFall, Barbara 208
McGinley, Karen 208
McGonigle, Bill 229
McRee, Patsy 154
Mead, Phil 142
Medea 162, *photo*
Medoff, Mark 249, *photos*
Medoff, Vicki 222, 229
Meier, Sharon 208
Men in White 109
Mexico City, earthquake 149; theatre 145, 149, 243
Meyerhold, Vsevolod 152
A Midsummer Night's Dream 158, 167, *photo*
Milam, Mike 161
Miles, Lee 207
Miles Fife 249
Miller, Arthur 135, 137, 144, 158, 210, 215, 242, 256, 263, 265
Miller, James 173
Miller, Joy 137, 141, 147
The Miracle Worker 200
Moliere 105, 148, 176
Molinari, Juan 239, 245
Moore, Jeff 216
Moore, Laura 208
Moscow, theatres today 252
Moscow Art Theatre 63, 104, 111, 228, 241, 252
Muni, Paul 61, 67, 164
My Fair Lady 131

Myers, Kathryn (Deedie) (see also Harry, Kathryn) 208, 216
Myers, Michael 172, 184, 207-9, 261, *photo*

Nash, N. Richard 154
National Play Bureau 76
Nazimova, Alla 153
Neumann, Alfred 229
Neville, Terryl 149
New Kaleidoscope Players 257
New Mexico College of Agriculture & Mechanic Arts (A&M) (see also NM State Univ.) x, 115, 119, 121ff; drama department & groups 123ff
New Mexico State University (NMSU), new theatre 197ff
New York City, education 2ff; finding work 50ff; immigrant life 47ff; jeweler's apprentice 55; pushcart deli 50ff; theatres 60ff
New York Public Library x; Theatre Collection 75
New York Times 75, 166
New York Tribune 166
New York University 106ff
The Night Thoreau Spent in Jail 240
No Exit 176
Northwestern University 114
Nugent, Elliott 136
Nusbaum, Mrs. Louise 169, 287

O'Connell, Richard L. 207
Odd Couple 222
Odets, Clifford 74, 141
Odom, Tom 239
O'Donnell, William 156
Oedipus Rex 208, *photo*
O'Keeff, John 264
Oliver, Irene 222, 229, *photos*
Olivier, Sir Laurence 154, 261
one-man shows 258, 262, 266
O'Neill, Eugene 168
Opatashu, David 68
Othello xi, 123, 211, *photo*
Owen, Gordon 205

Palmer, Phillip 246, *photo*
Papp, Joseph 217
Patrick, John 134, 161, 254
Pattison, Judith, 208, 210, 222, *photos*
Pavlova, Anna 60
Peace on Earth 103
Pearl Harbor attack 81
Phelps, William Lyon 232
A Phoenix Too Frequent 140
The Physicists 209
Pickard, Frank 250
Pierce, Patricia 149
Pille, Judy 167, 168, 176, *photo*
Piscator, Erwin 229

Index

Pitoniak, Anne 264
Playboy of the Western World 161
Players Inc., Mexico City 149, 243
Playmakers, productions 277; South Pacific tour 178; school tours 127, 131
Plowright, Joan 261
Plumbley, Pauline 132, 134, *photo*
pogroms 16, 23, 29
Porter, Bob 222
Post, James 246, *photo*
Prague, theatres today 255
Preciado, Willie 156
Princess Turandot 253
The Prisoner of Second Avenue 246
Procaccino, John 264
Prokofiev, *War and Peace* ballet 254
Prufer, Guntram 229
Pygmalion 130, *photo*

Quarm, Joan 204, 210, 214, 239, 260, 288
The Queen and the Rebels 213

Rabinowitz, Solomon (see also Sholom Aleichem) 236
The Rainmaker 154
Ratigan, Terrence 142
Red Rocks Ampitheater 110
The Red Ryder Trilogy 249
Reed, Neuman 145, 155, 205
Reid, Janice 222
Remarque, Eric Maria 82
Reuth, Lois 208
Rhinoceros 179, *photo*
Rhome, Frances 205
Richardson, Frank 120, 129, *photo*
Richardson, Shirley 208
Riegel, Marcia 244, *photo*
Riesen, Al 172
Rocky Mountain News 111
Rodwell, David 169, 281ff
Roederer, Gordon 165, 168
Roether, Dianne 208
Roman, Richard 245
Romeo and Juliet 124, 204, *photo*
Roosevelt, Franklin D. 74, 98
The Round Up 133, 136, 165, 170, 171, 175, 178, 262
Royal Gambit 222
Russian Revolution 11ff, 23ff

Sackler, Harry 64
Sage, Mrs. June 121
Sano, Seki 145, 243
Santa Fe Festival Theatre 264
Santa Fe New Mexican 257, 264
Santa Fe Railroad 94
Saroyan, William 175, 217, 291
Sartre, Jean-Paul 176
Satz, Ludwig 45
Scarbrough, Janeice 250

Schlamme, Martha 229
Schneider, Benny 68
School for Scandal 214
Schuldt, John 222, 229
Schwartz, Maurice 61, 71, 107
Schweid, Mark 66
Schweiss, Rose *photo*
Schwengel, Mary 208
Scofield, Susan 208
The Sea Gull 105, 149, 159, 246, 252, *photos*
Seamans, Herbert 239, *photo*
The Seer Sees His Bride 64
The Seven Who Were Hanged 107
Shabtsai Zvi 107
Shakespeare, William 109, 141, 158, 167, 170, 199, 204, 211, 236
Shakespeare Festival 203ff
Shamel, Bruce 207, 216, 222
Shamel, Dorothy 208
Shaw, George Bernard 119, 128, 130, 155, 163
Sheridan, Richard B. 214
Sholom Aleichem 64, 236
Shook, Ada *photo*
Showdown 81
Silbiger, Norbert 110
The Silver Whistle 130
Simmons, Ernest J. 226
Simon, Neil 206, 216, 222, 246, 254, 261
Singer, I.S. 71
Sinyava, Ukraine 3ff, 36, 47; education 8ff; influenza epidemic 28; return to 275; Sabbath 7; village life 14ff; wedding customs 13, 19
Sironi, Edmond 119, 129
The Skin Of Our Teeth 148
Smith, Dianne 238, *photo*
Smith, Jolly 208
Sophocles 208, 243
Soules, Jack 159, 163, 167, 170, 213, 260, *photos*; Shirley 260
Southwest Regional Festival 246
Southwest Theatre Conf. 217
Spanish Civil War 76, 78, 95
Sparger, Nancy 216
Spencer, Shorah 216
Spitz, Robert 179
Stanislavski, Konstantin x, 68, 104, 109, 228, 241, *photo*; methods 63
Stein, Joseph 236
Stillwell, Charles 157, 161-2, 165, 170, 172
Stobie, Harold 141, 173
Story of the Yiddish Theatre 64, 73
Stratford Theatre, Connecticut 160; Ontario, Canada 160
Striezhnov, O.A. 253
Strindberg, August 205
Stubing, Charles 132
Summers, Cherie 172, 184

Sutherland, Ann 168
The Swan Song 111
Sydow, Helen 208
Synge, John Millington 161, 205

Tanner, Robin 208
Taylor, John 184
Tea and Sympathy 164
Teahouse of the August Moon 161, *photo*
The Tempest 236
Tennanholtz, Malka 63-65, *photo*
The Testament 267
That All May Learn 123
Theatre Abroad magazine 76
theatre of the absurd 179
The Thieves' Carnival 212
Thomas, Gerald W. 259, *photo*
Thompson, Glorietta 246, *photo*
Thoteron, Dan 110
Three Penny Opera 201, 206, *photo*
Thurber, James 136
Todd, Larry 246
Tolstoy, Leo 82, 226, 229, 241
Tom Sawyer 216
A Touch of the Poet 168
Travis, David 147, *photo*
Treakle, Gayle 262
Troyat, Henri 224ff
Twain, Mark 237
Twelfth Night 141, 158, 257, *photo*
Tyszka, Walter 175

USO 185, 193
Uncle Vanya 213, *photo*
United States Army, discharge 99; experience 84ff; furloughs 92ff
University of Denver 108ff
University of Texas at El Paso (UTEP) 141, 210, 260

Vakhtangov, Eugene 68; methods 63; Theatre in Moscow 252
Valach, Cornelia (see also Easterling) 262, 265
Valdez, Corry 238, *photo*
Van Antwerp, John 132
Vardi, David 63, *photo*
Vardi-Yoalit Theatre Studio 63ff, *photo*
Veitch, Ray 142, 159, 176, 245, 262
A View from the Bridge 210, 263
Villard, Paul 82
Volpone 178

Waiting for a Lefty 74
Want, Valeria 208
War and Peace 82, 229ff, *photos*
Ward, C. O. *photo*
Ward, Nancy 208
Warren, Robert Penn 169
The Warrior's Husband 124

The Warsaw Melody 253
Watts, Lloyd 222, 229
Webb, Charles 229
Wedding, Phil 184, *photo*
The Wedding 111, 140
Weiler, Pat 157
Weill, Kurt 143, 201
Weiselman, David 262
Weisenfreund, Muni (see also Muni, Paul) 61
What You Will 141
Whiting, Dr. Frank 185
Wichert, Bob 132
Wiesel, Elie 266
Wild Oats
Wilde, Oscar 124
Wilder, Thornton 149, 171
Williams, Betty 163
Williams, Frances 239
Williams, Tennessee 157, 205
Wilson, Bill *photo*
Wilson, Duane 184
Wings 264
The Winslow Boy 142
Wiseman, Lou 148
Wolfe, Lazar 239
Wolpe and Folson 222
Wood, Carroll 216
Works Progress Administration (WPA) 74ff; New York Public Library 74; workers group 70
World War II x, 124; drafted 81ff; prelude to 78; ends 98
Wright, Monte 222, 229, 239, 245

Yerma 79
Yiddish Art Theatre x, 61, 67, 71, 107, 230
Yiddish theatre 45, 67, 75, 113, 175
Yiddish writers, Stalin executes 267
Yoalit, Eva 63, *photo*
Yoshe Kalb 68, 71
The Yucca Players 123

Zalmen or the Madness of God 266
Zefferelli, Franco 261
Zhulavsky, I. 107
Zohn, Ann 148, 167, 168, 170, 173, 175, 176, 198, 201, 259, 262, 264, *photo*
Zohn, Bella (Mama) 4ff, 36ff, 47ff, *photo*; Esther 12, 32; family 11ff; Feige (Fanny) 12, 45; Haye (Khaike or Ida) 12; Malka (Mollie) 12, 33, 45; Sholem (Tate) 3ff, 36ff, 47ff, *photo*
Zohn, Hershel, tenth anniv. 169, 281ff, *photos*
Zohn Theatre, Hershel dedication xi, 259, 267, 288ff, *photos*
Zorin, L. 253
Zweig, Stefan 178